FARMHOUSE KITCHEN
Cooking for One & Two

A fifth book of recipes based on
the Independent Television series.

The main contributor to
this recipe collection
is the programme presenter

GRACE MULLIGAN

Edited by MARY WATTS

YORKSHIRE
TELEVISION

First published in Great Britain, 1988, by
YORKSHIRE TELEVISION ENTERPRISES LTD
Television House, 32 Bedford Row, London WC1R 4HE

ISBN 0 946064 02 4

Design and production: Joy Langridge

Front cover illustration: 'Peeling Vegetables' by
Fanny Fildes, courtesy of Fine Art Photographs.
Back cover illustration: Alan Harbour, Yorkshire TV
Text illustrations: Mary Evans Picture Library,
'Food and Drink Collection' and '1800 Woodcuts'
both published by Dover Publications.

Printed in Great Britain by
Richard Clay Ltd, Bungay, Suffolk

CONTENTS

ACKNOWLEDGMENTS

The compilation of recipes for *Farmhouse Kitchen* books is a rewarding task. There are many viewers who take the trouble to write out and send in recipes and stories about dishes they have made for their family and friends, sometimes over generations. In fact, nearly a third of the recipes in this book have come from viewers, some of whom claim to have been watching *Farmhouse Kitchen* since the series began in 1970. Although I hope we've written to each of them about the recipes chosen for this book, now is my chance to make public my indebtedness and gratitude to all who have contributed or participated in its preparation.

Grace Mulligan is well aware of our viewers' requests and has a wide-ranging selection of recipes in every chapter. Her guest cooks – some who are already familiar faces in the programmes, some who will be introduced in the next year or so – have given recipes to suit their particular interests. They are Yvonne Coull, Head Home Economist of the Sea Fish Industry Authority; Dilwen Phillips from South Wales, well known throughout the Women's Institute, whose current interest is in fresh fast food, with the emphasis on fresh; Jilly Myers, from the British Diabetic Association; Jennie Siew Lee Cook whose dishes first appeared in her charity publication *My Favourite Chinese Recipes*; Nirmal Singh from Nuneaton whose Indian dishes will be a new feature in the programmes and David Shepperdson, manager of Winn's Fish in Huddersfield market, who brings some everyday fish and some less-so to our attention, and who has forgotten more than some of us ever knew about the handling of fish.

My thanks are due to Joan Tyers, who has been our microwave expert for the last few years, and to Yvonne Hamlett – also an expert in the field – who has done the microwave conversions in this book and who will be seen in forthcoming programmes. Angela Henderson has contributed at least three special-occasion meals and also hopes to be a guest. Angela shared much of the early work with me by writing up recipes for testing. Three more special meals, *A Three-Course Dinner for Two*, have come from the from the winner and two runners-up in the *1987 Junior Cook of the Year* competition conducted by the Young Cooks Club of Great Britain, whose organisers Anna Best and Peta Brown readily agreed to our sharing their recipes. Janet Horsley has given a couple of recipes again; since her last contribution to *Farmhouse Kitchen*, she has produced several more books of her own including *The New Fish Cook Book*, (Piatkus and Futura) and *The Weekend Cook Book* (Collins).

When the idea for this book was announced, we were also invited to choose recipes from *The June Hulbert Cook Book*. June Hulbert, who made and published this collection in aid of Finchale Training College for the Disabled in Durham, is Women's Page Editor of Newcastle Upon Tyne's *Evening Chronicle*. Due recognition must also be given to *Saga Magazine*, whose editor kindly agreed to let us use material from Grace's cookery column.

Margaret Heywood has not only given at least twelve recipes to this book, but has been Grace's much-valued helper in the background of *Farmhouse Kitchen* for five years. She and Debbie Woolhead – a recent recruit to that arduous task and who has also dropped in two or three recipes to fill gaps – have with Judith Adshead, Yvonne Hamlett, Angela Henderson and Bunty Johnson, shared nearly all the testing of the recipes in this book. Their valued comments have been the 'Yea' or 'Nay' to many offerings, and their skill at getting worthwhile but incomplete ideas to work is hereby acknowledged with all my admiration and respect.

Almost the last but *never* the least to be admired and thanked are those who type, retype and type again. Julie Cookson has organised this tirelessly; her helpers at YTV have been Joyce Town, Amanda Finney, Hilary Robinson and Kashmir Kaur. And finally, thanks are due to design editor Joy Langridge, whose diplomatic and energetic attention helped the book through its final stages at production.

Thanks and thanks again – to you all.

Mary Watts
Spring 1988

FOREWORD

by Grace Mulligan

Cooking in smaller quantities after a lifetime of feeding a growing, hungry family, is awkward. It took me ages to get used to preparing just enough potatoes and vegetables for my husband and me: three potatoes looked lost in my big pan when I had been used to doing enough for six. Now a large loaf of bread lasts – and lasts! I know you can bake and buy smaller loaves but we do like big slices for our morning toast, so now I divide my wholemeal loaf and repackage it in small plastic bags for the freezer.

The planning and preparation of meals for just one or two is so different. One has to think it all out in a new way. Why cook if you don't have to? What can you make that will last for a day or two? Can one chicken last a week without becoming boring? Can the whole meal be cooked on top of the stove? Is there reason enough to heat the oven when the amounts are so small? Can you *ever* enjoy cooking a whole roast dinner again? If you live alone, I can see why the incentive to cook at all is sometimes missing – but I *do* think it is important to sit comfortably at a properly laid table so that your main meal is something to look forward to and enjoy. A wobbly tray on your knees is no substitute.

This is the first book in which Mary Watts and I have tried to think out quite specifically for the needs of ones and twos. In the programmes it is easy enough to say, 'Just make half-quantities of this family-sized recipe', but quite a few requests – enough in fact to get us moving – have now come in saying, 'Couldn't you do some recipes just for me, just for us two?' Some want it plain, simple and cheap; others are happy to be a bit extravagant, and both young and old have requested dinners for two for special occasions. I am not the only one who knows that for the cost of eating at a restaurant you can dine far more lavishly at home. (See page 179 for Special Occasion Menus.)

I hope our new recipes will remind you that fresh food and home cooking are best in the long run, and often the cheapest. I also hope our recipes will show you different ways of shopping, planning and cooking, to get the best possible value. In some cases we suggest you make up enough for two or three meals and divide it into portions to freeze away for future use. Try filling small containers with just enough for one serving, or making individual pies rather than one large one. Nothing is more depressing than eating your way through a pie which you *know* will last two or three days!

A pot of good home-made soup is easily divided into single portions to come out fresh and tasty just when you need it, and if you haven't much room in your freezer for plastic boxes you can always freeze liquid or semi-liquid food in plastic bags. Just stand the empty bag in a small bowl or − better still − a small, square plastic box. Pour whatever you wish into the plastic bag and put both the bag and box in the freezer. When the soup or casserole is frozen solid, take the box away and seal up, label and store the bag. The square frozen parcel is easier to stack than a round-bottomed one.

Our viewers often tell me that one of the things they most enjoy about our series is all the tips and suggestions I give as I go along. The tips all come from the experience of doing the recipe many times. All our recipe testers make suggestions about the recipes too as they try them out and we have included their comments to help you as well.

I do hope our new book gives you real pleasure. I love the expression *'Bon Appétit'* but since we *always* go in for plain speaking I will wish you *'Good cooking!'*

Grace Mulligan

INTRODUCTION

If you are looking for recipes that make just one helping for one person then, at a glance, you may think we have not provided enough. However, if you look again I hope you will see that in nearly all recipes where two or more helpings are derived, we have explained whether the dish is good served hot then cold, whether it will keep for a day or two, whether it will freeze well, and if so, how best this is done.

Though it may seem extravagant, I believe a freezer is one of the most important pieces of equipment for a small household. Likewise, a microwave cooker – though a luxury gadget – is ideal if only because you do not have to decide before you go out in the morning what you are going to eat in the evening. The two together, plus your conventional cooker and hob, give maximum flexibility for just one or two to eat what you like – when you like.

I regard this as sufficient reason for quite substantial pastry and baking chapters. There are times, however, when one feels guilty using the amount of fuel it takes to bake one small dish, so to ease your conscience and ours we have included in the book what we call 'All In The Oven' lists. You can see how to fill the oven with a variety of dishes that will cook happily together at the same temperature.

Whatever kitchen equipment you have, I hope you will find plenty of dishes to make. Some recipes require no cooking at all; many can be done entirely on top of the stove, and there are simple snacks on toast to elaborate party pieces.

For microwave cooks
If you decide to compare the results of a recipe cooked first the conventional way and then by microwave, don't be surprised if they look and taste different – sometimes like completely different recipes! Microwave cooking just *is* different for many foods and we have not pretended otherwise. What we have done in the conversions and testing is to satisfy ourselves that the finished dish is pleasant to look at and good to eat.

The timing given relate to microwave cookers of **650 to 700 wattage**. Even if yours is a 600-watt model you may well find that the timings given are suitable. If yours is a 500-watt model, then you should *add 15 seconds in every minute given in the recipe.*

I hope you will approve of the use of **different power levels** in this book compared with our original *Microwave Cook Book* in which we confined ourselves to **Full Power** and **Defrost**, because at that time there were more 2-power-level microwave cookers than variable power models on the market. I have found results infinitely better since I learned how to use the various **Medium** settings on my microwave as well as **High** and **Defrost**.

However, if you have a 2-power microwave cooker you will find we have given details where necessary on dealing with the different power settings recommended by Yvonne Hamlett.

Are you worried about the use of 'clingfilm'?
In my opinion this is the most useful name for the stuff which-ever brand you favour, but Grace and I have both gone over to the brand which fits the current scientific notions about toxic substances. So 'clear film' seems to be the handiest name to give to it in this book and, short of advertising, I can only say that one or two manufacturers do offer the purer product as well as the one about which the fuss arose.

Some expert advice about microwaving follows.

Mary Watts

Yvonne Hamlett's Microwave Hints

1 A microwave cooker is just another source of heat, so don't feel you have to cook *everything* in it. There are some foods that cook well in a microwave; with others the results are just not acceptable. The grill is used in many of the recipes in this book to brown and crisp the surface of foods, expecially those with cheese toppings, which might otherwise stay pale and look unappetising.
Meats should roast to an acceptable colour, and it is not always necessary to brush with melted butter before cooking, nor to sprinkle the surface with microwave seasonings or browning mixtures.
Do not salt food to be cooked in the microwave as salt draws the moisture out of the food and cause it to toughen. It causes specks of brown on cauliflower, tough skins on vegetables and a dry surface on meat. Always season at the end of cooking. You can, however, lightly salt sauces and stocks for casseroles and stews as the salt is dissolved in the cooking liquids and not concentrated on the surface of the food.

2 **Timing:** always start checking the results after the minimum cooking time given. Remember that the texture, initial temperature of the food and even the cooking container – its shape, size and the materials of which it is made – will all affect the cooking time. It is all too easy to add extra time but do resist: once overcooked, most foods are irretrievably ruined! Overcooking simply dehydrates and hardens food beyond 'repair'.
Always allow food to stand at the end of cooking. This stand time allows the heat to carry on cooking through the food. If you test it *before* the stand time, it may seem undercooked and you may be tempted to put it back in the cooker for a little longer, thus resulting in overcooking. Meat and poultry need to stand for 5 minutes per 450 g/lb. During this time, the temperature at the centre actually increases; wrapped in foil, shiny side in, the meat stays hot for a good 15 to 20 minutes. In that time, you can be cooking the vegetables to go with the main dish.
Foods with a high fat or sugar content cook very quickly, so check regularly during cooking. Shorten cooking times when using *polyunsaturated fats* as they heat up more quickly than other fats.
Foods with a light airy texture heat more quickly than those with a dense texture.

3 **Dishes:** soup and cereal bowls are ideal for cooking 1 to 2 portions. Make sure they do not have a gold or silver pattern on them.

Generally speaking, Pyrex, ceramic, china and dishwasher-proof plastics are ideal. In fact, any dish that is dishwasher-proof should be fine in the microwave. There are many special microwave dishes available in various shapes and sizes, but check what dishes you already have before buying lots of extras. If you want to buy special dishes, here are the ones to look out for:

'*Cook 'n' Roast*' sets made from a plastic which can be used in the conventional oven, up to 410 °F, 210 °C. (*NB: Do not put plastic dishes under the grill.*) The plastic rack is ideal for roasting joints, cooking bacon or for reheating pastry items. This is one of the most popular and versatile sets available.

Microwave Tender Cooker This is one of the very latest 'active' cookware accessories: it is a special microwave pressure cooker which will cook and tenderise a stew or casserole in 20 to 25 minutes. It is excellent for chicken, chops and small joints and will even cook a steak and kidney pudding from raw ingredients in just 25 minutes.

4 When cooking: remember that foods arranged in a large flat dish will cook more quickly than those in a smaller deeper dish. Foods in a large flat dish will need stirring quite often to prevent the edge from overcooking.

Arrange items such as chicken portions with the *meatiest parts* to the outside of the dish. This will save turning or shielding the thinner parts. Do not stack foods on top of each other as this will give uneven cooking results.

Cover dishes as recommended in the recipe. It is not always necessary to pierce clear film as it is porous at 212 °F, 100 °C, and will allow the steam to pass through it. In some auto-sensor microwave cookers you must **not** pierce the clear film. Check with your manufacturer's instructions.

Always release the clear film with a fork on the side of the dish farthest away from you. Lids should always be lifted using oven gloves, and then always lifted *away* from you to avoid steam burns.

5 Cooking complete meals: the secret of cooking complete meals is to have everything ready prepared before beginning to cook so that it is then just a succession of dishes in and out of the microwave.

Always cook jacket potatoes before the main course as these can be wrapped in foil and they will stay very hot for about 25 minutes.

Choose vegetables with similar cooking times so that they can be cooked together. Good combinations are:

Sprouts, carrots, leeks, cauliflower, baby corn.

Or, potatoes, swede, parsnip.

Or, peas and sweetcorn kernels.

Do not mix fresh and frozen vegetables; however, two frozen vegetables can be cooked together.

Vegetables cook better in a flat-bottomed dish rather than a bowl or basin, but if you only have a basin – that will be fine. Boiled potatoes, though may need to be stirred during cooking or those on top will go waxy.

Add two to three 15 ml tablespoons cold water to fresh vegetables. Always cover the dish with a lid or with clear film.

When cooking fish dinners it is better to cook all the vegetables before the fish, as the fish cooks quickly and needs little or no stand time. Vegetables reheat quickly and with better results than fish.

6 Reheating meals on plates: complete servings can be covered with clear film and chilled until required. For successful reheating, make sure to place the foods around the outside of the plate. Do not pile everything in the centre. Flatten piles of mashed potato and dot with a little butter. Pour a little gravy over the meat to keep it moist. If you do not like gravy, then sprinkle a few drops of water on the meat to keep it moist. Small, delicate items such as peas which reheat quickly can be put at the centre of the plate.

Reheat meals on plates one at a time on full power for 2 to 3 minutes. Feel the bottom of the plate and, if this is warm, the meal should be hot enough to eat.

7 Casseroles and stews: a small plate placed on top of the meat and vegetables in a casserole will keep them under the gravy and prevent overcooking of the pieces that would normally rise above the surface of the gravy. It will also eliminate the need to stir food during cooking.

For slow cooking, always use 600 ml/1 pint stock to 450 g/1 lb meat and vegetables. Allow an extra 300 ml/$\frac{1}{2}$ pint of stock for each extra 450 g/1 lb meat or vegetables.

Use hot stock rather than cold. This saves more time. Cook the casserole on full power for 10 minutes, then on Simmer (or Defrost in a 2-power microwave cooker) for 60 to 90 minutes. This timing may sound quite long for a microwave but remember the only way to tenderise a tough cut is by long, slow cooking. This is equivalent to 3 hours in the conventional cooker. The microwave also uses less fuel.

Stews and casseroles are always best thickened at the end of cooking.

Vegetables used in a stew should be cut into small dice or slices.

8 Individual steamed sponge puddings can be cooked in teacups, as you will see in the recipes. Allow 1 to 1$\frac{1}{2}$ minutes for 1 pudding. For two cups, allow 2 to 2$\frac{1}{2}$ minutes on full power.

13

9 Decreasing recipe servings: if you wish to reduce a recipe from 4 to 2 helpings, halve all the ingredients listed. To reduce 4 to 1 helping, quarter all the ingredients listed. Choose a dish that is proportionately smaller than the one recommended in the recipe. Do take care to see that it is deep enough for the food not to boil over.

Use the power setting recommended in the original recipe. For one serving, allow a quarter to one-third of the time recommended for four. For two servings, allow one-third to two-thirds of the recommended time.

If the original recipe states *stir frequently*, one stir for the reduced amounts is all that is required. For most recipes, providing you use the correct dish and your microwave cooker has a turntable, you will not need to stir. For cookers without a turntable, stir the food or turn the dish through 90° halfway through the cooking time.

10 Lastly, do not try to cook the following in your microwave as they won't be successful:

Yorkshire puddings and batter mixes. They require hot air to crisp and brown them which can only be provided in a conventional cooker.

Choux pastry. This can be made but not baked in the microwave because it needs hot air to crisp and brown it.

Deep fat frying. There is no temperature control.

Reheating in narrow-necked bottles, e.g. tomato sauce bottles, as they easily shatter when the contents expand unevenly – as they can do in a microwave.

Chapter 1

Breakfast

PROPER PORRIDGE

Enough for 1 large or 2 small portions, this is the way it is made and eaten by all Scots!

40 g/1½ oz medium oatmeal
300 ml/½ pint water
2 generous pinches of salt

1 To shorten the cooking time, soak the oatmeal overnight in the cold water.
2 Next morning, bring the porridge up to boiling point, turn the heat down and cook gently until it is thick. Stir often to make sure there are no lumps.
3 Add the salt and serve with cold milk or cream – never with sugar, nor treacle, God forbid!

Grace Mulligan

1 In a 1-litre/1¾-pint basin, soak the oatmeal overnight in the cold water.
2 Next morning, heat the porridge on full power for 2½ minutes, stirring halfway through and then again at the end of cooking.
3 Let it stand for 5 minutes, then add salt and stir well. Serve with cold milk or cream.

PORRIDGE WITH ROLLED OATS

For 2.

50 g/2 oz rolled oats or porridge oats
300 ml/½ pint cold water
Salt to taste

Traditional method
1 Stir the rolled oats into the cold water in a saucepan. Add salt to taste.
2 Bring up to a boil, stir well, then lower the heat and simmer for 5

minutes, stirring occasionally. Serve with cold milk.

'Fast' method
1 Stir the rolled oats into 240 ml/8 fl oz boiling water. Add salt.
2 Boil for 1 minute, then remove from the heat and leave, covered, for 5 minutes. Stir well before serving.

Grace Mulligan

PORRIDGE FOR ONE

25 g/1 oz porridge oats
240 ml/7 fl oz water
A pinch of salt

1 Combine all the ingredients in a deep cereal bowl or small basin. Cook on full power for 4 to 5 minutes, stirring once during cooking and once at the end.
2 Let it stand for 2 minutes before eating – or it will burn your tongue!

HOME-MADE BREAKFAST CEREAL

Delicious served with stewed or fresh fruits, yoghurt and milk or fruit juice to moisten. If you find this muesli 'chewy', try soaking each helping in a little apple juice overnight. Makes 700g/1½ lb.

50 g/2 oz dried apricots
25 g/1 oz nuts
75 g/3 oz raisins
300 g/12 oz porridge oats
50 g/2 oz wheatmeal, or flaked wheat, barley or rye
25 g/1 oz bran (optional*)
50 g/2 oz soft brown sugar (optional*)

* *If you are not fond of bran, which is simply the husk of ground grains like wheat, oats, barley and rye, it can be left out. When the cereal already*

*contains whole rolled or flaked grains,
as this one does, there is no dietary need
for extra bran. As for sugar – it would
be better to manage without it or add a
very little to taste when serving.*

1 Cut apricots in small pieces. Chop nuts.
2 Mix all ingredients together and store in a covered jar or tin. It keeps for several weeks.

Mrs Margaret Walkinshaw
Ballymena, Co. Antrim, N. Ireland

FARMHOUSE KITCHEN SCRAMBLED EGG

For 1.

1 large egg
1 large tablespoon of milk
Salt and pepper
15 g/½ oz butter or margarine
1 round of hot buttered
  wholemeal toast

1 Beat the egg and milk together with a fork and add salt and pepper.
2 Melt the butter or margarine in a small, heavy pan, pour in the beaten egg and stir gently over a moderate heat until the egg is creamy.
3 Pile the creamy egg on to the toast.

Variation: for a more substantial dish for later in the day, add any of the following as the egg is cooking:

50 g/2 oz chopped and grilled
  bacon
50 g/2 oz cooked prawns
40 g/1½ oz chopped boiled ham
1 tablespoons chopped chives or
  parsley
1 anchovy fillet, finely chopped

Grace Mulligan

 Microwave

*As eggs differ in size, and the
temperature varies depending on
whether they are stored in the
refrigerator or at room temperature, and
taking personal preferences into account,
it's hard to give precise cooking times
for microwaving scrambled egg.
However, you will soon learn how long
to allow to suit your taste.*

1 In a small basin, beat together the egg and milk. Season with a little salt and pepper. Put in the butter.
2 Heat on full power for 30 seconds and then stir well. Heat on full power for a further 15 to 30 seconds, then stir. The scrambled egg should be quite creamy as it will continue to cook slightly and firm up after it is taken out of the cooker.
3 Pile the egg on to the toast.

For a more substantial dish, add bacon, prawns etc as above. Add them to the egg when it is stirred after the first 30 seconds. You may need to give an extra 15 seconds to the cooking time. Sprinkle with chopped parsley.

POACHED EGG

*For a really tender, softly cooked egg,
use this old foolproof method.*

Water
A generous pinch of salt
A few drops of vinegar
1 egg, as fresh as possible
1 slice of thick hot buttered toast

1 Put the water, salt and vinegar into a pan and heat to boiling point.
2 Break the egg into a wetted saucer, then slide the egg into the water.
3 Bring back to boiling point, remove the pan from the heat, cover with a lid and leave for 2 minutes until the egg is set.

4 Drain on a fish slice, shaking off as much water as possible. Serve on hot buttered toast.

Variation: for a change, when it's not for breakfast, spread the toast with a little butter and one of the following before adding the egg:

Yeast extract (e.g. Marmite)
Mango chutney
Good-flavoured pickle
Cheese spread

Grace Mulligan

Like scrambled eggs by microwave, you gradually get used to knowing how long it will take. The size of the egg and the temperature at which you store them both affect the timing.

1 Lightly butter a ramekin dish and half-fill it with boiling water. Add a shake of salt and 1 teaspoon vinegar. Heat on full power for 30 seconds until the water is just boiling.
2 Crack an egg into the boiling water and, with a wooden cocktail stick, pierce the yolk once and the white several times. This is to prevent it exploding. Cover the dish with clear film and heat on full power for 30 to 60 seconds, but check it every 30 seconds. If the egg is very large or very cold it will take longer. The white should just be set when you stop the cooking.
3 Leave it covered for 2 minutes then drain away the water and have it on toast as Grace suggests.

SPICED APPLE AND YOGHURT DRINK
A pleasant, creamy drink for 1.

A 150-g/5-oz carton of natural yoghurt
About 100 ml/3 fl oz unsweetened apple juice
A tiny pinch of ground cloves or nutmeg

1 Use chilled yoghurt and apple juice, whisk together with spice and drink while it is still frothy.

Mrs Powell
Enfield, Middlesex

Chapter 2

Soups, Starters and Snacks

SMOKY BACON AND SWEETCORN SOUP

This quickly made soup is a nourishing snack when served with fresh crusty bread rolls. Freezes well, before yoghurt and bacon are added. For 2.

2 rashers rindless smoked
  streaky bacon
15 g/½ oz butter or margarine
1 onion, finely chopped
450 ml/¾ pint milk and water,
  mixed
1 chicken stock cube
1 bay leaf
A 325-g/12-oz can of creamed
  sweetcorn *
Salt and pepper
2 tablespoons cornflour mixed
  with 2 tablespoons cold water
2 tablespoons natural yoghurt

* *If you cannot buy this, make your own by putting drained canned sweetcorn kernels through the liquidiser.*

1 Grill the bacon until crisp. Allow to cool, then crush into little pieces.
2 Melt butter or margarine in a saucepan, adding a little of the melted bacon fat, if you like. Add onion, then cover and cook very slowly so the onion just sweats for 5 minutes – until soft but not brown.
3 Pour milk and water into the pan, crumble in the stock cube, add the bay leaf, sweetcorn, salt and pepper.
4 Stir in the cornflour mixture and bring the soup to the boil, stirring all the time. Boil for 1 minute.
5 Remove the bay leaf and ladle the soup into hot bowls.
6 Spoon yoghurt over each bowl and scatter with crumbled bacon.

Grace Mulligan

CHICKEN AND SWEETCORN SOUP

A delicately flavoured and nourishing soup. It takes a bit of practice to master the addition of the egg! For 2.

1 small chicken breast,
  uncooked, on the bone
450 ml/¾ pint chicken stock
1 dessertspoon cornflour mixed
  with 1 tablespoon cold water
100 g/4 oz creamed sweetcorn (see
  previous recipe)
Salt and pepper to taste
1 large egg
1 spring onion, trimmed and
  chopped

1 Remove skin and bone from chicken and use to make the stock (or use a stock cube).
2 Chop chicken flesh, then mince or process it.
3 Put the stock in a saucepan with the cornflour mixture, sweetcorn, salt and pepper and stir continuously until it boils. Cook for 2 minutes.
4 Add the minced chicken and reheat until the soup boils. Cook for 1 minute.
5 Lightly beat the egg and pour it into the boiling soup in a fine stream, pulling the strands of egg over the surface of the soup with chopsticks or the prongs of a fork in a slow, circular movement. Do not stir vigorously!
6 When the egg has set, ladle soup into hot bowls and scatter with chopped spring onion.

Jennie Siew Lee Cook
York

FISHERMAN'S CHOWDER

This substantial fish soup makes a filling main meal served with hot, crusty French bread. Makes enough for 2 or 3.

15 g/½ oz butter or margarine
1 small onion, thinly sliced
25 g/1 oz rindless bacon, chopped
2 sticks celery, trimmed and
  chopped
Half a small red pepper, cored
  and diced

125 g/4 oz potatoes, peeled and cut
  into 7-mm/$\frac{1}{4}$-inch dice
300 ml/$\frac{1}{2}$ pint fish or chicken
  stock
350 g/12 oz smoked and white
  haddock (or whiting), skinned
  and cubed
150 ml/$\frac{1}{4}$ pint semi-skimmed
  milk
A 15 ml tablespoon cornflour
Salt
Freshly ground black pepper
Chopped parsley for serving

1 Melt the butter or margarine in a
large saucepan and fry the onion,
bacon, celery, red pepper and potato
for 5 minutes.
2 Pour in the stock, lower the heat
and simmer until potatoes are just
tender, then add the fish.
3 Mix together the milk and
cornflour and stir it into the soup.
Bring to the boil, stirring
continuously, then simmer for 5
minutes. Season to taste and serve.

Yvonne Coull
Sea Fish Industry Authority,
Edinburgh

Microwave ≈≈≈≈≈≈≈

1 Put the butter, onion, bacon,
celery, pepper and potato into a 1.4-
litre/3-pint casserole dish. Cook on
full power for 5 minutes, stirring
once.
2 Add the fish and stock, stir well.
Cover with a lid or clear film and
cook on full power for 4 to 5
minutes. The potatoes should then be
tender and the fish cooked.
3 Mix the cornflour to a paste with a
little of the milk. Uncover the fish,
stir in the cornflour paste and the
remaining milk. Cook, uncovered, on
full power for 3 to 5 minutes, stirring
once. The soup should have
thickened.
4 Season lightly, sprinkle with
chopped parsley and serve.

TIP
Instead of using stock and milk with
cornflour to thicken, use a 300 g/10
oz can of condensed asparagus soup.
Stir the soup into the fish, cover and
cook on full power for 5 to 6
minutes. Stir, then serve.

Yvonne Hamlett
Haddenham, Buckinghamshire

CARROT AND
ORANGE SOUP

*Enough for 4: 2 hot servings on the first
day, 2 cold the next. Especially good
liquidised, it freezes well for 2 or 3
weeks. Serve with croûtons or
wholemeal bread.*

15 g/1$\frac{1}{2}$ oz butter or
  margarine
1 small onion, chopped
A clove of garlic, crushed
325 g/12 oz carrots, peeled or
  scrubbed and chopped
1 teaspoon dried chopped
  tarragon *or* 2 teaspoons fresh
  chopped tarragon
600 ml/1 pint chicken stock
Finely grated rind and juice of 1
  orange
Salt and pepper
2 tablespoons natural yoghurt

1 In a fairly large saucepan, melt the
butter or margarine and cook the
onion over a low heat until soft but
not browned.
2 Add the garlic and carrot and cook
slowly for a few minutes.
3 Sprinkle in the tarragon, then
pour in the chicken stock, add orange
rind and juice and seasoning.
4 Bring the soup to the boil, then
cover and simmer for 30 minutes or
until the carrots are soft.
5 Serve the soup as it is, or purée in
a liquidiser or food processor.
6 Pour the soup into warmed bowls
and spoon over the yoghurt.

Grace Mulligan

1 Put the butter and onion in a 1.4–litre/3-pint dish. Heat on full power for 3 minutes.
2 Add the garlic and carrot. Pour over orange juice. Cover with a lid or clear film and cook on full power for 6 minutes.
3 Tip the cooked carrots into a liquidiser or processor and blend with 150 ml/$\frac{1}{4}$ pint chicken stock until smooth.
4 Tip back into the dish. Stir in the tarragon, orange rind and remaining stock. Heat on full power for 6 minutes. Stir, then lightly season and serve in warm bowls, with yoghurt.

CREAM OF LENTIL SOUP

This makes 6 helpings, but it freezes well for 2 to 3 weeks. You'll find a liquidiser useful.

225 g/8 oz red lentils
2 sticks of celery
2 large carrots, scrubbed but not peeled
2 medium onions
A clove of garlic, peeled
2 tablespoons safflower or other good-quality oil
2 tablespoons soy sauce
Salt and pepper
1.25 litres/2 pints water

1 Wash lentils and pick them over for stones.
2 Chop vegetables and fry in the oil in a large saucepan for 5 minutes.
3 Add all the remaining ingredients, bring to the boil, then lower the heat and simmer for 45 minutes. Or pressure-cook for 8 minutes.
4 Liquidise the soup – it should be thick and creamy. Adjust seasoning to taste and serve.

Janet Horsley
Leeds, Yorkshire

MUSHROOM SOUP

For this you need a liquidiser or processor. Serve with hot crusty rolls, or croûtons. Enough for 2.

350 g/12 oz dark flat mushrooms, washed and finely chopped
1 onion, finely chopped
25 g/1 oz butter
25 g/1 oz flour
450 ml/$\frac{3}{4}$ pint chicken stock
Salt
Freshly ground black pepper
2 tablespoons cream

1 Put the mushrooms into a saucepan with the onion and butter. Cover and cook very gently over low heat for 10 minutes, shaking the pan from time to time.
2 Stir in the flour, then add the stock. Bring to the boil and simmer for 10 minutes.
3 Allow the soup to cook a little longer, then liquidise.
4 Reheat the soup, season to taste and serve in warm bowls with a swirl of cream in each.

Julie Cookson
Leeds, Yorkshire

 Microwave

Use hot stock for this.

1 Put the mushrooms, onion and butter into a 1.5-litre/3-pint casserole; heat on full power for 5 minutes.
2 Stir in the flour and gradually blend in the hot stock. Heat on full power for 2 minutes, stir, then continue to heat on full power for a further 3 minutes. Allow to cool slightly.
3 Put the soup in a processor or liquidiser and blend until smooth.
4 Tip the soup back into the casserole. Season and heat for 1 to 2 minutes on full power.
5 Serve as above.

22

PARSNIP SOUP

Very sustaining; keeps a day or two in the fridge. It freezes well. Makes 2 to 3 helpings.

25 g/1 oz butter or margarine
1 large onion, finely chopped
½ level teaspoon curry powder
225 g/8 oz parsnips, scrubbed and diced
125 g/4 oz potato, peeled and diced
600 ml/1 pint hot light stock – a chicken or vegetable stock cube will do
Pepper and salt
Single cream (optional)

1 Melt the butter or margarine in a saucepan and fry onion gently until just softening.
2 Stir in the curry powder and cook gently for 2 or 3 minutes.
3 Toss the parsnip and potato with the onion over gentle heat for 2 or 3 minutes more.
4 Add stock, bring to the boil and simmer soup for about 20 minutes or until vegetables are tender.

The soup is nice to have in its chunky state. For a soft, creamy soup, liquidise and reheat, adding pepper and a little salt if necessary. Add a swirl of cream to each bowlful. Alternatively, strain off liquid into a jug, mash vegetables with a potato masher, then stir stock back in, adjusting seasoning to taste.

Mrs Thelma E Boyne
Aberdeen

Microwave

1 Put the butter and onion into a 1.5-litre/3-pint casserole dish. Heat on full power for 2 minutes.
2 Stir in the parsnip and potato. Add 150 ml/¼ pint hot stock and cover the dish with a lid. Cook on full power for 10 minutes, stirring once.

2 Put the vegetables and stock into a liquidiser or processor and blend until smooth. Return to the casserole.
3 Stir in the curry powder and the remaining hot stock. Season and heat on full power for 4 to 5 minutes, stirring once.
4 Serve in warm bowls with a swirl of cream.

ONION SOUP WITH CHEESE TOAST

This nourishing soup freezes well: a use for stock derived from boiling a Ham Shank (page 67). Makes 4 to 5 helpings.

40 g/1½ oz butter or margarine
1 tablespoon oil
450 g/1 lb onions, peeled and thinly sliced
900 ml/1½ pints ham stock
1 teaspoon yeast extract (e.g. Marmite)
Freshly ground black pepper
1 tablespoon pasta shells or alphabet letters
2 slices wholemeal bread
50 g/2 oz grated Cheddar cheese

1 In a large pan, melt the butter, add the oil and fry the onion very slowly until soft and light brown, stirring often. This will take about 15 minutes.
2 Add the stock, yeast extract and a little black pepper.
3 Bring to the boil, cover with a lid, then simmer for 20 minutes.
4 Add the pasta 5 or 10 minutes before the end of cooking time.
5 To serve – toast the bread under the grill on one side only. Cover the untoasted sides with the cheese and cook under the grill until the cheese has melted and browned. Cut in fingers and serve with the soup.

Grace Mulligan

PEA AND MINT SOUP

For 2: this soup makes a refreshing start to a meal; it needs quite a lot of mint, but at least this is easy to grow. Dried mint could be used. The soup may be served chilled, and it also freezes well.

15 g/½ oz butter
1 small onion, finely chopped
225 g/8 oz frozen peas
2 potatoes, peeled and diced
600 ml/1 pint chicken stock
12 stems of fresh mint, or try 2
    teaspoons dried mint
Salt and pepper
A pinch of sugar
Whipped cream and sprigs of
    mint to garnish

1 Melt the butter in a saucepan, add the onion and cook until soft.
2 Add the peas, potatoes, stock, mint and seasonings and bring up to the boil. Cover with a lid and simmer for 25 minutes.
3 Purée the soup in a blender or food processor, then sieve it to remove the mint stems and to ensure it is completely smooth.
4 Reheat the soup and decorate each bowl with a spoonful of whipped cream and a sprig of fresh mint.

Angela Henderson
Fleet, Hampshire

SPICED VEGETABLE SOUP

The flavour of ginger in this soup is delicious. Serve it hot with croûtons or garlic toast and a dash of Tabasco sauce. Freezes well, and makes plenty for 2 or 3.

100 g/4 oz chopped mixed
    vegetables, fresh or frozen
1 small onion, chopped
A 7-mm/¼-inch piece of fresh
    ginger, peeled and chopped
A clove of garlic, crushed
A 200 g/8 oz can of tomatoes
600 ml/1 pint water
1 vegetable stock cube
2 teaspoons ghee or butter
½ teaspoon cumin seeds
Salt and pepper
Lemon juice to taste

1 Put the mixed vegetables in a saucepan with the onion, ginger, garlic, tomatoes and water. Crumble in the stock cube and bring to the boil. Cover with a lid and simmer for 30 minutes.
2 Purée the soup in a liquidiser or processor and return it to a clean saucepan.
3 Heat the ghee or butter in a frying pan and when very hot, quickly fry the cumin seeds.
4 Add the cumin to the soup, season and add lemon juice to taste before serving.

Nirmal Singh
Nuneaton, Warwickshire

WATERCRESS SOUP

This is a beautiful green, with a delicate flavour –good enough for a special occasion. It freezes well. For 2.

1 small onion, finely chopped
15 g/½ oz butter
1 to 2 bunches of watercress, well
    washed
15 g/½ oz flour
450 ml/¾ pint chicken stock,
    made from a cube if necessary
Salt
Freshly ground black pepper
A grating of nutmeg
A little cream for serving

1 Fry the onion gently in the butter until soft.
2 Add the watercress, put a lid on the pan, lower the heat and let it cook just to sweat it for 5 minutes. Shake the pan from time to time.
3 Stir in the flour and stock, bring to

the boil and cook for 5 minutes more.

4 Liquidise the soup until it is quite smooth, then return it to the pan to reheat.

5 Season to taste with salt, pepper and nutmeg.

6 Serve the soup in hot bowls, pouring in a swirl of cream at the last moment.

Mary Watts

CHILLED TOMATO AND APPLE SOUP

Always serve a chilled soup in smaller bowls than your usual everyday ones. Make this when fresh tomatoes are plentiful and taste the flavour of real tomato soup. It makes 4 helpings and freezes well.

450 g/1 lb fresh ripe tomatoes, chopped
225 g/8 oz onion, chopped
450 g/1 lb cooking apples, peeled, cored and chopped
600 ml/1 pint chicken stock
Salt
Freshly ground black pepper
Finely chopped basil or chives to garnish

1 Put all the ingredients, except the basil or chives, into a saucepan. Bring to the boil, then lower the heat and simmer together for 20 minutes, or until the onions are soft.

2 Purée the soup in a liquidiser or processor, then sieve it to remove the tomato skins and pips and to ensure the soup is completely smooth. (Alternatively, you can skin the tomatoes and remove the pips before cooking them. See Tip, page 26.)

3 Leave to cool, then garnish the soup with the basil or chives.

TIP

If you don't have a liquidiser or food processor, mash up the soup in the pan with a potato masher, then sieve it.

Grace Mulligan

 Microwave

1 Put the onion in a large mixing bowl with four 15 ml tablespoons of the stock. Heat on full power for 3 minutes, stirring once. The onions should be soft.

2 Add the tomatoes and apples. Cover the dish with clear film and cook on full power for 8 to 10 minutes.

3 Purée the soup in a liquidiser or processor and then sieve it into the cleaned bowl. This will ensure it is completely smooth.

4 Stir in the chicken stock. Chill, then serve the soup garnished with basil or chives.

QUICK CHILLED TOMATO SOUP

For 2. Easy as well as quick to make – but you do need a liquidiser or processor for this one. Serve it with wholemeal bread.

25 g/1 oz canned sweetcorn kernels, drained
25 g/1 oz green pepper or courgette
100 g/4 oz tomatoes, peeled (see next page)
1 teaspoon wine vinegar or lemon juice
1 tablespoon oil
1 shallot or half a small onion, chopped
210 ml/7 fl oz tomato juice
Salt and pepper
Chopped fresh parsley or mint to garnish

1 Put all the ingredients, except the parsley or mint, into a liquidiser or processor and work until well blended. If you want a completely

smooth soup, sieve it.
2 Chill, then serve the soup garnished with parsley or mint.

Dilwen Phillips
Gileston, South Glamorgan

CHILLED SOUP WITH AVOCADO

This variation on the classic Spanish Gazpacho has a very pleasant avocado flavour. It keeps in the refrigerator for a day or two; you'll need a liquidiser or processor for the right consistency. Makes 2 or 3 generous helpings.

450 ml/¾ pint chicken stock, either home-made or from a stock cube
Half a small onion, chopped
Half a small green pepper, flesh only, chopped
2 small tomatoes, skinned (see below), and quartered
A 2.5-cm/1 to 2-inch piece of cucumber, peeled and sliced
Half a ripe avocado, peeled and sliced
1 teaspoon white wine vinegar
2 large tablespoons natural yoghurt
Salt and pepper

1 Prepare the stock and let it cool.
2 Put onion, green pepper, tomato, cucumber, avocado, vinegar, yoghurt and half the stock in the liquidiser or processor and run it until smooth.
3 Empty the soup into a large serving bowl or a jug and stir in the remaining stock. Season to taste and serve chilled with hot rolls and butter.

Grace Mulligan

TIP
To skin tomatoes, put them in a basin, cover with boiling water and wait 30 seconds. Then drain and cover with cold water. After a minute, the skin should easily peel off.

26

MINTED CUCUMBER MOUSSE

Simon Dunn, 14, came third in the 1987 Junior Cook of the Year competition organised by the Young Cooks' Club of Great Britain with this delicious starter. (See page 179 for his complete, three-course menu.) This keeps for a day in the fridge; serve it with brown bread and butter or rolls. For 2.

7.5 cm/3 inches of cucumber, peeled and finely diced
Salt
1½ level teaspoons gelatine
60 ml/2 fl oz chicken stock
100 g/4 oz cream cheese
A small pinch of ground mace
1 tablespoon chopped fresh mint
2 teaspoons wine or cider vinegar
1 teaspoon caster sugar
60 ml/2 fl oz double cream
1 egg white
A little oil
Cucumber curls and sprigs of mint to decorate

1 Put the cucumber in a sieve over a bowl and sprinkle with salt. This will draw out some of the liquid. Leave it for 30 minutes, then rinse the cucumber pieces very thoroughly in cold water and drain well on kitchen paper.
2 In a small saucepan, sprinkle the gelatine over the chicken stock, leave it for a few minutes, then gently warm it until all the gelatine has dissolved. Let it cool a little.
3 Beat the cream cheese with the mace, mint, vinegar, sugar and the gelatine mixture. Stir in the cucumber and put aside until it begins to set slightly.
4 Whip the cream until just thick, then fold it into the cucumber mixture.
5 Whisk egg white stiffly and fold into the mousse.
6 Lightly oil a small ring mould or 2 ramekins, pour in the mousse and chill until set.

7 Turn it out and decorate with cucumber curls and sprigs of mint.

Simon Dunn
Bickley, Kent

EGGS IN A FOREST

This luxurious starter, with the other two dishes listed on page 179, won Sally Wilson, 14, the title of Junior Cook of the Year, 1987. It makes a good light meal with crusty rolls or toast. For 2.

3 tablespoons good olive oil
2 garlic cloves, crushed
1 large green pepper, chopped
225 g/8 oz chopped courgettes
½ teaspoon grated nutmeg
Freshly ground pepper
Salt
Half a small cauliflower
Juice of half a lemon
A pinch of chilli powder
1 rounded teaspoon caraway seeds
2 eggs
Parsley to garnish

1 Heat half the oil over a medium heat. Add garlic and green pepper, cook over low heat until the pepper has softened, stirring often.
2 Add courgettes and cook for 3 to 5 minutes, stirring carefully, until soft but still bright green.
3 Pour into a liquidiser or processor and process until smooth. Add nutmeg, pepper and salt. Spoon purée into a large, shallow serving dish.
4 Divide cauliflower into small florets; boil until just tender.
5 Put the lemon juice, chilli powder, caraway seed, salt and 4 teaspoons olive oil into a bowl. Add hot cauliflower and coat with the dressing. Leave to cool.
6 Soft-poach the eggs (page 17).
7 When everything is cold, place the eggs on the green purée surrounded by cauliflower florets. Garnish with parsley.

Sally Wilson
Pinner, Middlesex

 Microwave

1 Put half the oil in a basin with the garlic and green pepper; heat on full power for 3 to 5 minutes, until soft.
2 Add the courgettes and heat on full power for 2 minutes.
3 Pour into a liquidiser or processor and blend until smooth. Season with the nutmeg, pepper and salt. Pour the purée into a large shallow dish.
4 Divide the cauliflower into florets. Put it into a small bowl and sprinkle with three 15 ml tablespoons cold water. Cover with clear film and cook on full power for 4 minutes.
5 Put the lemon juice, chilli powder, caraway seed, salt and 4 teaspoons olive oil into a bowl. Drain cauliflower and add to the dressing, stirring well so that it is coated. Leave to cool.
6 Meanwhile poach the eggs, following instructions on page 17, but heating the dishes for 30 to 60 seconds, and cooking the eggs for 1 to 1½ minutes, checking every 30 seconds. The whites should just be set. Remove film and cool. Drain off the water.
7 When everything is cold, slide the eggs on to the green purée. Surround with cauliflower florets and garnish with parsley.

PEAR WITH STILTON SAUCE

A sophisticated starter for 2. The sauce can be made in advance, but prepare the pear and assemble the dish at the last minute.

50 g/2 oz blue Stilton cheese
1 to 2 tablespoons cream or top-of-the-milk
1 large ripe pear
Toasted flaked almonds*
Lettuce leaves and brown bread and butter or Melba Toast (page 29) to serve

* Flaked almonds can be toasted under the grill but watch them as they easily burn.

1 Grate the cheese and mix in enough cream or milk to make a thick sauce.
2 Peel the pear, cut it in half and remove the core with a teaspoon.
3 Place each pear flat-side down and cut it into thin slices.
4 Arrange the slices like a fan on 2 small plates and spoon over the Stilton sauce. Scatter the almonds on top.
5 Garnish the plates with lettuce leaves and serve with brown bread and butter or toast.

Grace Mulligan

SMOKED MACKEREL AND LEMON DIP

For 2 or more.

225 g/8 oz 'hot' smoked
   mackerel fillets *
15 g/½ oz butter or
   polyunsaturated margarine

Half an onion, finely chopped
1 teaspoon horseradish relish
1 teaspoon lemon juice
3 to 4 tablespoons soured cream
   (natural yoghurt is a suitable
   substitute)
Freshly ground black pepper
Lemon slices to garnish

* Hot smoked mackerel means that the fillets have actually been cooked during the smoking process.

1 Remove skin and bones from the fish.
2 In a small saucepan, melt the butter or margarine. Add the onion and cook until soft.
3 Stir in the mackerel, horseradish and lemon juice, and heat gently for 1 to 2 minutes.
4 Allow to cool, then blend with the soured cream and ground black pepper in a liquidiser or processor until smooth and creamy. Spoon into a serving dish and chill before serving with chunks of colourful fresh vegetables and fingers of toast.

Yvonne Coull
Sea Fish Industry Authority,
Edinburgh

Microwave

1 Remove the skin and bones from the fish.
2 Put the butter or margarine in a bowl with the onion and cook on full power for 3 minutes until the onion is soft.
3 Stir in the mackerel, horseradish and lemon juice, and heat on full power for a further 1½ minutes.
4 Cool, then blend with the soured cream and ground black pepper in a food processor until smooth and creamy. Spoon into a serving dish and chill before serving with chunks of colourful fresh vegetables and fingers of toast.

QUICK LIVER PATE

For 1 or 2, but easy to make more. Particularly nice made with chicken livers.

15 g/½ oz butter
50 g/2 oz liver
25 g/1 oz cooked ham
Salt and pepper
A few drops of soy sauce

1 Melt the butter in a small pan and fry the liver until cooked, but not dry.
2 Put the liver and butter into a food processor or liquidiser and add the remaining ingredients. Process until smooth.
3 Put the pâté into a small dish, cover with clear film and chill slightly in the refrigerator.
4 Serve with toast, Melba toast (see right) or rolls.

Dilwen Phillips
Gileston, South Glamorgan

Microwave

1 Cut the liver into small pieces. Put it with the butter into a small 600-

ml/1-pint basin. Cover with clear film and cook on full power for 1 minute; allow to cool slightly.
2 Tip the liver and butter into a food processor or liquidiser with the remaining ingredients. Blend until smooth.
3 Put the pâté in a small dish, cover with film and chill.

The pâté can also be topped with a little melted butter — this will stop the surface from drying.

TUNA FISH PATE

The pâté freezes well. It tastes best served at room temperature, with toast, rolls or oat cakes. For a change it may be served in lemon shells. For 2.

85 g/3½ oz can of tuna fish in oil
50 g/2 oz butter, softened
2 teaspoons lemon juice
½ teaspoon anchovy essence
2 tablespoons cream or top-of-the-milk
A pinch of cayenne pepper
Salt and pepper
Cucumber slices for decoration

1 Drain the tuna and mash it in a bowl, gradually working in the softened butter.
2 When thoroughly mixed, stir in the lemon juice, anchovy essence, cream and seasonings. Alternatively, place all the ingredients in a liquidiser or processor and blend until thoroughly mixed and smooth.
3 Put the pâté in a small bowl or individual ramekins and decorate with twists of cucumber.

Angela Henderson
Fleet, Hampshire

MELBA TOAST

Lovely with pâté or soups.

2 large slices white or
  wholemeal bread

1 Toast both sides of the bread until nicely golden, then carefully trim off the crusts.
2 Hold the toasted bread flat down on a wooden board with the palm of your hand and, using a sharp knife, cut through horizontally to make two slices.
3 Return to the grill and toast the uncooked sides until crisp and golden.
4 Cool and store in an airtight tin until needed.

Grace Mulligan

STUFFED MUSHROOMS

For 2.

10 medium mushrooms
75 g/3 oz smooth pâté (try Quick Liver Pâté, page 29)
Seasoned flour
1 egg, lightly beaten
Dried breadcrumbs
Oil for frying
Tartare sauce, lemon wedges and slices of tomato and cucumber to serve

1 Wipe the mushrooms and remove the stalks. Using a knife, spread the pâté into the hollows, making it level with the caps.
2 Dip the mushrooms in seasoned flour, then coat with the beaten egg and finally the breadcrumbs.
3 Heat the oil and deep-fry the mushrooms for a few minutes until golden brown. Drain on kitchen paper, sprinkle lightly with salt and serve immediately.
4 Garnish with lemon wedges and slices of tomato and cucumber and serve the tartare sauce separately.

TIP
These mushrooms may be fried earlier in the day and reheated in the oven or microwave just prior to serving. The stalks from the mushrooms may be used in soups, stocks or casseroles.

Angela Henderson
Fleet, Hampshire

HOT SAVOURY TOASTED SNACKS FOR ONE

HAM

1 slice of bread, preferably wholemeal
Butter
1 small slice of cooked ham, finely chopped
1 pickled onion, chopped
25 g/1 oz grated cheese

1 Toast the bread on one side under the grill.
2 Turn the bread over and butter lightly, then cover first with the chopped ham, then the pickled onion, lastly the cheese.
3 Replace under the hot grill to reheat and melt the cheese. Eat at once.

FRANKFURTER

1 slice of bread, preferably wholemeal
Butter
1 Frankfurter sausage, cut in 1-cm/½-inch slices
1 mushroom, finely sliced
25 g/1 oz grated Edam cheese

1 Toast the bread on one side under the grill.
2 Turn the bread over and butter it lightly. Cover with sliced Frankfurter sausage, then the finely sliced mushroom and lastly the grated cheese.
3 Replace under the hot grill to reheat and melt the cheese. Eat at once.

CORNED BEEF

1 slice of bread, preferably
    wholemeal
Butter
1 finely sliced spring onion or 1
    teaspoon finely grated raw
    onion
1 tablespoon finely chopped sweet
    apple
1 slice corned beef
25 g/1 oz Edam cheese, grated

1 Toast the bread on one side under
the grill.
2 Turn it over and butter lightly,
then cover with the onion, the apple,
the corned beef and lastly the grated
cheese. Replace under the hot grill to
reheat and melt the cheese. Eat at
once.

FAST GARLIC TOAST
Rub a cut clove of garlic vigorously
over a slice of toast and butter. Eat
hot.

CREAM CHEESE AND CELERY
Beat finely chopped raw celery and
celery leaves into a well-seasoned
cream cheese and spread on cold
squares of toast. This makes a nice
savoury end to a meal.

Grace Mulligan

EGG-IN-A-NEST
*For 1: hot, quick, nourishing and
filling. Only the grill used.*

A thick slice of white or
    wholemeal bread
Grated Cheddar cheese
1 size 3 egg

1 Toast the bread on one side only.
2 On the untoasted side, make a
'wall' of grated cheese, leaving a well
in centre. Press cheese a little so that
the wall is firm enough to hold the
egg in.

3 Break the egg into the nest, then
return to a moderately hot grill until
the egg is lightly cooked and cheese
has melted. If grill is too hot, the top
of the egg goes hard before the rest
of it is cooked.

Mrs Mary Potts
Bedlington, Northumberland

HAM TITBITS
For 1 or 2 or more . . .

Slices of wholemeal or white
    bread
Thick slices of ham
Rings of well-drained canned
    pineapple
Grated Cheddar cheese

1 Toast the bread lightly on both
sides, then cut rings about 9 cm/3½
inches across with a biscuit cutter.
2 Now cut rings of ham.
3 Lay slices of ham on the toast.
(The offcuts can be tucked in, too.)
4 Place a pineapple ring on each
piece of ham and cover with grated
cheese.
5 Grill until cheese bubbles and
browns. Serve at once on warm
plates.

Save the toast offcuts to make
croûtons or breadcrumbs. For another
recipe using canned pineapple rings,
see page 55.

Mrs Riseborough,
Widdrington Station,
Northumberland.

CHEESE AND
SARDINE FINGERS
*For 2 but easy to make for 1. Nice
served with grilled tomatoes.*

A 120 g/4½ oz can of sardines
    in oil
25 g/1 oz fresh breadcrumbs,
    wholemeal or white
½ teaspoon made mustard

1 teaspoon Worcestershire sauce
50 g/2 oz grated cheese
Salt and pepper
4 slices of buttered toast

1 Drain oil from sardine can and mix
some of it with breadcrumbs,
mustard, sauce and cheese to form a
crumbly mixture.
2 Mash sardines and season well with
salt and pepper.
3 Spread sardines on toast, top with
crumbly mixture and grill.

Mrs Margaret Heywood
Todmorden, Yorkshire

WELSH RAREBIT
For 2, but easy to make for 1.

2 slices of wholemeal bread,
    toasted and warm
25 g/1 oz butter
100 g/4 oz strong Cheddar cheese,
    grated
1 teaspoon dry mustard
2 tablespoons beer
Salt and pepper

1 Put the slices of toast on to
heatproof plates.
2 In a small pan, melt the butter,
then add all the other ingredients,
stirring all the time with a wooden
spoon.
3 When the cheese mixture is hot,
but not boiling, pour it over the slices
of toast.
4 Put the toast under a very hot grill
to give a brown bubbly finish. Serve
at once.

Variation: top the cheese with a
poached egg or crispy bacon.

Grace Mulligan

SWEET TOASTED SNACKS

HOT CINNAMON TOAST

1 teaspoon ground cinnamon
2 teaspoons caster sugar
40 g/1½ oz soft butter
Toast

Mix together the cinnamon, sugar and
butter, then spread it on slices of hot
toast. This spiced butter can be kept
in the refrigerator for several days if
it is not all used up at once.

HOT DEMERARA TOAST

Toast
40 g/1½ oz soft butter
Demerara sugar

1 Butter warm slices of toast and
sprinkle over some Demerara sugar.
2 Cut into fingers and serve while
the sugar is still crunchy. Children
love this if coloured sugar crystals are
used instead of Demerara.

BANANA TOAST

Mash a banana with a dusting of
sugar and a dash of rum. Spread on
hot buttered toast. Eat instead of
pudding.

Grace Mulligan

CHICKEN PASTE
*Eat this like a pâté with fingers of
toast, or make a softer spread for
sandwiches. Excellent in sandwiches
with sliced cucumber. Keep refrigerated.*

75 g/3 oz very finely chopped or
    minced cooked chicken
1 tablespoon soft butter
Salt and pepper
Pinch of sage
Extra butter, melted, to seal pots

33

1 Mix all the ingredients, except melted butter, together until smooth.
2 Spoon into two small pots, smooth the surface and cover with a film of melted butter.
3 To make a softer paste, add a very little chicken stock.

Grace Mulligan

SMOKED FISH SPREAD

Can be spread on toast as a light meal or used as a sandwich filling. Keeps in refrigerator for several days. Makes enough for 2 or 3.

200 g/8 oz smoked fish fillet
2 tablespoons milk
50 g/2 oz margarine or butter
75 g/3 oz cream cheese
35 g/1½ oz fresh breadcrumbs
Grated rind and juice of half a
   lemon
Pepper

1 Cut fish into small pieces and put it in a small pan with the milk and margarine or butter. Cook gently for about 5 to 7 minutes, then mash with a fork and leave to cool.
2 Beat in the cream cheese, breadcrumbs, finely grated lemon rind and juice. Add pepper to taste but no salt.

If you think the fish may be too salty for you, put it in a pan, cover with water and bring to the boil. Then drain off the water and start at step 1.

Mrs Margaret Heywood
Todmorden, Yorkshire

 Microwave

1 Put the fish on a plate. Cover with clear film and cook on full power for 2 minutes. Cool slightly, flake with a fork, removing any skin or bones, then mash well.
2 Beat in the cream cheese, breadcrumbs, lemon rind and juice. Add pepper to taste but it is unlikely to need salt.

HAM SANDWICH SPREAD

This works well with meat from a Ham Shank (page 67). The proportions for this recipe don't really matter, but as a guide you need about twice as much ham as butter.

Cooked ham, very finely cut or
   minced
Soft butter
Freshly ground pepper
A little ham stock

Mix all the ingredients together until you have a moist, spreading consistency.

TIP
If you have a food processor you can make this ham spread in only a few seconds. It is delicious in sandwiches or rolls with a few slices of cucumber and it will keep for several days in a refrigerator.

Grace Mulligan

Chapter 3

Fish and Shellfish

SHRIMP-STUFFED TOMATOES

For 1 or 2, delicious!

2 large tomatoes
225 g/8 oz shrimps which, when
  peeled, give 50 g/2 oz for this
  recipe
25 g/1 oz white or wholemeal
  breadcrumbs
A little beaten egg, to bind
Salt and pepper
A little chopped parsley

1 Preheat over to moderate, Gas 4,
350°F, 180°C.
2 Cut tomatoes in half, scoop out a
little of the flesh and place them in
an ovenproof dish.
3 Mix the scooped-out tomato with
shrimps and breadcrumbs and use
just enough beaten egg to bind the
mixture. Season with salt, pepper and
parsley and fill the tomato halves.
4 Cook for 15 to 20 minutes until the
tomatoes are tender.

Mrs A. M. Taylor
Boyton, Suffolk

SEAFOOD WITH TAGLIATELLE

For 2. Make this for a special occasion.
Frozen cooked mussels may be used.

25 g/1 oz butter or margarine
Half an onion, finely chopped
Half a red pepper, deseeded and
  chopped
1 teaspoon chopped fresh basil
Freshly ground black pepper
A 400 g/14 oz can of tomatoes,
  chopped
1 wineglass of red wine
1 dessertspoon of tomato purée
A clove of garlic, crushed
125 g/4 oz tagliatelle verde
50 g/2 oz peeled prawns
125 g/4 oz white fish fillet, skinned
  and cut in 1.5-cm/¾-inch cubes

125 g/4 oz cooked shelled mussels
Chopped fresh basil to garnish

1 In a large saucepan, melt the butter
or margarine and fry the onion until
soft.
2 Add all the other ingredients except
the tagliatelle, fish and shellfish.
Simmer for 30 minutes with the lid
off.
3 Add the tagliatelle to the sauce and
simmer for a further 10 minutes, or
until the pasta is cooked.
4 Add the prawns, cubed white fish
and mussels, and continue to simmer
with the lid on for a further 3 to 4
minutes, until the white fish is
cooked.
5 Serve sprinkled with chopped fresh
basil.

Yvonne Coull
Sea Fish Industry Authority,
Edinburgh

 Microwave

1 Put the butter or margarine and
onion in a medium-sized bowl and
cook on full power for 2 minutes,
stirring halfway through.
2 Add all ingredients, except the fish,
cover and cook on full power for 5 to
6 minutes until the pasta is cooked.
3 Add the prawns, cubed white fish
and cooked shelled mussels; cover and
cook on full power for 2 minutes
more.
4 Serve sprinkled with fresh basil.

SPAGHETTI WITH MUSSELS

Delicious for 2.

900 g/2 lb fresh mussels,*
  scrubbed
175 g/6 oz spaghetti
2 to 3 tablespoons oil
1 medium onion, chopped
A clove of garlic, crushed

A 200 g/8 oz can of tomatoes, drained and chopped
½ teaspoon dried oregano
2 tablespoons chopped fresh parsley
Pepper and a little salt

225 g/8 oz frozen or canned mussels can be substituted.

1 If using fresh mussels, make sure that they are all tightly closed before cooking and discard any that do not shut when the shell is tapped. Put the cleaned mussels into a pan with 1 cm/½ inch of water, put on the lid and steam them for 6 to 7 minutes until they are open. If any do not open, discard them. Remove the meat from the shells.
2 Cook the spaghetti in plenty of boiling salted water with 1 tablespoon oil until tender. When cooked, drain and keep warm.
3 Heat 2 tablespoons oil and fry the onion and garlic until lightly browned. Pour in the tomatoes and cook for about 5 minutes, mashing them down so the mixture resembles a sauce.
4 Add the oregano and mussels and allow to warm through. Season to taste.
5 Pile the spaghetti on to a warmed dish and pour the mussels and sauce over the top. Sprinkle with chopped parsley.

David Shepperdson
Huddersfield, Yorkshire

SQUID WITH GREEN PEPPERS IN A BLACK BEAN SAUCE

The black bean sauce in this unusual recipe goes particularly well with squid. It is sold in Chinese and Oriental food shops. Serve this with boiled rice. For 2.

325 g/12 oz cleaned squid tubes
A clove of garlic, crushed
3 tablespoons water
2 tablespoons light soy sauce
1½ tablespoons black bean sauce
2 tablespoons oil
1 green pepper, deseeded, and cut into 2.5 cm/1 inch squares
6 spring onions, cut into 5 cm/2 inch pieces
1 teaspoon cornflour mixed with 2 teaspoons water
Pepper and a little salt

1 Cut the squid into pieces 2.5 cm/1 inch square and put them into a bowl with the garlic. Cover the bowl and leave it in a cool place for at least half an hour.
2 Mix together the water, soy sauce and black bean sauce and set aside.
3 Put the oil into a frying pan or wok and heat until very hot. Add the squid and fry for about 4 minutes.
4 Remove the squid from the pan, drain well, and set aside.
5 Wipe out the pan and then heat 1 tablespoon fresh oil. Stir in the pepper and cook for 2 minutes. Add the onions and cook for about 1 minute, then return the squid to the pan.
6 Pour the black bean sauce mixture and cornflour into the pan and stir until the sauce thickens. Season if necessary with pepper and a little salt.

David Shepperdson
Huddersfield, Yorkshire

COD WITH NOODLES IN A LEEK AND CHEESE SAUCE

For 2, but can be made in separate dishes for two different meals for 1 person.

225 g/8 oz cod, skinned
25 g/1 oz butter
75 g/3 oz noodles, pasta shells or macaroni

The white part of 1 leek, well
washed and cut in fine rings
15g/½ oz flour
150 ml/¼ pint milk
Pepper and a little salt
50 g/2 oz (or 1½ tablespoons)
grated cheese

1 Lay cod in a shallow flameproof
dish and dot with half of the butter,
cut in tiny pieces.
2 Cook it under a medium-hot grill.
3 Meanwhile cook the noodles or
pasta shells in boiling water until just
done. Drain and spread over cooked
fish. Keep warm.
4 Melt remaining butter, add leek,
cover pan and cook gently for 5
minutes.
5 Stir flour into leeks and then
gradually add milk, stirring over
gentle heat as sauce thickens. Let it
simmer for 1 minute. Season with
pepper and a little salt.
6 Pour sauce over noodles, cover with
grated cheese and return to grill to
brown the top.

If making two individual dishes, the
second can be kept covered in the
refrigerator overnight. Reheat in a
moderately hot oven, Gas 5, 375°F,
190°C for 20 minutes.

Mrs Ivy Hopes
Oxford

1 If using macaroni or pasta shells,
put them in an 18-cm/7-inch soufflé-
type dish. Cover with boiling water
and add a 15 ml tablespoon oil. Heat
on full power for 5 to 6 minutes.
Drain.
2 Put the leeks and butter in a 600
ml/1 pint jug. Heat on full power for
3 minutes.
3 Stir in the flour, then gradually
blend in the milk. Cook on full power
for 1 minute then stir in the salt and
pepper and cook for a further 30
seconds on full power.

4 Arrange the fish in a single layer
in a shallow 18-cm/7-inch flan dish.
Cover with clear film and cook on
full power for 2 minutes. Drain off
any juices.
5 Tip the pasta over the fish, then
pour the sauce over the pasta.
Sprinkle over the grated cheese. Heat
on full power for 2 minutes then
brown the cheese under a hot grill if
desired.

COD BAKED WITH SWEETCORN

*For 1, wrapped in foil like a parcel and
baked in the oven. However, to make
larger quantities, layer the ingredients in
a casserole, cover and bake for 30
minutes.*

50 g/2 oz canned or frozen
sweetcorn
1 tomato, skinned (page 26) and
sliced
Salt and pepper
100 g/4 oz fillet of cod or haddock,
or a cod steak
1 teaspoon lemon juice
A few sprigs of parsley or
watercress
25 g/1 oz Cheddar cheese, grated

1 Preheat oven to moderately hot,
Gas 6, 400°F, 200°C.
2 Spread out a piece of cooking foil
and on it make a layer of sweetcorn,
then tomato and season it.
3 Place fish on top, sprinkle with
lemon juice and a little more salt and
pepper.
4 Coarsely chop parsley or watercress
and lay it over fish.
5 Finally, cover with cheese.
6 Close the foil tightly and put the
parcel on a baking tray. Cook near top
of oven for 20 minutes.

Mrs J. Macdonald
Aberfeldy, Perthshire

1 Put the fish in a small dish – a cereal bowl is ideal. Sprinkle the sweetcorn over and arrange two tomato slices on top.
2 Sprinkle with lemon juice. Coarsely chop the parsley or watercress and scatter over the tomato slices.
3 Sprinkle with the cheese. Cover the dish with clear film and cook on full power for 1½ minutes. If the fish is thick it may take another minute or two.

TASTY FISH PIE

For 2. A good recipe and very tasty, especially if you use new potatoes. Cod, haddock, coley and whiting are all suitable.

3 medium potatoes
2 teaspoons flour
Salt and pepper
225 g/8 oz cod fillet, skinned and
    cut into 2 portions
A little butter or margarine
150 ml/¼ pint milk
100 g/4 oz grated Cheddar cheese
50 g/2 oz prawns (optional)
4 medium mushrooms, chopped
25 g/1 oz diced red pepper

1 Slice potatoes thickly and parboil them for 6 minutes, then drain.
2 Meanwhile, preheat oven to moderately hot, Gas 6, 400°F, 200°C.
3 Season flour with salt and pepper and toss the fish in it to coat.
4 Grease an ovenproof dish quite liberally with butter or margarine and put in the fish.
5 Pour in the milk and sprinkle fish with half the grated cheese.
6 Add prawns, mushrooms and red pepper and season with a little salt and pepper.
7 Arrange the potatoes on top and cover with the remaining cheese.

8 Cook near top of preheated oven for 30 minutes. Serve with whole green beans.

Mrs Kay Fussey
Denby Dale, Yorkshire

FISH TIKKA

For 2. Nice served with a green salad and the marinade.

2 cod steaks, each about
    225 g/8 oz

MARINADE
3 tablespoons natural yoghurt
A clove of garlic, crushed
A pinch of ground chilli
½ teaspoon garam masala
A pinch of ground ginger
1 dessertspoon lemon juice
Salt and freshly ground black
    pepper
1 to 2 drops of red food
    colouring (optional)

1 Place the fish in a shallow dish.
2 In a small bowl, mix together the remaining ingredients and pour over the cod steaks.
3 Cover and refrigerate for 2 to 4 hours.
4 Lift the fish out of the marinade and grill it under a low heat on both sides, for 15 to 20 minutes in all. Serve with the marinade as a cold sauce.

1 Place the fish in a shallow dish.
2 In a small bowl, mix together the remaining ingredients and pour over the cod steaks.
3 Cover and refrigerate for 2 to 4 hours.
4 Cook on full power for 3 to 4 minutes. Serve with the marinade.

Yvonne Coull
Sea Fish Industry Authority,
Edinburgh

SMOKED HADDOCK AND CHEESE SAVOURY

For 2. Serve this with fresh toast and halved tomatoes, sprinkled with a little sugar and grilled.

225 g/8 oz smoked haddock
Pepper and a little salt

SAUCE
25 g/1 oz margarine or butter
25 g/1 oz flour
300 ml/½ pint milk
2 teaspoons capers
50 g/2 oz cheese, cut in slices

1 Sprinkle fish with pepper but not too much salt. Place between two plates to steam over a pan of simmering water. It will cook in about 15 minutes.
2 Make a sauce by melting margarine and stirring in flour with a wooden spoon. Allow to cook for 1 minute.
3 Remove pan from heat and gradually stir in half the milk until blended and smooth.
4 Return pan to heat and stir continuously as sauce thickens, gradually adding remaining milk. Bring to the boil and stir as it cooks for 2 to 3 minutes more.
5 Add capers and season with a little salt and pepper.
6 Now flake the cooked fish and mix it into sauce. Pour into a warmed ovenproof serving dish and cover with the thin slices of cheese.
7 Place dish under a hot grill until cheese bubbles and browns nicely.

H. R. Kelman
Aberdeen

1 Put the fish on a plate and cover with clear film. Cook on full power for 2 minutes.
2 Put the margarine in a 600-ml/ 1-pint jug, heat on full power for 1 minute.
3 Stir in the flour and gradually blend in the milk. Cook on full power for 1 minute, then stir. Cook for a further 1 minute.
4 Then stir in the capers and season with a little salt and pepper.
5 Flake the fish into the sauce and tip into a shallow 600-ml/1-pint pie dish, cover with thin slices of cheese and grill until the cheese browns.

SMOKED HADDOCK IN A CREAM SAUCE

For 2, but easy to make just for one.

2 fillets smoked haddock, about
    175 g/6 oz each
60 ml/2 fl oz single cream
120 ml/4 fl oz milk
2 eggs
2 tomatoes, skinned (page 26)
    and chopped
A knob of butter or margarine
Salt and pepper
Finely chopped fresh parsley

1 Poach the haddock fillets in a pan in the cream and milk until cooked, 10 to 15 minutes.
2 Poach the eggs (page 17).
3 Warm the tomatoes through in a little butter, then spread them on a warmed serving dish. Put the drained haddock on top and finally top with the poached eggs.
4 Boil the milk and cream mixture to reduce it slightly, add salt and pepper to taste, then strain it over the fish. Garnish with parsley and serve.

David Shepperdson
Huddersfield, Yorkshire

SMOKED FISH SOUFFLÉ

For 2.

225 g/8 oz smoked haddock, cod
    or halibut

Water
Pepper
2 large eggs, separated
1 teaspoon chopped parsley

1 Preheat the oven to moderate, Gas
4, 350°F, 180°C.
2 Poach the fish on top of the cooker
in a covered pan in just enough water
to come halfway up the thickest part
of the fish. The fish is cooked when
it looks opaque (about 5 to 8
minutes).
3 Drain the fish and break into small
pieces, removing any bones.
4 Season the fish with pepper and
beat in the two egg yolks and the
parsley.
5 In another bowl, whip the egg
whites until stiff and fold them into
the fish mixture.
6 Tip this mixture into a buttered
ovenproof dish. Ensure that the dish
or tin is big enough to allow the
soufflé to rise. A 20-cm/8-inch
casserole is nicely filled.
7 Bake for 20 minutes. Serve
immediately with a good salad or just
crusty bread.

Grace Mulligan

Soufflés cannot be made in the
microwave but you can use it to cook
the fish. At step 2 above: put the fish
on a plate, cover with clear film and
cook on full power for 2 to 2½
minutes. It is cooked when it is
opaque and flakes easily.

SALMON PARCEL

*For 2. Serve with Herb Sauce (page
51), Casseroled Potatoes (page 114),
and peas, courgettes or a salad.*

450 g/1 lb tail piece of salmon
25 g/1 oz butter, softened but not
    melted
Juice of half a lemon

½ teaspoon chopped chives
½ teaspoon chopped parsley
Salt and pepper
175 g/6 oz flaky or puff pastry
Milk or beaten egg to glaze

1 Skin the salmon and bone it. This
will give you two fillets.
2 Mix together the butter, lemon
juice, chives, parsley and seasoning.
3 Spread half of the butter mixture
on one salmon fillet, cover with the
other fillet and spread the remaining
butter mixture all over the fish.
4 Roll out the pastry and wrap the
fish in it, damp and seal the edges
well, keeping the join on top. Cut the
pastry trimmings into small leaf
shapes. Put the parcel on a baking
tray.
5 Glaze the pastry with milk or
beaten egg. Arrange the pastry leaves
on top and glaze them. Make a small
hole in top of the pastry to allow the
steam to escape. Leave the salmon
parcel to rest for 10 minutes in a cool
place.
6 Preheat the oven to hot, Gas 7,
425°F, 220°C.
7 Bake the parcel towards the top of
the oven for 30 minutes.

Dilwen Phillips
Gileston, South Glamorgan

SEA FISH CAKES

Enough for 2.

225 g/8 oz white fish fillet,
    skinned
225 g/8 oz potatoes, peeled
1 egg yolk
Salt and freshly ground black
    pepper
Milk
2 tablespoons wholemeal flour
1 egg, beaten
4 tablespoons fresh wholemeal
    breadcrumbs

1 Finely dice the fish, or put it
through a liquidiser or processor.

41

2 Put the potatoes in a saucepan with a little lightly salted water and cook until tender.
3 Drain and mash with the egg yolk and seasoning. Allow to cool, then mix into the fish.
4 Form into 2 large or 4 small fish cakes. If the mixture is too stiff add a few drops of milk. Coat the fish cakes in flour, then beaten egg and breadcrumbs. Chill for 30 minutes.
5 Grill the fish cakes for 5 minutes on each side.

Yvonne Coull
Sea Fish Industry Authority,
Edinburgh

CRISP-FRIED FISH PIECES WITH A PIQUANT SAUCE

Enough for 2 generous helpings. If quantities are increased, this makes a good party dish with the sauce as a dip. Use an assortment of filleted fish, e.g. cod, haddock, plaice, sole, whiting, even a few prawns.

250 g/8 oz fish, boned, skinned
15 g/$\frac{1}{2}$ oz seasoned flour
A little beaten egg
50 g/2 oz fine dried breadcrumbs
Oil for deep frying

DRESSING
2 large tablespoons mayonnaise
$\frac{1}{4}$ teaspoon each of English and French mustard
$\frac{1}{2}$ level teaspoon each of chopped capers, gherkins and fresh parsley
A pinch of chervil

1 Make dressing well in advance to allow flavours to blend. Thoroughly mix all ingredients.
2 Cut fish into bite-sized strips and dust with seasoned flour.
3 Dip strips in egg, then pat on breadcrumbs.

42

4 Drop into deep hot fat, moving them around with a draining spoon to keep pieces separate.
5 When evenly browned and cooked through – 3 minutes will be enough – lift out on to kitchen paper to drain. Do not overcook.
6 Serve piping hot with the cold dressing in a separate bowl.

TIP
If serving this for a party, fish strips can be 'egged and crumbed', then fried at last minute.

Anne Wallace
Stewarton, Ayrshire

CRISP AND BUTTERY HERRINGS

For 2. The wholemeal coating is delicious and the brown butter sauce is very rich.

2 herrings, heads and gut removed
Wholemeal flour
1 small egg, beaten
50 g/2 oz fresh wholemeal breadcrumbs
25 g/1 oz butter

SAUCE
25 to 50 g/1 to 2 oz butter
1 tablespoon vinegar
$\frac{1}{2}$ teaspoon mustard
Lemon slices and wholemeal toast for serving

1 Using the back of a knife, scrape off the scales, then rinse the herrings and dry well.
2 Toss each fish first in flour, then beaten egg, and finally coat with the breadcrumbs.
3 Melt the butter and gently fry the herrings for about 5 to 6 minutes on each side. When cooked, remove from the pan, drain well and set aside to keep warm while preparing the sauce.
4 Melt the butter in a small pan and allow it to brown a little. Mix the

vinegar and mustard together and add
to pan. Stir as it heats, season with a
little salt and pour the sauce over the
herrings.
5 Serve with lemon slices and toast.

Grace Mulligan

HERRING KEBABS WITH REDCURRANT JELLY

For 2.

2 herring fillets, 175 g/6 oz
   each
8 bay leaves
1 small onion, halved and
   quartered
Salt and freshly ground black
   pepper
3 tablespoons redcurrant jelly,
   melted

1 Cut each herring into 4 and thread
on to skewers, alternating with the
bay leaves and onion pieces.
2 Season with salt and black pepper
and cook under a moderate grill for 8
to 10 minutes, turning the kebabs
once and brushing over with some of
the redcurrant jelly.
3 Heat the remaining redcurrant jelly
but do not let it boil.
4 Serve the kebabs on a bed of
brown rice and pour the sauce over
the top.

1 Cut each herring into 4 chunks and
thread on to wooden skewers along
with the bay leaves and onion pieces.
Arrange them on a plate in a single
layer.
2 Cook for 2 to 3 minutes on full
power. Set aside, covered.
3 Put the redcurrant jelly in a small
bowl and heat in full power for 1
minute.

4 Serve the kebabs on a bed of
brown rice and pour the sauce over.

Yvonne Coull
Sea Fish Industry Authority,
Edinburgh

PICKLED HERRINGS

*Often served cut into strips and mixed
with a potato salad. Delicious as a
starter on their own with brown bread
or rolls. Can be frozen after pickling –
best to pack individual fillets with a
little liquor in small containers – so it's
worth making a quantity.*

3 herrings
Salt

PICKLING LIQUOR
120 ml/4 fl oz white vinegar
120 ml/4 fl oz wine or tarragon
   vinegar
120 ml/4 fl oz water
75 g/3 oz granulated sugar
1 small onion, thinly sliced or
   finely chopped
Freshly ground black pepper
3 allspice berries
3 cloves
A pinch of fennel seed

1 Clean the herrings (or ask the
fishmonger to do this for you) and
divide fish into several fillets,
removing as many bones as possible.
2 Sprinkle a layer of salt (about 1
tablespoon) into an earthenware or
Pyrex casserole. Arrange a layer of
fillets on top. Add another layer of
salt, then fish, ending with a layer of
salt. Cover and leave in a cool place
(bottom of the refrigerator) for 1 to
2 days.
3 Remove the herrings from the salt
and carefully peel away the skin.
Leave to soak in cold water for about
an hour, changing the water if very
salty.
4 Prepare the pickling liquor by
mixing together the remaining
ingredients.
5 Lift the fillets out of the water, pat

43

dry, replace in a clean dish and pour over the pickling liquor. Cover and leave at least 48 hours in a cool place.

Margaret Heywood
Todmorden, Yorkshire

CITRUS MACKEREL

For 2; try them served hot with a green salad.

Half a small red apple, cored
  and chopped
Half a small orange, peeled and
  chopped
1 teaspoon chopped fresh tarragon
  or $\frac{1}{2}$ teaspoon dried tarragon
1 tablespoon lemon juice
15 g/$\frac{1}{2}$ oz butter or margarine
50 g/2 oz porridge oats
Salt and black pepper
2 mackerel fillets, 225 to 275 g/8 to
  10 oz each

1 Put the apple, orange, tarragon, lemon juice and butter or margarine in a saucepan and gently heat through, until the apple has softened.
2 Stir in the oats and seasoning and divide the filling in two.
3 Place the mackerel on a board, skin side down, spread the filling over the mackerel and roll up each fish from the head end. Secure with cocktail sticks and place in a shallow dish.
4 Preheat oven to moderately hot, Gas 6, 400°F, 200°C.
5 Cover the dish and cook the mackerel for 10 to 15 minutes. Serve with salad.

Microwave

1 Put the apple, orange, tarragon, lemon juice and butter or margarine into a bowl. Cover and cook on full power for 1 minute until the apple has softened.
2 Stir in the oats and season with salt and pepper. Divide into 2 portions.

3 Place the mackerel on a board, and follow the rest of step 3 above.
4 Cover and cook on full power for 3 minutes.

Yvonne Coull
Sea Fish Industry Authority,
Edinburgh

CRISP LEMON SOLE

For 2.

2 skinned fillets of lemon sole
  or plaice, about 225 to 275 g/8 to
  10 oz each
2 rindless rashers back bacon
Salt and black pepper
Lemon juice
A knob of butter or margarine
25 g/1 oz Cheddar cheese, grated
A few potato crisps, slightly
  crushed

1 Preheat the oven to moderately hot, Gas 6, 400°F, 200°C.
2 Place each fillet on top of a rasher of bacon, season with salt and black pepper and sprinkle with a little lemon juice.
3 Roll up the fillets from head to tail and place in an ovenproof dish, ensuring that the tails are secured underneath. Dot with butter.
4 Bake in the preheated oven for 15 minutes.
5 Remove the dish from the oven, sprinkle with cheese and the crisps, then bake for a further 5 minutes until golden brown.

Yvonne Coull
Sea Fish Industry Authority,
Edinburgh

SOLE WITH CREAM AND PARMESAN

For 1 or 2. Can also be made with haddock or whiting. For one person, this simple, delicious recipe can be eaten from the dish in which it has been cooked.

A little butter
1 or 2 fillets of sole, haddock or
    whiting, skinned*
Salt and freshly ground black
    pepper
4 tablespoons double cream, but
    single will do
About 6 teaspoons Parmesan
    cheese

*For instructions to skin fish, see Fish
Pie in Puff Pastry, page 121, step 2.*

1 Preheat grill to moderately hot.
2 Butter a shallow flameproof dish
and put in the fish. Season with salt
and pepper.
3 Spoon over the cream and sprinkle
well with Parmesan.
4 Grill slowly until fish is cooked and
the cream and cheese turn into a
lovely sauce.

Mrs J. B. Morrison
Elgin, Grampian

POACHED SALMON WITH TWO SAUCES

*Here's the main course cooked by Simon
Dunn, who won third place in the 1987
Junior Cook of the Year competition.
You'll find a liquidiser or processor is
needed for the sauces. The dish is for 2.*

250 ml/½ pint water
A quarter of a Spanish onion,
    sliced
Half a stick of celery, sliced
1 bay leaf
Juice of a lemon
Salt and pepper
2 fresh salmon steaks

FRESH TOMATO SAUCE
25 g/1 oz butter
1 small onion, finely chopped
A clove of garlic, crushed
2 large tomatoes, skinned (page
    26) and deseeded
A pinch of oregano
Salt and pepper
A pinch of sugar
1 tablespoon dry white vermouth

45

WATERCRESS SAUCE

Half a bunch of watercress,
  washed
2 tablespoons double cream
2 tablespoons natural yoghurt
2 twists of sliced lemon and
  sprigs of watercress to
  garnish

1 For the tomato sauce: melt butter
in a pan and cook onion and garlic
until transparent. Add remaining
ingredients and cook quickly for 4
minutes. Liquidise and set aside to
reheat when salmon is ready to serve.
2 For the watercress sauce, which is
served cold, liquidise the watercress
with the cream and yoghurt, adding
salt if necessary. Keep cool.
3 Now for the salmon. Put water,
onion, celery, bay leaf, lemon juice,
pepper and a little salt in a saucepan.
Bring to the boil, reduce heat and
simmer for 15 minutes.
4 Add the salmon, placing the steaks
carefully in the pan. Cover and
simmer for 10 minutes. Lift out
carefully so they do not break.
5 Serve the salmon on individual hot
plates with a spoonful of each sauce
alongside. Hand the rest of the sauces
in two small bowls.

Simon Dunn
Bickley, Kent

*For microwaving, choose salmon steaks
weighing 175 g/6 oz each; substitute a
squeeze of lemon juice for the juice of a
whole lemon and disregard the rest of the
ingredients for poaching the fish. You
should need only one large tomato for
the Fresh Tomato Sauce. Otherwise, the
sauce ingredients are the same.*

1 Arrange the salmon steaks on a
plate, thickest parts to the outside.
Sprinkle with lemon juice and a good
grind of black pepper. Cover with
clear film and set aside while you
make the sauces.

2 First, make the tomato sauce: put
the butter, onion and garlic in a small
basin and heat on full power for 3
minutes. Stir in the rest of the
ingredients and heat on full power for
2 minutes. Liquidise and set aside to
reheat when the salmon is ready to
serve.
3 Make the watercress sauce,
following step 2 of the main method.
Keep it cool.
4 Cook the prepared salmon steaks on
full power for 3 to 4 minutes, then
stand for 5 minutes.
5 Meanwhile, reheat the tomato
sauce on full power for 30 seconds to
1 minute. Serve and garnish as
above.

TEIFI SALMON IN A SAUCE

(Saws Ellog Teifi)

*This main course for 2 was cooked by
Lucy Barton-Greenwood when she won
second place in the 1987 Junior Cook of
the Year competition. See page 179 for
her full menu. We suggest serving this
with new potatoes and mange-tout
peas.*

2 salmon steaks
25 g/1 oz butter
A liqueur glass of port or sweet
  sherry
A dash of tomato ketchup
1 fillet from a can of anchovies
Pepper and salt
Lemon rings and tiny hearts cut
  from tomato skins to garnish

1 Preheat oven to moderately hot,
Gas 5, 375°F, 190°C.
2 Wash and dry the salmon and put
it in an ovenproof dish.
3 Melt the butter and add the port,
ketchup and anchovy; stir over a low
heat until hot and it becomes a
smooth sauce. Season with pepper
and salt. Pour over the salmon.

4 Cover dish and bake for about 35 minutes – the time depends on the thickness of the salmon.
5 Carefully remove the skin from the salmon steaks, put them on a serving dish, and pour over the sauce. Garnish with lemon rings and tiny tomato hearts.

Lucy Barton-Greenwood
Radyr, Cardiff

 Microwave

1 Wash and dry the salmon steaks. Arrange in a shallow dish with the thickest parts to the outside.
2 Put 50 g/2 oz butter in a jug and heat on full power for 1 to 1½ minutes until melted. Stir in two 15 ml tablespoons port, 1 tablespoon tomato ketchup and the anchovy. Stir until well combined.
3 Pour the sauce over the salmon. Cover the dish with clear film and cook on full power for 4 to 5 minutes.
4 Serve with the sauce poured over, garnished as above.

SEA BASS WITH CLAMS AND HERBS

This main course was cooked by Sally Wilson, 14, when she became Junior Cook of the Year, 1987. (See page 179 for the other dishes in her 3-course menu.) This recipe is also very successful with salmon instead of sea bass and prawns instead of clams. For 2.

300 ml/½ pint hot court bouillon (see step 1)
275 g/10 oz clams in shells, washed
40 g/1½ oz butter
1 shallot, chopped
A clove of garlic, chopped
Two 150 g/6 oz fillets of sea bass
Sea salt

A bouquet garni (or small bunch of fresh herbs)
1 tablespoon chopped fresh parsley
Juice of half a lemon
1 large tomato, skinned (page 26) and diced

FOR THE BASIL CRUST
25 g/1 oz pine nuts, ready-roasted and chopped
1 tablespoon olive oil
5 leaves of fresh basil, chopped, or a pinch of dried basil
25 g/1 oz fresh white breadcrumbs
Salt and pepper

1 A simple court bouillon is made by simmering together gently for 20 minutes 300 ml/½ pint water, 1 small sliced carrot, half an onion, 1 bay leaf, a pinch or sprig of thyme, 1 or 2 sprigs of parsley, a pinch of salt, 3 peppercorns and 2 tablespoons cider or white wine vinegar. Strain and use.
2 Cook the clams by putting them into a pan of boiling, lightly salted water and cooking over moderate heat just until the shells open. Drain.
3 Melt 25 g/1 oz of the butter, put in the shallot and garlic and fry gently for 1 or 2 minutes just to soften.
4 Put the sea bass into the pan and sprinkle over the clams and a little salt. Add the hot court bouillon and bouquet garni. Bring just to boiling point, cover pan and let it simmer for 5 minutes.
5 Meanwhile prepare the basil crust. Liquidise the pine nuts (or put them through a food processor) with the olive oil; transfer to a bowl and mix in basil, breadcrumbs, pepper and salt.
6 Lift the sea bass carefully out of the pan into a heatproof dish, spread each piece with basil crust and grill until golden brown.
7 Remove the clams from pan and keep them warm. Remove the bouquet garni.

8 Strain the cooking liquid and then return it to the pan to boil and reduce the quantity until there is just enough to make a sauce for 2 people.
9 Add parsley and whisk in remaining butter. Add lemon juice, salt, pepper and lastly the diced tomato.
10 Spoon the tomato mixture into the hot serving dish. Carefully lift the sea bass fillets and place them on top. Serve at once with the clams arranged prettily around the dish.

Sally Wilson
Hatch End, Middlesex

 Microwave

The only changes to the ingredients given above is that the bouquet garni is not required and the court bouillon has been adjusted.

1 To make the court bouillon put 150 ml/¼ fl oz hot water into a 1.1 litre/2 pint basin. Add 1 small sliced carrot, 1 onion, peeled and cut in half, 1 bay leaf, a pinch each of thyme and salt, 2 to 3 sprigs of parsley, 2 to 3 peppercorns and 2 tablespoons cider or wine vinegar. Heat on full power for 5 minutes then let it stand for 5 minutes. Strain into a jug and use.
2 Put 15 g/1 oz of the butter, the shallot and garlic into a shallow 20-cm/8-inch round dish. Heat on full power for 2 minutes.
3 Arrange the sea bass over the onion mixture. Put the clams on top of the sea bass. Sprinkle over four 15 ml tablespoons court bouillon and cover the dish with a piece of clear film. Cook on full power for 4 to 5 minutes. The clam shells should have opened and the sea bass should be opaque.
4 Meanwhile prepare the basil crust. Put the pine nuts and olive oil into a liquidiser or food processor and blend until smooth. Mix in the breadcrumbs

and basil and season with a little salt and pepper.
5 Carefully lift the sea bass out of the dish, leaving the clams behind. Spread each fillet with the basil crust and grill until golden brown.
6 Drain the cooking juices from the dish of clams into a 600 ml/1 pint jug, heat on full power for 3 to 5 minutes or until the juices are reduced to half. Add the parsley and whisk in the remaining butter. Add the lemon juice, diced tomato and season to taste with salt and pepper.
7 Re-cover the dish of clams and heat on full power for 30 to 45 seconds. Spoon the sauce on to a hot serving dish. Carefully lift the sea bass fillets and place them on the sauce. Arrange the clams prettily in the dish.

MUSHROOM-STUFFED PLAICE
For 2, but easy to make just for 1.

2 whole plaice, pocketed* or
   whole white fish, cleaned, 225 to
   275 g/8 to 10 oz each

STUFFING
100 g/4 oz mushrooms, finely
   chopped
25 g/1 oz walnuts, finely chopped
2 teaspoons chopped parsley
25 g/1 oz butter or margarine
2 tablespoons fresh brown
   breadcrumbs
50 g/2 oz sweetcorn
Freshly ground black pepper
Lemon juice

* *'Pocketed' means filleted down the backbone. Ask your fishmonger to do this for you, if necessary.*

1 Preheat the oven to moderately hot, Gas 6, 400°F, 200°C.
2 Heat the mushrooms, walnuts, parsley and butter or margarine together in a saucepan. Stir in the breadcrumbs, sweetcorn and pepper.

3 Divide the mixture equally between the two whole plaice, filling the pockets. Put them in an ovenproof dish. If there is spare stuffing, put it between fish. Sprinkle with lemon juice.
4 Cover the dish and cook in the preheated oven for 15 to 20 minutes. Serve with plain boiled potatoes and green beans.

1 Cook the mushrooms, walnuts, parsley and butter or margarine in a covered bowl for 1 minute on full power. Stir in the breadcrumbs, sweetcorn and pepper.
2 Divide the mixture equally between the two whole plaice, filling the pockets. Sprinkle with lemon juice.
3 Put each fish on a separate plate, cover and cook separately on full power for 1 to 2 minutes each.

Yvonne Coull
Sea Fish Industry Authority,
Edinburgh

BAKED GREY MULLET
For 2.

450 g/1 grey mullet, gutted and scaled
2 rashers smoked bacon
4 fresh sage leaves, finely chopped, or 1 teaspoon dried sage
25 g/1 oz fresh breadcrumbs
Butter
$\frac{1}{2}$ glass dry white wine or dry cider
60 ml/2 fl oz double cream

1 Make 4 or 5 cuts on each side of the fish.
2 Lightly grill the bacon, then chop it up finely almost to a paste.
3 Mix the bacon with the sage and put a little of this mixture into the cuts in the fish. Add the breadcrumbs to the remaining sage and bacon. Season with salt and pepper and use it to stuff the gut cavity.
4 Put the fish into a thickly buttered dish and cook in a moderately hot oven, Gas 6, 400°F, 200°C for 15 minutes.
5 Pour over the wine or cider and cook for a further 10 to 15 minutes.
6 Pour over the cream and cook for just 2 minutes more. Serve.

David Shepperdson
Huddersfield, Yorkshire

1 Make 4 or 5 cuts on each side of the fish.
2 Put the bacon on a rack set over a drip tray and lightly cover with a piece of kitchen paper. Cook on full power for 2 to 3 minutes until crispy – the time will vary depending on the fat content in the bacon so check after half of the cooking time.
3 Finely chop the bacon and mix it with the sage, so that it is almost a paste. Put a little of this mixture into the cuts in the fish. Mix the remainder with the breadcrumbs, season with a little salt, if needed, and black pepper. Use this to stuff the cavity of the fish.
4 Put the fish into a shallow oval dish, pour over the wine or cider and cover with clear film. Cook on full power for 5 to 6 minutes.
5 Lift the fish on to a warm serving plate. Stir the cream into the cooking juices and heat on full power for 1 minute. Stir well then pour the sauce over the fish and serve.

TROUT WITH HAZELNUTS

For 2. Rainbow or brown trout can be used.

2 trout, gutted
Seasoned flour
50 g/2 oz butter and 1 tablespoon oil
25 g/1 oz hazelnuts, skins removed,* roughly chopped
Juice of 1 lemon
2 tablespoons chopped parsley
Salt and pepper
A few lemon slices to garnish

* To remove skins from hazelnuts, put them under the grill for 5 minutes turning often. Then rub the skins off.

1 Dip the prepared trout in seasoned flour and shake off any excess.
2 Heat the butter and oil together and gently fry the trout for about 7 minutes on each side (the time will vary according to the size of the fish). When cooked and nicely browned, remove them from the pan and place on a warmed serving dish.
3 Add the roughly chopped hazelnuts to the frying pan and cook until lightly browned, then scatter them over the trout.
4 Add the lemon juice and chopped parsley to the remaining butter in the pan, season, warm through and pour over the fish. Garnish with slices of lemon.

Angela Henderson
Fleet, Hampshire

SALMON SAVOURY

For 1 or 2. Serve hot, sliced in wedges with mashed potato and vegetables, or cold with salads.

A 213 g/7½ oz can of red or pink salmon, drained
1 large egg
50 g/2 oz fresh breadcrumbs
Salt and pepper
A little milk
A little lemon juice (optional)
1 tomato, sliced

1 Mash salmon with a fork, adding egg, breadcrumbs, salt and pepper. If it is dry, moisten with a little milk or lemon juice.
2 Spoon mixture into a greased shallow ovenproof dish, level it and mark the top with the fork. Decorate with tomato slices.
3 Cook in a moderately hot oven, Gas 6, 400°F, 200°C for 20 minutes until firm and just lightly browned.

Mrs S. Joules
Croydon, Surrey

 Microwave

1 In a bowl, mash the salmon with a fork. Mix in the egg, breadcrumbs, salt, pepper and lemon juice.
2 Spoon the mixture into 2 ramekin dishes. Smooth over the surface and decorate with tomato slices.
3 Cook on full power for 2 to 3 minutes until just firm to the touch.

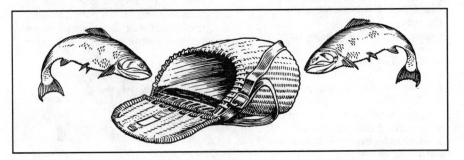

SALMON AND POTATO BAKE

Another recipe which uses canned salmon, though tuna fish or 175 g/6 oz grated cheese can be used instead. Makes 2 helpings.

175 g/6 oz boiled or steamed
  potatoes
A good 15 g/½ oz margarine or
  butter
175 to 225 g/6 to 8 oz canned pink
  salmon
1 tablespoon chopped parsley
A squeeze of lemon juice
Salt and pepper
150 ml/¼ pint milk
2 eggs, separated

1 Preheat oven to moderately hot,
Gas 5, 375°F, 190°C.
2 First cook the potatoes and keep
them hot.
3 Meanwhile, use a little of the
margarine or butter to grease a 1.2-
litre/2-pint pie dish or soufflé dish.
4 Chop fish finely, removing any
bone, and mix in parsley, lemon juice,
salt and pepper.
5 Mash the hot potatoes until
smooth, beating in margarine or
butter and milk until light and
creamy.
6 Mix in the salmon and parsley
mixture.
7 Beat in the egg yolks.
8 Whisk egg whites until stiff and
fold them in.
9 Bake in the preheated oven until
risen and golden brown, about 35
minutes.

Mrs Powell
Enfield, Middlesex

SARDINES FOR TEA

For 2. Easy and very tasty. See also Sardine Pasties (page 122).

A 120 g/4 oz can of sardines in
  oil

1 small onion, finely chopped
A small cup of rice, about 120 g/
  4 oz weighed when cooked
Pepper and salt
1 hard-boiled egg, sliced
1 tomato, sliced

1 Preheat oven to moderately hot,
Gas 6, 400°F, 200°C.
2 Pour oil off sardines and mash
them, adding onion and cooked rice.
Mix well and season to taste.
3 Divide mixture between two
individual ovenproof dishes.
4 Chop the hard-boiled egg and
spread it over. Cover with tomato
slices. Brush tomato with oil.
5 Cook in middle of preheated oven
for 30 minutes. Serve with fresh
salad.

Mrs M. Lownds
Uttoxeter, Staffordshire

 Microwave

15 g/½ oz butter is needed in addition to the ingredients given above. Cook the sardines in two individual dishes.

1 Put butter and onion into a bowl.
Cook, uncovered, on full power for 2
minutes to soften the onion.
2 Drain the sardines and mash them
and mix with the onion and rice.
Divide the mixture between two
dishes.
3 Chop the egg and spread it over the
sardines. Then cover with tomato
slices.
4 Cook on full power for 3 to 4
minutes.

HERB SAUCE

Makes about 300 ml/½ pint. Serve with the Salmon Parcels, or any firm-fleshed white fish.

25 g/1 oz butter
25 g/1 oz flour
300 ml/½ pint milk

1 teaspoon chopped chives
1 teaspoon chopped parsley
Salt and pepper
1 egg yolk
2 tablespoons cream

1 Melt the butter in a saucepan, add
the flour and cook for 1 minute.
2 Stirring all the time, gradually pour
in the milk.
3 Heat up the sauce and boil for 1
minute, then stir in the chives, parsley
and seasoning. Remove the pan from
the heat.
4 Mix together the egg yolk and
cream and stir them into the sauce, do
not re-boil or the yolk will curdle.

Dilwen Phillips
Gileston, South Glamorgan

1 Put the butter into a 600 ml/1 pint
jug. Heat on full power for 1 minute.
Stir in the flour and gradually blend
in the milk.
2 Heat on full power for 1½
minutes, then stir in the chives,
parsley and seasoning. Continue to
heat on full power for a further 30
to 60 seconds until the sauce has
thickened.
3 Mix together the egg yolk and
cream. Stir into the sauce and serve.

Reheating by microwave

If the sauce is to be made in advance
and reheated, cover the surface of the
sauce with clear film after step 2 –
this will prevent a skin forming.
Reheat the sauce on full power for 1
to 1½ minutes, stirring once, then stir
the egg yolk and cream into the hot
sauce.

If the completed sauce needs
reheating, once the egg and cream are
added to the sauce take care not to
overheat as they will curdle. Reheat
on full power in 10 second bursts,
stirring after every 10 seconds.

52

SHARP MUSTARD SAUCE

This sauce goes very well with poached, grilled or baked fish.

75 g/3 oz butter
1 large egg yolk
3 dessertspoons water
1 teaspoon dry mustard
White pepper and salt
1 dessertspoon lemon juice or
    wine vinegar
1 teaspoon finely chopped fresh
    parsley

1 Put the butter in a hot bowl and
melt it over a pan of hot water. Leave
it to cool slightly.
2 Put the egg yolk into a small pan
and, using a small wire whisk, add the
water and whisk the mixture over a
gentle heat until it begins to thicken.
3 Stir the mustard into the cool
butter and season with white pepper
and a grain or two of salt.
4 Beat the buttery mixture into the
egg yolk, a little at a time, and it will
begin to thicken.
5 Add the lemon juice or vinegar and
parsley and serve as soon as possible.

Grace Mulligan

1 Heat the butter in a jug on full
power for 1 to 2 minutes till melted.
2 Put the egg yolk into a small basin
and whisk in the water with a small
wire whisk. Stir in the mustard.
3 Whisk in the butter in a steady
stream.
4 Heat the sauce on full power for 10
seconds, then whisk well. Repeat
twice until the sauce has thickened
slightly.
5 Season with salt and pepper. Add
the lemon juice or vinegar and parsley
and serve as soon as possible.

Take care not to overheat or the sauce
will curdle.

Chapter 4

Poultry and Game

TO POACH A CHICKEN

Sometimes it makes good sense to buy more than you need particularly if there is a special offer or an exceptional bargain. Here are instructions for poaching, then recipes for using the lovely moist meat. Not only do you have the meat but also a delicious, jellied, strongly flavoured stock.

A 1½ kg/3 to 3½ lb chicken
1 small onion
A piece of carrot
1 bay leaf
4 peppercorns
Salt and pepper

1 Put the chicken into a close-fitting pan with the vegetables, bay leaf, peppercorns, salt and pepper, and add enough water to cover.
2 Cover with a lid, bring to the boil, then lower the heat and simmer for about 1½ hours or until the meat is falling from the bones.
3 Remove from the heat and allow to cool. Remove the chicken, strain the stock into a jug and put it in a cool place overnight.
4 Strip all the chicken from the bones, keeping the pieces as large as possible. Keep in the refrigerator until needed.
5 Remove the layer of solidified fat from the surface of the stock – which can then be used for making soups or sauces.
6 A little more stock can be made by returning the bones, skin etc. to a pan with more onion, carrot, herbs and seasoning and simmering as before.

Grace Mulligan

Chicken cooked in the microwave has a delicious flavour and is exceptionally moist. It is an ideal way of cooking chicken which is then to be used in other dishes. If you allow the dripping to set you can discard the fat and underneath you will have a jelly which can be used for stocks and soups.

A 1½ kg/3 to 3½ lb chicken
15 g/½ oz butter, melted

1 Place the chicken on a microwave roasting rack (or an upturned plate) set in a shallow dish. Brush with the melted butter. Cover with a roasting-set lid or with a roaster bag, which has been split up one side and then tented over the bird. Cook on Medium for 28 minutes. Allow to stand covered, or wrapped in foil, shiny side in, for 15 minutes.

In 2-powered microwave cookers:
Cook chicken on full power for 24 minutes, then stand as above.

CHICKEN MOULD

For this recipe you need a firm well-flavoured stock. If your stock hasn't set to a firm jelly, put it in a saucepan and boil it up to reduce the volume and strengthen the flavour.
For 1 or 2.

100 g/4 oz cooked chicken,
    diced
1 tablespoon cold cooked peas
2 tablespoons cold cooked mixed
    vegetables, diced
Salt and pepper
Jellied chicken stock

1 Put the chicken into a bowl or dish, add the peas and other vegetables and season.
2 Bring the jellied stock to the boil, allow to cool and then pour it over the mixture so that it just covers the ingredients.
3 Put into the refrigerator to set.
4 When chilled, serve with a salad of crisp lettuce; in winter, it is nice with hot mashed potatoes.

Grace Mulligan

CHICKEN SALAD

For 2. This salad goes well with new potatoes tossed in a French Dressing (page 106)

1 small red eating apple, cored
  and diced but not peeled
2 spring onions, chopped
1 stick of celery, chopped
100 g/4 oz cooked chicken, diced
3 tablespoons mayonnaise or
  salad cream
1 teaspoon chopped fresh
  chives
25 g/1 oz walnuts, chopped
Lettuce leaves for serving

1 Put all the ingredients, except the lettuce leaves, into a bowl and mix thoroughly.
2 Adjust the seasoning, then arrange the chicken salad on a few lettuce leaves.

Grace Mulligan

HONOLULU CHICKEN

Serves 2. A rice salad and a tomato and cucumber salad make excellent accompaniments.

20 g/¾ oz butter
50 g/2 oz whole blanched almonds
225 g/8 oz cooked chicken
2 sticks of celery
2 rings of canned pineapple
150 ml/¼ pint mayonnaise
1 teaspoon lemon juice
Salt and pepper
A pinch of sugar
Lettuce leaves to garnish

1 Melt the butter in a pan, add the nuts and cook until golden brown. Drain on kitchen paper, then sprinkle with a little salt and leave to cool.
2 Cut the chicken into bite-sized pieces and chop up the celery and pineapple.
3 Put the mayonnaise and lemon juice in a bowl and add the chicken, celery, pineapple, nuts and seasonings.

4 Toss all the ingredients together and serve in a bowl lined with lettuce.

Angela Henderson
Fleet, Hampshire

CREAMY CHICKEN AND MUSHROOMS

For 1. Known as Chicken à la King in restaurants and recipe books, this is delicious, quick and easy to make. Nice with Boiled Rice (page 88) and green peas or beans for colour, or a salad.

20 g/¾ oz margarine
15 g/½ oz flour
150 ml/¼ pint milk
50 g/2 oz button mushrooms,
  sliced
Salt and pepper
2 teaspoons sherry
150 g/5 oz cooked chicken, diced
1 tablespoon double cream
Chopped parsley to decorate

1 Melt the margarine in a saucepan, then stir in the flour and cook for 1 minute.
2 Gradually pour in the milk, stirring all the time, and heat until the sauce boils.
3 Add the mushrooms, seasoning, sherry and chicken, bring to the boil and cook gently for 3 minutes. Then stir in the cream and serve immediately, sprinkled with parsley.

 Microwave

1 Melt the margarine for 30 seconds on full power.
2 Add flour and gradually whisk in the milk. Cook on full power for 1 minute, whisk again and cook 1 minute more.
3 Add mushrooms, seasoning, sherry and chicken and cook, covered, on full power for 3 minutes.
4 Stir in the cream and serve.

Joan Tyers
Wingate, Co. Durham

CREAMED CHICKEN WITH RICE

For 1. Quick and easy!

50 g/2 oz long grain brown* or
   white rice
100 g/4 oz cooked chicken
A 295 g/10 oz can of condensed
   chicken soup
Half a 410 g/14 oz can of mixed
   vegetables*
A pinch of salt (optional)

*The exact timing for brown rice
depends on the type. Some have been
pre-fluffed and take only 12 minutes;
others may take as much as 20 minutes.
125 g/4 oz frozen mixed vegetables or
even frozen peas make an ideal and
more colourful alternative to canned.*

1 Cook rice by dropping it into 600
ml/1 pint of boiling water. Boil it
gently: brown rice for 20 to 25
minutes, white rice for 12 to 15
minutes, then drain it. (To cook
Boiled Rice by the absorption
method, see page 88.)
2 Cut chicken into fairly large pieces
and warm it carefully in the soup
with the vegetables, stirring so that it
does not stick to the pan. Add salt.
Allow the mixture to simmer for 5
minutes to be sure the chicken is
thoroughly heated through.
3 Make a ring of the rice on warm
plate and put the chicken in the
centre.

Miss M. Leafe
Wetherby, Yorkshire

 Microwave

*Use 125 g/4 oz frozen mixed vegetables,
cooked, instead of canned.*

1 Put the rice into an 18 cm/7 inch
soufflé-type dish with 300 ml/½ pint
water and a pinch of salt. Cover the
dish with the serving plate and cook
on full power for 8 minutes for white

long grain rice, 12 to 15 minutes for
brown rice. Brown rice will need
stirring once during cooking.
2 At the end of cooking, leave it to
stand, still covered, while you make
the sauce. The rice will continue to
absorb the water and stay hot.
3 Cut the chicken into 2.5-cm/1-inch
pieces. Put it into a basin with the
cooked vegetables and soup. Heat on
full power for 3 minutes, stirring
once.
4 Drain any excess liquid from the
rice and fluff up with a fork. Arrange
a circle of rice on the warm serving
plate and put chicken in centre.

QUICK CHICKEN IN A CREAM SAUCE

*For 1, but easy to make more. If you
do not like cream and wine, follow the
recipe to the end of step 4 and serve it
with lightly fried or steamed courgettes.*

1 chicken breast
1 teaspoon cornflour
Salt and pepper
1 tablespoon oil
50 g/2 oz mushrooms, sliced
2 tablespoons white wine or cider
75 ml/2½ fl oz whipping cream
Chopped parsley to garnish

1 Slice the chicken breast into thin
strips and toss the pieces in the
seasoned cornflour.
2 Heat the oil in a pan and fry the
chicken pieces until golden brown on
all sides, about 2 minutes.
3 Add the mushrooms and cook until
tender, about 2 minutes.
4 Remove chicken and mushrooms
and put on a warmed plate.
5 Pour the wine into the pan, bring
to the boil, add the cream and cook
for 1 to 2 minutes until the sauce is
thick and creamy. Season to taste.
6 Pour over the chicken. Sprinkle
chopped parsley over the top.

Dilwen Phillips
Gileston, South Glamorgan

This is an opportunity to use a browning dish. If you do not have one, cook this recipe on top of your stove (it will actually be just as quick). Do not cover the browning dish at any stage or the results will be soggy.

1 Put the empty browning dish in the microwave and heat on full power for 6 minutes (or according to the manufacturer's instructions).
2 Slice the chicken breast into thin strips and toss the pieces in seasoned cornflour.
3 Immediately the browning dish is ready, add the oil and chicken. Pressing the chicken well down so that it browns, cook on full power for 1 minute. Then turn the chicken, add the mushrooms and cook for a further 1 to 2 minutes on full power.
4 Stir in the wine, then add the cream. Cook on full power for 2 minutes, season and serve sprinkled with parsley.

CHICKEN FOR ONE ✓

Almost a meal in itself. Serve with green peas or beans.

One chicken joint
Seasoned flour
25 g/1 oz butter
1 small onion, chopped
2 fresh tomatoes, skinned (page 26) and chopped
1 large potato, cut into 7-mm/ $\frac{1}{4}$-inch pieces
Salt and pepper
75 ml/2 to 3 fl oz stock
1 teaspoon chopped parsley

1 Remove the skin from the chicken, then coat the joint with the seasoned flour.
2 Melt the butter in a pan and fry the chicken to brown it well all over.

3 Take out the chicken and fry onion until soft.
4 Put back the chicken along with the tomatoes, potato, seasoning and stock if it seems dry. Cover the pan and cook over low heat until the chicken is tender, about 20 minutes.
5 Sprinkle the parsley over the chicken and serve.

1 Remove the skin from the chicken and coat the joint with seasoned flour.
2 Heat 15 g/$\frac{1}{2}$ oz margarine in a shallow dish on full power for 30 seconds. Put in the chicken upside down and cook for 2 minutes on full power.
3 Turn the chicken over, surround it with the onion, tomatoes, potatoes, seasoning and a little stock if it seems too dry.
4 Cover the dish and cook on full power for a further 6 minutes or until the chicken is tender.
5 Serve sprinkled with parsley.

Joan Tyers
Wingate, Co. Durham

CHICKEN FINGERS

Nice either as snacks or as a meal for 2, served with vegetables such as peas, corn or French beans, or with salad and Yoghurt Chutney (page 111) or tomato ketchup.

2 chicken breasts, skinned and boned
2 cloves of garlic, crushed
Juice of half a lemon
Salt and pepper
A pinch of cayenne pepper
1 small egg, beaten
Freshly made white or brown breadcrumbs
About 6 tablespoons oil

1 Wash and dry chicken and cut into

57

thin fingers about 8 cm/3 inches long
and 2 cm/¾ inch thick.
2 Mix crushed garlic and lemon juice
and dip the fingers in. Then
sprinkle them with salt, pepper
and cayenne.
3 Now dip the fingers into beaten
egg and coat with breadcrumbs.
Then leave in the refrigerator for
at least an hour.
4 Heat oil in frying pan and fry the
fingers on medium heat for 5
minutes on each side, until crisp
and golden brown.

Mrs Jaswant Chopra
Childwall, Liverpool

CHICKEN WITH ORANGE AND GINGER

For 2.

1 orange
½ teaspoon ground ginger
A pinch of salt
1 teaspoon cornflour
2 chicken joints
1 tablespoon oil
100 ml/3 fl oz dry cider
1 level dessertspoon golden syrup
1 teaspoon grated fresh root
    ginger

1 Cut the orange in half and cut a
fine slice off each half for decoration.
Squeeze the juice from the rest.
2 Cut the pith away from about a
quarter of the orange skin, then cut
the zest into fine strips.
3 Mix together the ground ginger,
salt and cornflour and rub this all
over the chicken joints.
4 Heat the oil in a pan, and brown
the chicken joints all over.
5 Add the cider, orange juice, syrup,
grated ginger and the prepared strips
of orange zest. Bring to the boil,
cover with a lid and simmer gently
for about 30 minutes, or until the
chicken is tender.
6 Remove the chicken pieces and, if

there is too much sauce, reduce it a
little by boiling over a high heat.
7 Pour the sauce over the chicken
and garnish with the orange slices.

Dilwen Phillips
Gileston, South Glamorgan

BAKED CHICKEN WITH PINEAPPLE

*For 1 or 2. Mrs Voce likes to have this
delicious dish with small jacket potatoes
which she bakes in the oven with the
chicken. Can be reheated satisfactorily
for another meal, and also works well
with turkey.*

4 chicken joints or breasts
A 225 g/8 oz can of sliced
    pineapple in natural juice
25 g/1 oz margarine or butter
1 level tablespoon plain flour
2 level tablespoons tomato
    ketchup
2 teaspoons dry mustard
¼ level teaspoon salt
Pepper
1 teaspoon Worcestershire sauce
1 tablespoon vinegar

1 Skin the chicken joints and put
them in a roasting tin.
2 Strain pineapple and keep the
juice to use in another recipe. Chop
pineapple finely.
3 Heat the margarine or butter, stir
in flour and allow to sizzle for 1
minute. Stir in juice from pineapple,
bring to the boil and cook for 2
minutes.
4 Remove pan from heat and mix in
the rest of the ingredients and the
pineapple. Allow to cool.
5 Spoon the cooked sauce over the
chicken, cover tin and chill in the
refrigerator for about 4 hours, for
chicken to absorb the flavours.
6 Preheat oven to moderate, Gas 4,
350°F, 180°C.
7 Cook near top of oven, uncovered,
for 45 minutes. Baste chicken several
times during cooking, spooning sauce

over to prevent both pineapple and surface of meat from drying out.

Mrs A. M. Voce
Hampton, Worcestershire

1 Skin the chicken and arrange the portions in a single layer in a shallow 18-cm/7-inch flan dish.
2 Put the butter in a 600 ml/1 pint jug and heat on full power for 40 to 60 seconds until melted. Stir in the flour. Drain the juices of the pineapple into the flour and mix well. Heat on full power for 1 minute.
3 Mix in the ketchup, mustard, salt, pepper, Worcestershire sauce and vinegar. Heat on full power for a further 30 seconds.
4 Finely chop the pineapple and stir into the sauce. Allow to cool.
5 Pour cooled sauce over the chicken, then chill for about 4 hours, so the chicken absorbs the flavour fully.
6 Cover the dish with clear film and cook on Medium for 8 to 10 minutes. Stand for 5 minutes before serving.

MANDARIN CHICKEN

Chicken breasts coated in mildly hot spices, contrasting with the fruit and Madeira-flavoured sauce, this dish is garnished with flaked almonds and finished with cream. This recipe won Mrs Roberts a place in the semi-finals of a microwave cooking competition held by Sharp. It works well by conventional methods also. It was served with boiled rice (page 88) and carrots.
For 2.

25 g/1 oz flaked almonds
25 g/1 oz sultanas
2 tablespoons Madeira or sherry
2 skinned chicken breasts
15 g/½ oz butter

A pinch each of salt and white pepper
¼ teaspoon paprika pepper
Half a 312 g/10 oz can mandarin oranges in natural juice
A clove of garlic, finely chopped
4 tablespoons chicken stock
1 tablespoon soy sauce
¼ teaspoon ground ginger
2 level teaspoons cornflour mixed to a paste with 2 tablespoons cold water
2 tablespoons double cream

1 Put the almonds on a piece of kitchen paper and heat on full power for 2 to 3 minutes, until lightly browned. Stir or re-arrange every minute by gently shaking the paper. Set aside for garnish.
2 Heat the sultanas in the Madeira or sherry on full power for 1 minute. Leave to plump up while you cook the chicken.
3 Wash and dry chicken breasts. Arrange skinned side up in a shallow 18-cm/7-inch flan dish. Put the butter in a small basin and heat on full power for 20 to 30 seconds, until melted, then brush over the chicken breasts.
4 Mix together the salt, pepper and paprika and sprinkle liberally over the buttered chicken.
5 Drain 120 ml/4 fl oz juice from the can of mandarin oranges. Add the garlic, stock, sultanas and any remaining Madeira to the measured juice. Carefully pour this around the chicken breasts, so as not to wash off the paprika. Cover with clear film and cook on Medium for 6 minutes.

For a 2-power microwave cooker: Cook on full power for 5 minutes.

6 Uncover the dish, lift out the chicken, cover with a piece of foil, shiny side in, to keep hot. Stir the mandarins, soy sauce, ginger and cornflour paste into the sauce. Heat on full power for 2 minutes, stirring halfway through.

59

7 Stir the cream into the sauce. Replace the chicken breasts in the sauce, spoon some sauce over, and heat on full power for 2 minutes. Then scatter over the flaked almonds and serve.

If serving with rice and carrots, cook the rice first (page 88) and leave, covered, to stand. Next, cook the carrots, and leave them covered while you cook the chicken.

To serve: drain any excess water from the rice and fluff up with a fork. Spoon it on to a warm dish. Reheat the carrots on full power for 1 minute while you arrange the chicken on the rice.

Mrs Ann Roberts
Tarporley, Cheshire

MANDARIN CHICKEN

CONVENTIONAL METHOD
(*see previous page for ingredients*)
1 Place sultanas and Madeira in a small pan, cover and simmer for about 10 minutes until sultanas have plumped up.
2 Wash and dry skinned chicken breasts, place a little butter in the centre of the folded breast. Mix salt, pepper and paprika together and sprinkle over the chicken breasts.
3 Put chicken in a large frying pan and brown all over in a little extra butter or oil, if liked.
4 Drain the mandarin oranges, measure 120 ml/4 fl oz of the juice and add this to the pan with the

garlic. Pour in the stock, cover the pan, bring to the boil and reduce heat; simmer for 20 minutes or until the chicken is tender.
5 Add the sultanas and Madeira in which they have been soaking. Cook for a further 5 minutes.
6 Remove the chicken breasts from the pan and keep warm.
7 Stir the cornflour mixture into the liquid in the pan. Bring to the boil, stirring until the mixture is thickened.
8 Add the soy sauce, ground ginger and most of the mandarin oranges (keep a few for decoration). Stir the cream into the sauce and cook for 4 to 5 minutes, stirring.
9 Place the chicken in a hot dish, pour the sauce over and garnish with flaked almonds and reserved mandarin segments.

STEAMED RICE WITH CHICKEN AND CHINESE MUSHROOMS

For this you will really need to visit a Chinese supermarket; you also need a steamer. For 2.

Half a small chicken or 2 chicken thighs
6 Chinese mushrooms
1 cup of rice
1½ tablespoons oil
A pinch of salt
1 cup boiling water

2 tablespoons light soy sauce
2 spring onions, cut into 2.5-cm/
   1-inch lengths
A little sesame oil

MARINADE
1 tablespoon finely chopped fresh
   ginger
1 tablespoon light soy sauce
1 tablespoon water
1 teaspoon ginger juice
1 teaspoon rice wine or dry sherry
1 teaspoon sugar
1 teaspoon cornflour
½ teaspoon salt
A pinch of ground pepper
A pinch of Five Spice powder

1 Remove the chicken from the
bones and cut it into bite-sized
pieces.
2 Mix the marinade ingredients in a
bowl, put in the chicken and leave
to marinate for at least 30 minutes,
stirring from time to time.
3 Soak the Chinese mushrooms in
warm water until soft, about 10 to 15
minutes.
4 Wash the rice in several changes of
cold water to remove excess starch,
then put it into a large heatproof
bowl. Stir in 1 tablespoon oil and a
pinch of salt. Pour over 1 cup of
boiling water. Place the bowl in a
steamer, put on the lid and let it
steam for 15 minutes.
5 Drain mushrooms, remove stalks
and shred mushrooms finely. Mix
with ½ tablespoon oil and a little
salt.
6 Remove lid from steamer, loosen
the rice a little and put in the chicken
and marinade with the mushrooms on
top. Then let it steam for 15 to 20
minutes, or until chicken is cooked.
Turn off heat and leave it to stand
for 5 minutes.
7 Just before serving, sprinkle
chicken with the soy sauce, spring
onions and a little sesame oil.

Jennie Siew Lee Cook
York

PATTI'S CHICKEN FOR TWO

*But easy to make for one. The
remaining soups mix well together for
another meal. Use a soup can for
measuring.*

2 chicken portions or breasts
Half a 300 g/11 oz can of
   mushroom soup
Half a 300 g/11 oz can of celery
   soup
Half a can of grated Cheddar
   cheese
Half a can of white wine

1 Place the chicken in an ovenproof
dish.
2 Mix together the soups.
3 Mix the cheese and wine into the
soup. Pour it over the chicken.
4 Bake for 1 hour in a moderately
hot oven, Gas 6, 400°F, 200°C.
During this time the mixture will
have turned into a delicious sauce.
Serve with jacket potatoes and green
beans.

TIP
The dish may also be cooked in a cool
oven, Gas 2, 300°F, 150°C for 2
hours.

Megan Mallinson
Fixby, Huddersfield

 Microwave

1 Place the chicken in a single layer
in a 1.4-litre/3-pint casserole.
Follow steps 2 and 3 above.
4 Cover with a lid and cook on
Medium for 15 to 18 minutes.

For a 2-power microwave cooker: Cook
on full power for 10 minutes, stirring
once. Stand for 5 minutes at the end
of cooking.

5 Serve the chicken on warm plates
with the sauce stirred and poured
over.

NUTTY LEMON STUFFING

*For chicken or duck, this stuffing
mixture is baked separately, not inside
the bird.*

50 g/2 oz butter
Finely grated rind and juice of
   one lemon
75 g/3 oz fresh wholemeal
   breadcrumbs
40 g/1½ oz chopped walnuts
3 tablespoons chopped parsley
A pinch of thyme or marjoram
Salt and freshly ground pepper

1 Melt the butter, add lemon juice
and rind. Remove from the heat.
2 Mix all the other ingredients
together and add the melted butter
and lemon. The mixture should be
moist but not wet.
3 Pack into a buttered ovenproof
dish. Cover with foil and bake with
chicken or duck for 20 to 25 minutes.
Do not overcook.

                Grace Mulligan

BACON AND PRUNE ROLLS

*An excellent accompaniment for a
festive bird, or may be served for pre-
dinner snacks or as a savoury finish to
a meal on slices of toast or fried bread.*

Pitted prunes – there will be 10
   to 12 prunes in 125 g/4 oz
Thinly sliced streaky bacon

1 Soak the prunes in hot water or hot
tea overnight. If they are not really
soft next day then cook them for 15
minutes in the liquid in which they
were soaked. Drain and pat them dry
with kitchen paper.
2 De-rind the bacon and cut into
pieces about 10 cm/4 inches long.
Stretch the pieces with the back of a
knife.
3 Wrap the bacon around the prunes
and thread on to skewers.
5 Bake in a moderate oven, Gas 4,
350°F, 180°C, or set under a hot grill
turning often.

                Grace Mulligan

CRISP ROAST DUCK WITH GRAPEFRUIT SAUCE

*Serves 2. It has been said that there
should be only two of you when sitting
down to roast duck – you and the
duck!*

1 duckling, about 1.3 kg/3 lb
1 onion, halved
Salt
1 small grapefruit
1 tablespoon flour
200 ml/6 fl oz strong stock made
   from giblets *
Freshly ground pepper
Sprigs of parsley

* *To make giblet stock simmer the
giblets and neck from the duckling with
375 ml/¾ pint water, a bunch of herbs
or parsley and a few slices of onion for
45 minutes. Then strain.*

1 After removing the giblets, dry the
bird inside and out with kitchen
paper. Prick the skin all over with a
skewer or sharp scissors. Put the
peeled onion inside the bird. Rub
salt over the outer skin – this helps to
make it crisp.
2 Set the bird on a wire rack or
trivet inside a roasting tin so the fat
runs out easily as it cooks.
3 Preheat the oven to moderate, Gas
4, 350°F, 180°C, then cook the duck

uncovered and without basting for 30 minutes per 450 g/1 lb. When the time is up, pierce the thickest part of the thigh with a skewer. If juice is clear the bird is done; if still pink, leave it for 15 minutes more.

4 Cut grapefruit in half and cut off a slice for decorating. Finely grate the zest and squeeze out all the juice.

5 Remove the duck to a heated dish and keep warm.

6 Pour off all but 1 to 2 tablespoons of fat from the roasting tin, keeping as much as possible of the juices underneath. Sprinkle in the flour and stir over a low heat. Add the giblet stock a little at a time, stirring as it thickens. Boil for a minute or two and add the grapefruit juice and rind. (Add a spot of gravy browning or gravy salt if it is too pale.)

7 Pour the sauce into a heated jug and keep warm. Decorate the bird with one or two slices of grapefruit and lots of parsley.

Grace Mulligan

TURKEY OR CHICKEN IN A CIDER SAUCE

For 1 or 2. This reheats well. The addition of cream makes it a special occasion dish.

200 g/½ lb apples (Bramley's are ideal), peeled and cored
2 turkey or chicken pieces (leg joints are best)
1 small onion, finely chopped
1 tablespoon finely chopped fresh parsley
150 ml/¼ pint dry cider
Salt and pepper
1 teaspoon brown sugar
2 tablespoons cream (optional)

1 Cut the apples into slices and put them in a casserole.

2 Remove skin from the chicken

pieces and put them on top of the apples.

3 Scatter the onion and half the parsley over the chicken, then pour in the cider.

4 Cover with a lid and cook in a preheated oven, Gas 4, 350°F, 180°C, for 1 hour, or cook on top of the stove, just letting it simmer until chicken is tender – 30 to 45 minutes.

5 Remove the chicken pieces to a warmed serving dish. Sprinkle sugar over apples and spoon both apples and sauce on top of chicken. Sprinkle with the remaining parsley.

6 To make the sauce extra rich, stir in cream at the last minute.

Reheat on top of stove, 5 to 8 minutes in a covered pan over low heat. To reheat in oven, preheat to moderately hot, Gas 5 to 6, 375° to 400°F, 190° to 200°C and heat for 20 minutes in a covered dish on the middle shelf.

Grace Mulligan

1 Slice the apples and put them into a 1.5-litre/3-pint ceramic casserole. Cut each chicken quarter in half at the leg joint and arrange the pieces on top of the apple.

2 Scatter onion and half the parsley over the chicken, then pour over the cider. Cover the dish with a lid or clear film and cook on Medium for 15 minutes. Allow to stand for 5 minutes.

3 Lift the chicken portions out on to a warm serving plate.

4 *For a smooth sauce*, put the apples and cider into a processor or liquidiser and blend until smooth. Sweeten with the sugar and add 1 level (5 ml) teaspoon cornflour mixed with 1 tablespoon water. Return sauce to the cleaned dish. Reheat on full power for 2 to 3 minutes to thicken. Then pour it over the chicken. Sprinkle with the remaining parsley.

TURKEY KEBABS

Makes about 6 kebabs. This recipe is useful for leftover cooked turkey. The kebabs freeze well before they are fried and can be cooked straight from the freezer. Chicken can be used instead. If you have no food processor, then it is a matter of chopping or mincing by hand.

2 cloves of garlic
Half a green chilli, seeds removed
A 7 mm/$\frac{1}{4}$ inch cube of fresh
  ginger
325 g/$\frac{3}{4}$ lb cooked turkey meat,
  skin and bones removed
1 small egg
$\frac{1}{2}$ teaspoon garam masala
$\frac{1}{2}$ teaspoon cumin powder
$\frac{1}{4}$ teaspoon ground nutmeg
$\frac{1}{2}$ teaspoon salt
Oil for deep frying

1 Put the garlic, chilli and ginger into a food processor and process until it is finely chopped.
2 Add the turkey, egg, spices and salt and process until everything is smooth and well mixed.
3 Brush your hands with a little oil and form shapes with the turkey mixture about 1 cm/$\frac{1}{2}$ inch thick. Put them on an oiled tray in the refrigerator for 2 hours. They are easier to fry when very cold.
4 Deep-fry the turkey kebabs in hot oil for a few minutes each side, then drain them on kitchen paper. Serve them hot with Tangy Tomato Sauce, (page 95) and salad, or as a snack with Yoghurt Chutney (page 111).

Nirmal Singh
Nuneaton, Warwickshire

GAUDY RABBIT

For 1 or 2. This delicious dish reheats well. By adding mushrooms and red pepper at the last minute along with a second lot of wine or cider, the flavours of all the ingredients are refreshed and distinct.

2 tablespoons oil, preferably
  olive oil
1 clove of garlic, finely chopped
450 g/1 lb rabbit joints
A wineglass of dry white wine or
  dry cider
1 tablespoon tomato paste
250 ml/8 fl oz light stock (a
  chicken stock cube will do)
125 g/4 oz button mushrooms
Half a red pepper or a green one
  which is beginning to colour
15 g/$\frac{1}{2}$ oz butter

1 Heat oil, add garlic and rabbit and cook over medium heat until rabbit is browned all over.
2 Add half the wine or cider, turn up heat and let it bubble to evaporate a little.
3 Stir in half the tomato paste with half the stock. Cover and cook over medium heat for 15 minutes.
4 Now turn the rabbit pieces over. Replace the lid and cook over low heat for 20 to 25 minutes – the sauce will be very much reduced.
5 Take pan off heat, lift out rabbit pieces and, when cool enough to handle, strip flesh from bones.
6 Meanwhile, cut mushrooms into thin slices and chop the pepper. Cook together very gently in the butter in another pan for 3 to 4 minutes, then add remaining wine or cider and simmer until pepper is tender.
7 Stir rabbit carefully back into sauce in pan in which it cooked. Mix in remaining tomato paste and stock.
8 Stir in mushroom mixture. Reheat gently and serve.

Dr Doug McEachern
Stirling, South Australia

64

Chapter 5

Main Course Meats

BACON RIBS

These can be bought at most butchers' who bone their own bacon. One sheet (half a rib cage) weighs approximately 1.1 kg/2½ lb. This should give about 350 g/¾ lb of meat and a good 1.2 litres/2 pints of stock. Very economical – very satisfying.

1 Cut ribs into 3 to 4 pieces and put them in a large pan. Cover with cold water, bring to the boil and then pour off the water. This gets rid of any excess salt.
2 Cover again with cold water and bring to the boil. Cover pan and cook gently until tender – about 1 hour.

Alternatively in a pressure cooker, it will take about 20 minutes. The result will be less quantity but a stronger stock which can be diluted for use.

3 Drain the stock into a bowl; leave until quite cold, then skim off the fat.
4 Strip the meat from the bones.

To use the Stock:

LENTIL SOUP WITH SAUSAGE

100 g/4 oz lentils
2 sticks celery, finely chopped
1 onion, finely chopped
A small piece of swede, or
　1 turnip, finely chopped
1 potato, peeled and chopped
1 small cooking apple, peeled and
　chopped
1 bay leaf
1.2 litres/2 pints stock from bacon
　ribs
225 g/8 oz smoked Continental
　sausage

1 Put all ingredients except the sausage into a large pan and cook gently for about ¾ to 1 hour (20 minutes in pressure cooker) or until vegetables are tender and lentils soft.
2 Liquidise the soup if you prefer it smooth. At this stage it can be cooled

and frozen if you're keeping some for another day.
3 Chop the sausage, add to the soup and heat to warm the sausage through.

To use the Bacon Meat:

1 BACON MOULD

This turns out nicely on to a plate and looks attractive.

225 g/8 oz meat from bacon
　ribs
150 ml/¼ pint stock from ribs
2 level teaspoons gelatine
Pepper

1 Mince the meat or put it through a food processor.
2 Heat stock and sprinkle on the gelatine. Stir until dissolved.
3 Stir gelatine mixture into meat, seasoning if desired, but no extra salt should be required.
4 Pour into a wetted mould or basin and leave to set. Turn it out on to a plate to serve.

2 BACON CAKES

100 to 150 g/4 to 6 oz meat from
　bacon ribs
100 g/4 oz cooked potato, mashed
Pepper and salt, if necessary
1 small egg, beaten
2 tablespoons fresh or dried
　breadcrumbs
25 g/1 oz fat or 1 tablespoon oil
　for frying

1 Mince the bacon meat, or put it through a food processor.
2 Mix it into the potato, seasoning to taste. Shape into 4 round cakes.
3 Coat in egg, then in crumbs.
4 Heat fat or oil and fry the bacon cakes until crisp and golden on the outside and nicely warmed through, about 3 minutes on each side. Serve with carrots, parsnips or beans.

Margaret Heywood
Todmorden, Yorkshire

HAM SHANK

*A ham shank is a cheap cut, but
rewarding if you are prepared to go to
a little trouble. It can be cooked in two
ways – conventionally simmered in a
good-sized pan until the meat is falling
off the bone, or in a pressure cooker. If
using a pressure cooker, it will take
barely half an hour but follow the
manufacturer's instruction and never fill
the cooker more than half-full of liquid.*

1 ham shank, about 1 kg/2 to
   2½ lb in weight, plain or
   smoked
About 1½ litres/3 pints water
1 small onion
1 piece of carrot
1 bay leaf
4 peppercorns

1 Put everything into a large pan.
Bring to the boil and skim off any
grey scum which rises to the surface.
At this point, taste the water and if
it is very salty, pour it away and add
fresh water, otherwise you will have
very salty stock.
2 Cook the shank for about 1½
hours, or until the meat is falling
from the bone. Remove pan from
heat and allow everything to cool until
you can handle it easily.
3 Strain off the stock and leave in a
cool place, preferably overnight.
Remove the top layer of fat before
using.
4 To prepare the ham meat: remove
all fat and gristle while it is still hot.
Allow to cool and store in refrigerator
until needed.

Grace Mulligan

SAVOURY HOT POT

*This is very good made with cooked
ham from a shank or bacon ribs. Also
good for cold beef, pork or lamb.
For 1.*

2 medium potatoes
A little butter
1 medium onion, finely chopped
1 large tomato, sliced
100 g/4 oz cooked meat,* sliced or
   minced
Pepper and salt
50 g/2 oz grated cheese
150 ml/¼ pint milk or stock

* *If using ham, make the dish without
the cheese and use stock instead of
milk.*

1 Preheat the oven to moderate, Gas
4, 350°F, 180°C.
2 Boil potatoes until nearly cooked,
then slice them thinly.
3 Butter an ovenproof dish and put
in layers of potato, onion, tomato and
meat. Season with pepper and a little
salt.
4 Repeat layers, finishing with
potato.
5 Cover with cheese. If not using
cheese, dot with butter. Pour in milk
or stock.
6 Cook in preheated oven for 40 to
45 minutes.

Mrs Catherine Sangster
Aberdeen

SWEET-AND-SOUR
PORK CHOP

For 1.

1 tablespoon oil
1 pork chop
1 small onion, chopped
2 teaspoons brown sugar
1 teaspoon finely chopped fresh
   ginger or a pinch of dry ginger
1 tablespoon light soy sauce
4 tablespoons cider
Salt and pepper

1 Heat the oil in a small frying pan
with a good lid. Quickly brown the
chop on both sides.
2 Remove the chop for a moment
and fry the onion for 2 minutes.
Then mix and add the rest of the
ingredients and reduce the heat to the
lowest possible.

3 Replace the pork chop, cover with a lid and simmer slowly for 15 to 20 minutes, or until the chop is cooked.

Grace Mulligan

SHERRIED PORK CHOPS

Creamed potatoes and courgettes, lightly fried with sliced green and red peppers, go well with this dish. For 2.

15 g/½ oz butter
2 pork chops
1 small onion, finely chopped
150 ml/5 fl oz apple juice
3 tablespoons dry sherry
1 teaspoon dried thyme or 2 teaspoons chopped fresh thyme
Salt and pepper
A pinch of sugar
100 g/4 oz mushrooms, wiped and thinly sliced

1 Melt the butter in a frying pan and brown the chops on both sides, then remove from the pan and set aside.
2 Add the onion to the remaining butter and fry for a few minutes, then pour in the apple juice, 2 tablespoons of the sherry, the thyme and seasonings.
3 Replace the pork chops and scatter the mushrooms over.
4 Bring to the boil, cover with a lid and cook for 25 minutes, or until the pork chops are tender.
5 Just before serving, stir in the remaining tablespoon of sherry and transfer the chops and sauce to a warmed serving dish.

Angela Henderson
Fleet, Hampshire

PORK STIR-FRY

For 2, but easy to make just enough for 1 person. Serve with Boiled Rice (page 88) or Vegetable Rice (page 90).

175 to 225 g/6 to 8 oz pork fillet, cut into thin strips

1 tablespoon cornflour, seasoned with salt and pepper
1 to 2 tablespoons oil
A clove of garlic, crushed
75 to 100 g/3 to 4 oz red cabbage, finely shredded
50 g/2 oz mushrooms, wiped and sliced
Half a green pepper, thinly sliced in strips
1 to 2 tablespoons soy sauce

1 Toss the meat in the seasoned cornflour.
2 Heat the oil in a large frying pan or a wok and cook the garlic for a minute, then stir-fry the meat until it is well browned, about 2 minutes.
3 Add the cabbage, mushrooms and green pepper and continue to stir-fry until the meat is cooked, about 5 to 8 minutes.
4 Stir in the soy sauce and serve at once.

Dilwen Phillips
Gileston, South Glamorgan

CELERY PORK STEAKS

This is delicious and a very easy recipe, ideal if you have a 'slow cooker'; simply cook on the low setting for 6 to 7 hours. Makes 2 helpings.

2 pork steaks
A can of condensed celery soup
1 tablespoon cold water
Chopped celery leaves or parsley (optional)

1 Put the pork steaks into a pan with a tight-fitting lid and pour the soup over. Add 1 tablespoon cold water to the empty soup tin to rinse it out, then pour this over too. Put on the lid.
2 Put the pan on a low heat and let it slowly simmer for 40 minutes.

Alternatively arrange the pork and soup in an ovenproof dish, put on a

tight-fitting lid and cook in a
moderately hot oven, Gas 6, 400°F,
200°C, for 40 to 45 minutes.

3 Garnishing with celery leaves or
parsley makes the dish look as nice as
it tastes. Serve with rice and green
vegetables.

Mrs A. M. Anderson
Stamford, Lincolnshire

1 Arrange the pork steaks in a single
layer in a small ceramic casserole.
Pour over the soup. Add cold water
to rinse out the can, then pour this
over the soup.
2 Cover the casserole with a lid or
clear film and cook on Low for 20
minutes. Allow to stand for 5
minutes.

For a 2-power microwave cooker:
Cook on Defrost.

3 Serve sprinkled with parsley.

PORK WITH CHESTNUTS

*For 2, but as this dish freezes and
reheats well it would make two
substantial meals for one person.
Remember to start this recipe the day
before you plan to eat the dish.*

125 g/4 oz chestnuts, whole or
    broken pieces
225 g/8 oz pork fillet or tenderloin
1 to 2 tablespoons oil
1 medium onion, chopped
1 medium apple, peeled, cored
    and chopped
300 ml/½ pint apple juice
300 ml/½ pint light stock
½ to 1 teaspoon dried marjoram
25 g/1 oz millet-flakes*
50 g/2 oz mushrooms, sliced
15 g/½ oz butter
25 g/1 oz raisins

* *Millet flakes can be bought from good
wholefood or health food shops.*

1 Soak the chestnuts in water
overnight; next day, pick out all the
brown flakes of skin that may still
adhere.
2 Trim the pork and cut it
into 2-cm/¾-inch cubes.
3 Heat a little of the oil and fry pork
briskly for only 2 to 3 minutes,
turning and stirring it so that all sides
are sealed. Then transfer to a
casserole.
4 Fry onion in remaining oil until
just turning golden. Add to casserole
with apple and chestnuts.
5 Stir in the apple juice and stock,
marjoram and millet.
6 Cover and cook in a moderately hot
oven, Gas 6, 400°F, 200°C, for 45
minutes.
7 Ten minutes before the end of
cooking time, lightly fry the
mushrooms in butter and stir them
into casserole with the raisins.
8 Serve with a green vegetable and
boiled potatoes.

Catriona Mulligan
Leatherhead, Surrey

*This dish turns out rather pale and
needs a bright-coloured vegetable to
accompany it.*

*See below for the microwave way to
peel chestnuts.*

You need no oil and only half the
stock, but increase the butter to
25 g/1 oz.
Follow steps 1 and 2 from the
previous method.
3 Put 25 g/1 oz butter into a 2.1
litre/4 pint casserole with the onions
and mushrooms and heat on full
power for 3 minutes.
4 Stir in the pork, apple, chestnuts,
raisins, apple juice, 150 ml/¼ pint
stock, the marjoram and millet. Cover
the casserole with a lid or clear film

and cook on Low for 30 minutes, stirring once.

For a 2-power microwave cooker:
Cook on full power for 5 minutes, then on Defrost for 25 to 30 minutes.

5 Let it stand for 10 minutes, then stir well and season to taste before serving.

A Microwave Tip

TO PEEL CHESTNUTS
Cut a cross in the top of each chestnut and place 8 at a time, in a circle, on kitchen paper in the microwave. Cook on full power for 1 minute. Cool slightly, then peel.

Yvonne Hamlett
Haddenham, Buckinghamshire

SWEET AND SOUR PORK

This is especially delicious if you can buy fresh ginger. Chicken, fish fillets or king prawns can be used instead of pork. Makes enough for 2.

225 g/8 oz pork, cut into 1-cm/
  ½-inch cubes
1 egg, beaten
2 tablespoons self raising flour
  mixed with salt, pepper and
  1 teaspoon cornflour
Oil for deep frying

SAUCE
1½ tablespoons oil
1 large onion, chopped roughly
1 clove of garlic, crushed
2.5 cm/1 inch fresh ginger, peeled
  and grated, or 1½ teaspoons
  ground ginger
2 tablespoons tomato ketchup*
1½ teaspoons cornflour mixed
  with 8 tablespoons water
2 tablespoons sugar
Salt and pepper
½ teaspoon vinegar

2 tomatoes, skinned (page 26) and
  cut into wedges
Sliced pickled cucumber and
  carrot shreds to garnish

* *Pineapple juice can be used as an alternative and gives a delicate and slightly richer flavour.*

1 Start by making the sauce: heat the oil in a saucepan and cook the onion until soft, then add the garlic and ginger and cook for a few minutes.
2 Mix in all the remaining ingredients, except the fresh tomatoes, and cook until the sauce thickens.
3 Now coat the pork in beaten egg, then roll the pieces in the seasoned flour and cornflour mixture.
4 Heat the oil and deep-fry the pork until golden brown. Drain well on kitchen paper.
5 Reheat the sauce, mix in the tomato wedges and pour the sauce over the cooked pork. Serve at once, garnished with pickled cucumber and carrot shreds.

Jennie Siew Lee Cook
York

BARBECUE SPARE RIBS
For 2.

450 g/1 lb pork spare ribs
½ tablespoon honey, warmed
1 teaspoon cornflour mixed with 1
  tablespoon water

MARINADE
1 small onion, chopped
1 clove of garlic, crushed
1 tablespoon light soy sauce
1 tablespoon dark soy sauce
1 tablespoon dry sherry
1 tablespoon golden syrup, or
  sugar
1 dessertspoon chilli sauce, or
  Worcestershire sauce
1 dessertspoon tomato ketchup, or
  Hoisin sauce

¼ teaspoon salt
A pinch of Five Spice powder

1 First mix together the marinade ingredients and put the pork ribs to marinate in this mixture for at least 2 hours. Turn them every now and then.
2 Remove the ribs and brush them lightly with the warmed honey.
3 Grill the chops, turning them frequently, until cooked – 15 to 20 minutes. Alternatively, they may be cooked on a barbecue or in a hot oven, Gas 7, 425°F, 210°C for about 20 minutes.
4 Put the remaining marinade into a pan with the cornflour and water and heat until it thickens. Add more water if necessary to make a tasty sauce to serve with the ribs.

Jennie Siew Lee Cook
York

BARBECUE SAUCE

This sauce will keep well in the refrigerator for about 2 weeks. Use with hot and cold food as a dip; good also hot with sausages or chops. Makes about 300 ml/½ pint.

300 ml/½ pint dry cider or dry
    home-made wine
1 dessertspoon cornflour
1 large teaspoon dry mustard
1 tablespoon soy sauce
1 level tablespoon brown sugar
125 g/4 oz canned pineapple
    pieces, drained and diced

1 Put all the ingredients into a saucepan and, stirring all the time, bring slowly up to the boil.
2 Cook for 3 minutes. The sauce is then ready to use.

Grace Mulligan

1 Put the cornflour in a 600-ml/ 1-pint jug. Mix to a smooth paste with a little of the cider.
2 Stir in the mustard, sugar and soy sauce. Blend in the remaining cider.
3 Stir in the pineapple pieces and cook on full power for 3 to 4 minutes, stirring once, halfway through cooking.

BELLY PORK WITH APPLE AND SAGE COATING

One hot plus one cold meal for two people. Ask the butcher for a single piece of belly pork.

A 675 g/1½ lb piece of belly
    pork
A little fat or oil

STUFFING
1 small onion, finely chopped
1 small dessert apple, grated
50 to 75 g/2 to 3 oz fresh
    wholemeal breadcrumbs
1 small egg

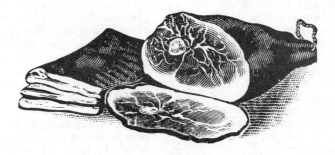

2 teaspoons chopped fresh sage or
$\frac{1}{2}$ teaspoon dried sage
$\frac{1}{2}$ teaspoon salt
Freshly ground black pepper

1 Preheat the oven to moderate,
Gas 3, 325°F, 160°C.
2 Prepare the pork, removing rind,
excess fat, bones and gristle. Lay the
piece of meat rough side up on a
board or plate.
3 Mix the stuffing ingredients
together, then pile it neatly on top of
pork, pressing it down gently.
4 Grease or oil a small roasting tin
and place the prepared pork in it.
Cover with a piece of greased foil.
5 Put it above the middle of the
preheated oven and cook it for 45
minutes.
6 Take it out and increase oven
temperature to Gas 4, 350°F, 180°C.
Remove foil, baste top of stuffing all
over with the dripping from the meat
and return it, uncovered, to the top
shelf of the oven for 30 minutes. The
stuffing will be nicely browned and
just crisp and firm, and the meat well
done, tender and moist.
7 Serve with plain boiled potatoes
and lightly steamed vegetables, such
as carrot and cabbage.

Mary Watts

Microwave

1 Trim the pork, removing the rind,
excess fat, bone and any gristle. Lay
the meat on an upturned plate in the
base of a 20-cm/8-inch pie dish.
2 Mix the stuffing ingredients
together and pile neatly on top of the
pork, pressing it down gently. Cover
with clear film and cook on Low for
35 minutes or until tender.
3 Remove the film, drain off any
excess fat, slide out the upturned
plate and then put the dish under a
moderate grill until the top is crisp
and brown.

ALL-IN-ONE SAUSAGE SUPPER

For 2, but easy to reduce for one.

4 to 6 sausages
15 g/$\frac{1}{2}$ oz fat, lard or dripping
1 onion, peeled and sliced
125 g/4 oz cabbage, finely
   chopped
225 g/8 oz potatoes, peeled and
   diced
A pinch of dried mixed herbs
1 carrot, peeled and sliced
A 230 g/8 oz can of tomatoes
Salt and pepper

1 Cut the sausages into chunks and
fry them in the fat until browned.
2 Remove sausages and all but 2
tablespoons of the fat. Fry the onion
until soft.
3 Add all the remaining ingredients,
mix well together and cook for 2 to 3
minutes.
4 Put the sausages back on top of the
vegetables, put on the lid and simmer
gently for 30 minutes, or until
potatoes and carrots are soft.

Miss Pauline Eddowes
Heworth, York

CIDER WITH SAUSAGES

For 2, but easy to make for 1.

225 g/8 oz pork sausages
50 g/2 oz streaky bacon, cut small
100 g/4 oz tiny onions or 1 small
   onion cut in 4 pieces
1 level tablespoon plain flour
225 ml/8 fl oz dry cider
$\frac{1}{2}$ teaspoon dried thyme
1 bay leaf
A small clove of garlic, peeled and
   crushed
Half a beef stock cube

1 In a frying pan, lightly brown the
sausages, bacon and onions.
2 Sprinkle in the flour and gradually

add the cider, stirring as it thickens. Add the thyme, bay leaf, garlic and stock cube and simmer, covered with a lid, for 20 minutes.

3 Remove the bay leaf before serving with potatoes and vegetables.

The June Hulbert Cookbook

SCOTCH EGGS

For 1 or 2. Hot one day, cold the next. Bake or deep-fry them. Nice with freshly made Tomato Sauce (page 175).

2 large sausages
A generous pinch of dried sage
2 small hard-boiled eggs, shelled
1 egg, beaten
Dried breadcrumbs
Oil

1 Skin the sausages, then work the dried sage into the sausagemeat.
2 Divide the sausagemeat in half and flatten each piece into a large circle. Mould the circles around the eggs, pressing firmly to ensure that there are no holes.
3 Chill the eggs for about 1 hour, then dip each one into the beaten egg and coat in breadcrumbs.
4 Heat the oil to 350° to 360°F, 180° to 185°C, and deep fry the Scotch Eggs for about 5 minutes, turning them frequently.
5 Drain well and serve hot or cold.

To bake the Scotch Eggs: leave out steps 3 to 5 above and simply put the sausage-coated eggs straight on to a greased baking tray. Preheat the oven to moderately hot, Gas 6, 400°F, 200°C, and bake for 20 minutes.

Grace Mulligan

CRISPY NOODLES WITH BEEF

For 2. This recipe is a meal in itself as it contains meat, noodles and vegetables.

175 g/6 oz rump steak
75 to 100 g/3 to 4 oz egg noodles
150 g/5 oz whole green beans, topped, tailed and cut into 5-cm/2-inch pieces
250 ml/8 fl oz oil
1 clove of garlic
150 ml/$\frac{1}{4}$ pint beef stock
1 teaspoon cornflour mixed with 1 tablespoon water
2 spring onions, cut in small pieces

MARINADE
1 teaspoon dark soy sauce
$\frac{1}{2}$ teaspoon sugar
$\frac{1}{2}$ teaspoon rice wine or dry sherry
$\frac{1}{2}$ teaspoon cornflour
Freshly ground pepper
90 ml/3 fl oz water
2 tablespoons oil

1 Cut the beef into thin strips. Mix the marinade, put in the beef and leave it for 30 minutes.
2 Plunge the noodles into boiling water for a short time to soften them, then rinse thoroughly and drain them.
3 Unless you like very crisp beans, put them in a pan with a little water and steam them for 2 or 3 minutes; otherwise add them at step 5.
4 Heat the oil in a wok or large deep frying pan and deep-fry the noodles, half at a time, until crisp on both sides. Transfer to 2 heated plates and keep warm.
5 Remove all but 3 tablespoons of oil from the wok. Add the garlic. Drain and add the beef. Fry over a high heat for about 30 seconds, then add the beans and mix well.
6 Pour in the stock and bring to the boil.
7 Stir in the cornflour mixture to thicken the sauce and lastly put in the spring onions.
8 Spoon the mixture evenly over the 2 plates of noodles and serve.

Jennie Siew Lee Cook
York

73

BEEF IN A TOMATO AND CREAM SAUCE

Nice with rice or potatoes and a green vegetable. For 2.

175 g/6 oz stewing beef
A little seasoned flour
1 to 2 tablespoons dripping or oil
Half a 300 g/10 oz can of
  condensed tomato soup
6 small pickling onions, or 1 small
  onion cut into 6 pieces
Half a red or green pepper,
  deseeded and sliced
150 ml/¼ pint beef stock
50 g/2 oz mushrooms, sliced
2 tablespoons soured cream *

* *See page 111 for another recipe using soured cream.*

1 Cut the beef into 1-cm/½-inch strips, toss in seasoned flour, then fry them in hot fat until browned.
2 Drain off the excess fat, add all the rest of the ingredients, except the mushrooms and cream, and bring gently to the boil. Cover with a lid and cook very slowly for 1 hour, or until the meat is tender.
4 Add the mushrooms and cook for a further 10 minutes, then remove from the heat and stir in the soured cream just before serving.

Mrs Jill Gouldstone
Wokingham, Berkshire

This works well by microwave using rump steak but you do need a browning dish.

A 15 ml tablespoon oil
1 onion, sliced
Half a red or green pepper,
  deseeded and sliced
50 g/2 oz mushrooms, sliced
175 g/6 oz rump steak
Half a 300 g/10 oz can condensed
  tomato soup
Half a beef stock cube dissolved
  in 2 tablespoons boiling water
2 tablespoons soured cream

1 Put the oil, onion, peppers and mushrooms into a small basin; cook on full power for 3 minutes.
2 Cut the beef into 1-cm/½-inch strips and stir into the onion mixture so that it is well coated in oil.
3 Heat the empty browning dish on full power for 6 minutes (or according to manufacturer's instructions). Immediately tip in the onion and beef mixture, stirring quickly so the beef is seared.
4 Cook on full power for 2 minutes, then stir in the soup and beef stock. Cook on full power for a further 2 to 3 minutes, stirring once.
5 Lastly, stir in the cream and serve.

A RICH BEEF STEW

For 1, 2 or more. This stew has a lovely flavour. It keeps for a day or two in the refrigerator, and freezes and reheats well.

450 g/1 lb braising steak
1 tablespoon cooking oil
1 medium onion, sliced
1 clove of garlic, crushed
1 medium carrot, peeled and cut
  in thick strips
4 or 5 lovage or celery leaves, cut
  up
Freshly ground black pepper
2 teaspoons tomato purée
150 ml/¼ pint best bitter beer
2 tablespoons chopped parsley

1 Cut the meat into 1-cm/½-inch cubes, trimming off excess fat and gristle.
2 Heat oil and gently fry onion and garlic until soft – about 5 minutes. Then add carrot and cook for another 5 minutes. Stir in lovage or celery leaves.

3 Add meat and keep stirring so it browns all over.
4 Stir in pepper, tomato purée and the beer, which will froth up at first, and stir occasionally as it comes to the boil. Turn heat very low, cover and let it simmer, stirring occasionally, for 1 to 1¼ hours until the meat is tender.
5 For the last quarter of an hour, remove the lid so that a little of the liquid evaporates and the meat is served in a rich sauce.
6 Check seasoning before serving and add the parsley at the last minute.

Mrs Charmaine McEachern
Hawes, North Yorkshire

 Microwave 〰〰〰〰〰〰〰〰〰〰

In addition to the above ingredients you need:

300 ml/½ pint hot beef stock
Two 15 ml tablespoons cornflour
Two 15 ml tablespoons cold water

1 Cut the meat into 1-cm/½-inch cubes. Trim away any excess fat and gristle.
2 Put the oil, onion and garlic into a 2-litre/4-pint casserole and heat on full power for 3 to 5 minutes until soft.
3 Add the meat, carrots and lovage or celery leaves. Stir well. Add the tomato purée, black pepper, stock and beer. Invert a small tea plate on top of the meat. This keeps the meat and vegetables under the stock and stops them dehydrating during cooking. It also means that the stew will not need stirring.
4 Cover the casserole dish with its own lid or with clear film. Cook on full power for 10 minutes to bring to the boil and then turn the power to Simmer for 60 minutes. This slow cooking will allow the meat to tenderise.
For a 2-power microwave cooker:
Cook the casserole on full power for

10 minutes and then on Defrost for 60 minutes.

5 At the end of cooking, remove the lid and lift out the plate. Blend the cornflour and water to a smooth paste and stir into the stew. Heat on full power for 5 minutes, stirring once. The stew should have thickened nicely.
6 Check seasoning and stir in parsley before serving.

STEAK AND KIDNEY PIE FILLING

This filling stores perfectly in a freezer and, if packed in small amounts, is ideal for turning into individual pies. Alternatively, the filling can be covered with mashed potatoes or just served by itself with boiled rice.

900 g/2 lb stewing steak
225 g/8 oz ox kidney
2 tablespoons oil
1 large onion, chopped
2 tablespoons wholemeal flour
450 ml/¾ pint beef stock
2 large teaspoons horseradish
  sauce or mustard
Salt, pepper and gravy browning

1 Prepare the steak and kidney, trimming it carefully and cutting into pieces as small as you like. Keep the trimmings (see Tip, below).
2 In a large pan, heat the oil and quickly brown the steak and kidney pieces. Remove from the pan and set aside.
3 If necessary, add more oil to the pan and cook the onion until soft.
4 Sprinkle in the flour, then add the stock and horseradish sauce, or mustard, and replace the meat.
5 Heat until the sauce boils, then cover and simmer very slowly, or transfer to a cool oven, Gas 2, 300°F, 150°C, for about 2 hours, or until the meat is tender.

6 Adjust the seasoning and add a little gravy browning if necessary.
7 Allow to cool, then pack in plastic bags in the freezer.

Grace Mulligan

TIP

The steak and kidney trimmings can be covered with water and cooked in a covered pan on top of the stove or in a covered ovenproof dish in the oven. Strain, leave the stock to go cold, lift off any fat and you have a good meat stock.

Margaret Heywood
Todmorden, Yorkshire

Use the same ingredients as above, omitting the oil and flour, but increasing the stock to 1 litre/1½ pints and using it hot. Add gravy browning, if necessary, when reheating after defrosting to serve.

1 Prepare the steak and kidney, trimming off any excess fat and gristle. Cut into even-sized pieces about 2 cm/¾ inch in size. Put into a deep 2.5-litre/4-pint casserole dish, with the onion.
2 Mix together the hot stock and the horseradish or mustard. Season with a little salt and plenty of ground black pepper. Pour the stock over the meat. Invert a small tea plate over the meat, pressing it down so that it keeps the meat under the stock. Cover the dish with a lid. Cook on full power for 10 minutes then on Simmer for 60 minutes, or longer. If the meat is not tender enough, allow up to an extra 30 minutes at Simmer. However do check and top up the liquid with HOT stock if required.

For a 2-power microwave cooker:
Use the Defrost setting instead of Simmer. Times will be the same.

3 Allow to cool, skim off any excess fat, then pack into plastic bags and freeze.

To defrost the pie filling:

Tip the frozen pie filling into a basin, heat on full power for 6 to 8 minutes, stirring and breaking up the block every 2 minutes. As the filling is already cooked, it is quite safe to defrost on full power as it is going to be fully reheated in any case.

Do not try to cook Steak and Kidney Pies in the microwave as the pastry stays soggy. However, the filling can be topped with mashed potato and reheated on full power for 5 minutes. Or it can be used as a casserole to serve with vegetables.

BEEF GOULASH

For 1, but easy to make more and larger quantities take no longer to cook. Freezes well before yoghurt is added.

1 tablespoon oil
1 onion, chopped
½ green pepper, deseeded and diced
110 g/4 oz chuck steak, cut into 1 cm/½ inch cubes
1 tablespoon tomato purée
2 fresh tomatoes, skinned (page 26) and chopped
1 small potato, diced
1 teaspoon paprika
Salt and pepper
300 ml/½ pint beef stock
1 teaspoon cornflour mixed with 1 tablespoon water
4 tablespoons natural yoghurt

1 Heat the oil and fry the onion and pepper until soft. Remove them from the pan and set aside.
2 Add the meat to the juices remaining in the pan. Seal the meat so that it is well browned, then stir in the tomato purée, fresh tomatoes, potato, paprika, salt and pepper. Return the onion and pepper to the

pan and pour in the stock.
3 Heat the goulash until it boils, then cover with a tightly fitting lid and simmer very gently for about 1 hour or until the meat is tender.
4 Stir in the cornflour mixture and cook until the sauce thickens, then mix in the yoghurt and serve at once.

Joan Tyers
Wingate, Co. Durham

BERKSHIRE MOUSSAKA

For 2.

225 g/8 oz potatoes, thinly sliced
1 small aubergine, sliced into rounds
225 g/8 oz raw minced beef or lamb
1 small onion, sliced
A 397 g/14 oz can of tomatoes
Salt and pepper
150 ml/¼ pint beef stock
150 ml/¼ pint Cheese Sauce (see below)

1 Place one third of the potatoes in an ovenproof dish, cover with half of the aubergine slices, then put half each of the mince, onion and tomatoes on top. Season with salt and pepper.
2 Cover with some of the remaining potato slices, then repeat the layers, ending with potato. Season again.
3 Pour over the stock, cover with a lid or foil and cook in a hot oven, Gas 6, 400°F, 200°C, for 1 hour.
4 Make the cheese sauce, pour it over the cooked dish and return to the oven, uncovered, for about 15 minutes or until the top is browned.

Mrs Jill Gouldstone
Wokingham, Berkshire

CHEESE SAUCE

Half quantity is suitable for Berkshire Moussaka. (Makes 300 ml/½ pint.)

25 g/1 oz butter
25 g/1 oz flour
300 ml/½ pint milk
Salt and freshly ground black pepper
½ teaspoon made mustard
¼ teaspoon freshly ground nutmeg
75 g/3 oz well-flavoured Cheddar cheese, grated

1 Melt butter over gentle heat. Stir in flour and cook for a minute.
2 Gradually blend in milk and bring to the boil, stirring until smooth and thickened.
3 Add seasoning, mustard, nutmeg and cheese. Stir well until cheese has melted. Serve straightaway.

Debbie Woolhead
Boston Spa, West Yorkshire

 Microwave

All-in-one method

1 Whisk the butter, flour, milk and seasonings together in a large jug. It does not matter if the butter does not combine at this stage.
2 Cook on full power for three 2-minute bursts, whisking thoroughly after each burst.
3 Stir the cheese in immediately. The sauce is so hot at this stage that the cheese will melt and the sauce will be ready to use without further cooking.

THREE-IN-ONE SAVOURY MINCE

Three meals for one person. Lee-anne Patterson lives alone and from the following recipe she prepares three separate meals: Spaghetti Bolognese for the first day, Cottage Pie the next, then there's a Savoury Crumble for the third meal.

3 tablespoons oil
2 onions, chopped
1 clove of garlic, crushed

450 g/1 lb minced beef
A 397 g/14 oz can of tomatoes
A pinch of dried oregano
100 g/4 oz mushrooms, sliced
1 green pepper, deseeded and cut
   into chunks
1 red pepper, deseeded and cut
   into chunks
Salt and pepper

1 Heat the oil in a large saucepan and
cook the onion until soft.
2 Add the garlic and mince and cook
over a moderate heat until the meat is
lightly browned.
3 Pour in the tomatoes and add the
oregano. Bring to the boil and simmer
gently for 20 minutes.
4 Mix the mushrooms and peppers
into the mince and cook for a further
15 minutes. If the meat looks a bit
dry, add a little water. Season to taste
with salt and pepper.

Lee-anne Patterson
Lockleaze, Bristol

*You may like to add 1 crumbled beef
stock cube to the ingredients listed
above.*

1 Put the oil, onions and garlic into a
2 litre/4 pint casserole with the green
and red peppers. Heat on full power
for 5 minutes.
2 Stir in the minced beef, tomatoes,
oregano, mushrooms and stock cube
and season with a little salt and
pepper. Mix, so that all the
ingredients are well combined.
3 Cover the casserole with a lid or
with film and cook on Medium for 15
minutes. Let it stand for 5 minutes
before serving.

For a 2-power microwave cooker:
Cook on full power for 10 to 12
minutes, stirring once after 6 minutes.
Stand for 5 minutes.

4 Stir and adjust seasoning before
serving.

SPAGHETTI BOLOGNESE

Make sure the spaghetti is not boiled
too long. A tablespoon of oil cooked
with it prevents the strands from
sticking together when drained. Serve
at once with 1 helping cooked
Savoury Mince on top and a
sprinkling of finely grated cheese.

This dish reheats well by microwave.
Put the prepared mince on top of the
cooked spaghetti. Cover and heat on
full power for 2 to 3 minutes.

COTTAGE PIE

1 helping cooked Savoury
   Mince
25 g/1 oz cooked mashed potatoes
125 g/4 oz cooked peas or beans

1 The dish can be assembled from
hot ingredients, in which case, put the
Savoury Mince in a small ovenproof
dish, sprinkle over it a layer of peas
or beans and cover with mashed
potato.
2 Fork up the top and brown it
under a hot grill.

For assembly from cold, the dish can
be reheated in a moderate oven, Gas
4, 300°F, 180°C, for 15 minutes. For
a change, cover the potatoes with a
layer of grated cheese.

*The potato for mashing can be cooked
by microwave – see page 117.*

1 To assemble: put the Savoury
Mince in a heatproof dish and put in
a layer of peas or beans. Cover with
a layer of potato, marking the top
with a fork.

2 If the ingredients are hot, simply brown the potato under the grill. If the ingredients are cold, reheat, covered, on full power for 3 minutes, then brown the potato under the grill as above.

SAVOURY MINCE CRUMBLE

It makes a change to have a crumble topping, and this good idea came from Mrs Susan Hersee of Hayling Island, Hampshire. Make more of the topping than you need for one meal, as it keeps well in the fridge. For 2 helpings:

100 g/4 oz plain flour, white or
    wholemeal
50 g/2 oz margarine
50 g/2 oz Edam cheese, grated
A pinch of cayenne pepper

1 Put the flour into a bowl and rub in the margarine until the mixture resembles breadcrumbs. Mix in the grated cheese and cayenne pepper.

2 Make a layer of cooked Savoury Mince in an ovenproof dish, cover with the crumble topping.
3 Cook in a preheated moderately hot oven, Gas 6, 400°F, 200°C, for 15 to 20 minutes. Serve with a good Onion Gravy (see below).

 Microwave ≈≈≈≈≈≈≈≈≈≈≈

For 1.

1 Sprinkle crumble topping over one helping of cooked Savoury Mince arranged in a layer in a heatproof dish.
2 Cover and cook on full power for 3 to 4 minutes, then finish under a hot grill to brown the top for 5 to 6 minutes. Serve with a good Onion Gravy (see below).

GOOD ONION GRAVY
Makes 300 ml/½ pint.

100 g/4 oz onion, finely
    chopped
20 g/¾ oz butter
20 g/¾ oz flour
300 ml/½ pint stock
Pepper and salt

1 Fry the onion in the butter until soft and lightly brown.
2 Add the flour and cook for one minute.
3 Add the stock and stir as it comes to the boil. Simmer for 5 minutes.
4 Season to taste. (Gravy browning can be added if too light in colour.)
Judith Adshead
Porth Colmon, Gwynedd

CHILLI CON CARNE
Serves 1 or 2 – freezes well. Serve with brown rice or a jacket potato.

100 g/4 oz lean minced beef
1 medium onion, finely chopped

A small clove of garlic, chopped
Half a 5 ml teaspoon chilli
  powder
Salt and pepper to taste
A 227 g/8 oz can of tomatoes
A 15 ml tablespoon tomato purée
A 213 g/7½ oz can of red kidney
  beans, drained

1 Brown the minced beef for 5
minutes in a large pan without added
fat. There is always enough fat even
in lean mince and no extra is needed.
2 Drain off any excess fat, then add
the onion, garlic, chilli and other
seasoning to taste.
3 Pour in tomatoes, add tomato purée
and bring to the boil. Cover and
simmer gently for 20 minutes. If the
mince looks a little dry, add a little
water.
4 Add the kidney beans and cook for
a further 5 minutes.

Jill Myers
The British Diabetic Association,
London

1 Put all the ingredients in a small
(1.5-litre/3-pint) casserole. Mix so
they are well combined. Cover with a
lid or with film.
2 Cook on Medium for 7 minutes.

For a 2-power microwave cooker:
Cook on full power for 3 to 4
minutes, stirring once.

Let it stand for 5 minutes, covered,
before you eat it.

QUICK PIZZA ROLLS

*A crusty wholemeal roll is sliced open to
form the pizza-type base to this tasty
dish. Enough for 2, but easy to make for
1. Serve with salad.*

1 long crusty wholemeal roll
50 g/2 oz reduced-fat Cheddar
  cheese, grated

75 g/3 oz lean minced beef
Half an onion, chopped
A 10 ml dessertspoon of tomato
  purée
A pinch of mixed herbs
Salt and pepper

1 Cut the roll in half lengthways.
2 Save half the grated cheese and
sprinkle the rest over the halved roll.
3 Cook the minced beef and onion
gently in a saucepan until the meat is
brown. It is not necessary to add fat
if you stir it carefully.
4 Add the tomato purée, mixed herbs
and seasoning and continue to cook
gently for 5 minutes. If the mixture
is too dry, add 1 to 2 tablespoons of
water.
5 Spread the minced meat on top of
the cheese rolls and cover with the
remaining cheese.
6 Grill until the cheese melts.

Jill Myers
The British Diabetic Association,
London

Follow steps 1 and 2 above.
3 Put the onion in a basin with one
(5 ml) teaspoon of water. Heat on
full power for 1 minute. Stir in the
minced beef, tomato purée, mixed
herbs and seasoning. Cook on full
power for 2 to 3 minutes, stirring
once.
4 Spread the mince on top of the
rolls and sprinkle with the remaining
cheese. Put under a hot grill until the
cheese bubbles and melts.

MEAT ROLLS

*For 2, but easy to make just for one
person.*

50 g/2 oz fresh breadcrumbs
½ teaspoon dried mixed herbs
1 tablespoon chives, chopped
1 egg
Salt and pepper

4 slices cold beef, or any cold
  meat
125 g/1 oz butter

1 Put the breadcrumbs, herbs, chives,
egg and seasoning into a bowl and
mix well.
2 Spread a quarter of the mixture
on each slice of meat, then roll up
and tie securely with thread or thin
string.
3 Melt the butter in a pan and fry
the rolls, turning them frequently,
until lightly browned. Serve with hot
vegetables and gravy. (See page 79
for Good Onion Gravy.)

Mrs Mary Potts
Bedlington, Northumberland

BAKED LAMB CHOPS WITH COURGETTES

*A complete main course for 2, served
with plain boiled potatoes or rice.*

2 lamb chops or lamb steaks
1 tablespoon oil
1 onion, chopped
225 g/8 oz courgettes, topped,
  tailed, and cut into slices
A 227 g/8 oz can of tomatoes
1 teaspoon finely chopped fresh
  rosemary or ½ teaspoon dried
  rosemary
A clove of garlic, crushed
A pinch of sugar
Salt and freshly ground black
  pepper

1 Trim off any fat from the chops,
leaving only a small amount around
the edges. Brush them with a little
oil.
2 Heat the oil in a flameproof
casserole and fry the onion quickly
for 1 minute. Then add the
courgettes, tomatoes, rosemary, garlic
and sugar.
3 Reduce the heat, mix well and
season with salt and freshly ground

black pepper. Make 2 hollows and
add the lamb, but make sure the meat
is not completely covered.
4 Put on the lid and cook in a
moderately hot oven, Gas 5, 375°F,
190°C for 20 minutes. Then remove
the lid and cook for a further 15
minutes.

Grace Mulligan

HONEY LAMB CHOPS

*For 1. Easy to make more. Nice served
with rice and peas.*

2 lamb chops
1 tablespoon thick honey
1 tablespoon oil
1 teaspoon lemon juice
½ teaspoon dried mixed herbs

1 Place the chops in an ovenproof
dish.
2 Put the honey, oil, lemon juice and
herbs into a small saucepan and stir
over a low heat until the honey has
melted. Pour this over the chops and
leave in a cool place for 30 minutes.
3 Preheat the oven to moderate, Gas
4, 350°F, 180°C and cook the chops
until tender, about 20 to 25 minutes.

Mrs A. Chapman
Hammersmith, London

LAMB KOFTA CURRY

*Serves 2. If you don't have a food
processor you can still make this, but it
will be a matter of grating the onion,
crushing the garlic and mixing it all by
hand. This curry can also be made with
minced beef.*

50 g/2 oz onions
2 cloves of garlic
225 g/8 oz minced lamb
¾ teaspoon salt
½ teaspoon cumin powder
¼ teaspoon chilli powder
¼ teaspoon garam masala
A pinch of ground nutmeg

SAUCE

3 tablespoons oil
125 g/4 oz onions, peeled and
 sliced
2 to 3 cloves of garlic, peeled and
 crushed
125 g/4 oz canned tomatoes,
 roughly chopped
$\frac{3}{4}$ teaspoon turmeric powder
$\frac{1}{2}$ teaspoon salt
$\frac{1}{2}$ teaspoon coriander powder
$\frac{1}{4}$ teaspoon cumin powder
$\frac{1}{4}$ teaspoon chilli powder
450 ml/$\frac{3}{4}$ pint water
Green coriander leaves or parsley
 to garnish

1 To prepare the meatballs, put the onion and garlic into a food processor and process until finely chopped. Add the meat, salt and spices and process again until everything is well blended.
2 Take small pieces of meat mixture and roll into balls about the size of a large walnut. Set aside in a cool place while making the sauce.
3 Heat the oil and fry the onion and garlic until dark brown, stirring most of the time.
4 Add tomatoes and 1 tablespoon of the juice, then add all the remaining ingredients. Cook, stirring, until the oil begins to separate. Drain the oil away. Then pour in 450 ml/$\frac{3}{4}$ pint water.
5 Bring the liquid up to boiling point, then put in the meatballs one at a time. Bring back to the boil, cover, then reduce the heat so the meatballs simmer gently for about 20 minutes.
6 Drain and place on a warmed serving dish. If the sauce is watery, boil it rapidly over a very high heat until it is reduced to a syrupy consistency. Pour over the meatballs.
7 Serve hot, sprinkled with coriander leaves or coarsely chopped parsley.

Nirmal Singh
Nuneaton, Warwickshire

SHEEKH KEBABS

These are delicious served with a green salad, or they may be cut into bite-sized pieces and served on cocktail sticks as a tasty snack with drinks. For this recipe you will need 4 skewers each at least 15 to 18 cm/6 to 7 inches in length. Notice also (step 3) that you need to start in very good time.

225 g/8 oz minced lamb or
 tender beef
$\frac{1}{2}$ teaspoon salt
1 dessertspoon lemon juice
1 tablespoon oil
1 small onion, finely chopped
$\frac{1}{4}$ to $\frac{1}{2}$ teaspoon chilli powder
$\frac{1}{4}$ to $\frac{1}{2}$ teaspoon garam masala
$\frac{1}{4}$ teaspoon ground nutmeg
2 tablespoons natural yoghurt

1 Put the meat into a bowl and mix in the salt and lemon juice. Leave it in a cool place for 20 minutes.
2 Heat the oil and fry the onion until it starts to turn a pale brown colour. Drain it very thoroughly on kitchen paper, then add the onion to the meat.
3 Mix all the remaining ingredients into the meat and leave it in the refrigerator for at least 4 hours, better still, for 24 hours.
4 Divide the meat into 4 pieces and firmly press it evenly around the 4 skewers in a long sausage shape, about 15 to 18 cm/6 to 7 inches. Make sure the meat is the same thickness throughout.
5 Preheat the grill to maximum heat. Pour a little water into the grill pan, and brush the rack with oil.
6 Put the skewers of meat on to the rack and grill on all sides until they are a light brown colour all over.
7 Serve at once, or wrap in foil to keep warm.

Nirmal Singh
Nuneaton, Warwickshire

MEATBALL SURPRISE
For 2.

225 g/½ lb minced beef
1 tablespoon tomato ketchup
1 small onion, finely chopped
½ teaspoon dried mixed herbs
Salt and pepper
1 egg, beaten
50 g/2 oz Cheddar cheese
25 g/1 oz flour seasoned with a
    little salt and pepper
Fat or dripping
150 ml/¼ pint beef stock, a stock
    cube will do
1 dessertspoon cornflour

1 Mix together the mince, ketchup,
onion, egg and herbs, seasoning well
with salt and pepper. Make into 8
even-sized portions.
2 Cut the cheese into 8 cubes.
3 Now make a ball carefully
surrounding each piece of cheese with
a coating of mince. Wet your hands
to make this easier.
4 Roll the meatballs in seasoned
flour.
5 Heat the fat in a pan and brown
the meatballs, then pour off any
excess fat.

6 Add the beef stock, bring up to the
boil, cover with a lid and simmer for
30 minutes.
7 Remove the meatballs to a hot
serving dish.
8 Mix the cornflour with 1
tablespoon cold water and stir it into
the liquid in the pan over moderate
heat until it thickens and comes to the
boil.
9 Pour this gravy over the meatballs
and serve with potatoes.

Catherine Sangster
Aberdeen

STIR-FRIED KIDNEYS AND BACON
For 2.

4 rashers smoked rindless
    streaky bacon, cut in strips
4 fresh or frozen lambs' kidneys,
    skinned, cored (use scissors)
    and quartered
1 level dessertspoon French
    mustard
1 tablespoon vinegar
1 tablespoon chopped parsley
1 tablespoon chopped chives
Salt and pepper

1 Cook the bacon in its own fat over a moderate heat until it is crisp. You will not need to add any oil.
2 Add the kidney pieces and fry until the kidneys are browned and just cooked.
3 Stir in the mustard, vinegar, parsley, chives and seasoning and mix well together. Serve on a bed of rice or on toasted wholemeal bread.

Grace Mulligan

LIVER AND BACON CASSEROLE
For 2.

225 g/8 oz lamb's liver
15 g/½ oz flour
1 tablespoon fresh white or wholemeal breadcrumbs
1 teaspoon chopped parsley
1 teaspoon chopped onion
25 g/1 oz mushrooms, sliced
Salt and pepper
300 ml/½ pint stock or gravy
2 rashers of bacon

1 Cut the liver into slices 7 mm/¼ inch thick and toss them in the flour.
2 Arrange in a greased ovenproof dish and sprinkle over the breadcrumbs, parsley, onion, mushrooms, salt and pepper.
3 Pour over the stock and cover with the rashers of bacon.
4 Cover with a lid and cook in a moderate oven, Gas 4, 350°F, 180°C, for 40 minutes. Before serving, put the dish under the grill to crisp the bacon.

Alternatively, this dish can be cooked on top of the stove. Assemble all the ingredients except the bacon in a saucepan and cook gently for 20 minutes. Grill the bacon at the last minute and put it on top of the liver as you serve it.

Mrs M. W. Kirk
Runcorn, Cheshire

 Microwave

1 Follow step 1 above.
2 Arrange the liver slices in a shallow 20-cm/8-inch round dish. Sprinkle over the breadcrumbs, parsley, onion, mushrooms and seasoning.
3 Pour over the stock and cover with the rashers of bacon. Cook, uncovered, on full power for 6 to 8 minutes, then let it stand for 5 minutes before serving.

LIVER BALLS IN TOMATO SAUCE

This is a good recipe for a food processor because of the number of ingredients that need chopping. Makes 2 helpings.

225 g/8 oz lamb's liver, skinned and chopped small
50 g/2 oz fresh breadcrumbs
1 onion, peeled and finely chopped
75 g/3 oz rindless bacon, cut in small strips
1 egg, beaten
A pinch of dried thyme
25 g/1 oz flour
25 g/1 oz dripping or 1 tablespoon oil
A 227 g/8 oz can of tomatoes, chopped

1 Mix together the liver, breadcrumbs, onion, bacon, egg and thyme. Roll the mixture into 6 balls and coat each one with flour.
2 Heat the fat in a frying pan and brown the liver balls evenly, then transfer to an ovenproof dish with a well-fitting lid.
3 Pour the tomatoes over the balls, sprinkle with a little extra dried thyme and put on the lid.
4 Cook in a moderate oven, Gas 4, 350°F, 180°C, for 20 minutes then

turn the balls over and cook for 20
minutes more.

Mrs Mary Potts
Bedlington, Northumberland

LIVER RISOTTO

*For 1. Serve with brown rice, or boiled
or baked potatoes and a green
vegetable.*

A 15 ml tablespoon of oil
1 small onion, finely chopped
100 g/4 oz lambs liver, skinned
and thinly sliced
A 15 ml tablespoon of wholemeal
flour seasoned with salt and
pepper
A 227 g/8 oz can of tomatoes
60 ml/2 fl oz water
A 15 ml tablespoon of dried
mushrooms
Half a chicken stock cube
A 15 ml tablespoon of frozen peas
or sweetcorn
Salt and pepper

1 Heat the oil in a pan and fry the
onion until soft.
2 Toss the liver in the seasoned flour
and fry with the onion until the liver
is lightly browned.
3 Add all the remaining ingredients
to the pan, bring to the boil, stirring
continously, then reduce the heat and
let it simmer gently for 10 minutes
before serving.

Jill Myers
The British Diabetic Association,
London

HEARTS BRAISED IN AN ORANGE SAUCE

*For 2. This dish can be cooked on top
of the stove or in the oven.*

1 or 2 lamb's or pig's hearts
Salted water for soaking
15 g/$\frac{1}{2}$ oz butter

1 tablespoon oil
125 g/4 oz onions, chopped
A clove of garlic, chopped
1 tablespoon flour
150 ml/$\frac{1}{4}$ pint meat stock
1 dessertspoon tomato purée
1 bay leaf
A sprig of thyme or a pinch of
dried thyme
The juice and 1 fine strip of peel
from a small orange
1 tablespoon bitter marmalade
Salt and freshly ground black
pepper
1 teaspoon lemon juice

1 Prepare the hearts by washing
under running water. With sharp
scissors, carefully cut away the
muscular artery walls and any outside
skin.
2 Soak hearts in lightly salted water
for 30 minutes. Drain and dry.
3 Heat butter and oil in a saucepan
or flameproof casserole. Fry hearts
for several minutes until brown all
over. Remove from pan.
4 Reduce heat, add onion and garlic
and fry for about 5 minutes until
soft.
5 Sprinkle in the flour, stirring all
the time. Stir in stock, tomato purée,
bay leaf, thyme, orange juice and
rind, and marmalade. Return to heat
and bring slowly to the boil. Season
with salt and pepper.
6 Cut the hearts diagonally into quite
thick slices and return them to the
pan or casserole. Cover and simmer
gently for 1 hour. Or cook in a
moderate oven, Gas, 3, 325°F, 150°C,
for 1 to 1$\frac{1}{2}$ hours.
7 Lift out the slices of heart and
arrange in a serving dish. Keep
warm.
8 Lift off fat from the cooking
liquid by tilting casserole and
spooning it away.
9 Add lemon juice and boil rapidly
until liquid is reduced to a thick
sauce. Pour over the hearts and
serve.

Grace Mulligan

Chapter 6

Rice, Pulses, Eggs

and Vegetable Dishes

BOILED RICE

The absorption method

Allow about 50 g/2 oz brown or white rice per person.

1 Put the rice into a measuring jug or cup to calculate the amount of water required: almost twice the volume of the rice. Heat the water until almost boiling.
2 Meanwhile, wash the rice thoroughly, shaking it in a sieve under the cold water tap.
3 Put the rice on to cook in the hot water. When it boils, stir, then let it boil steadily without the lid until the grains are almost breaking the surface.
4 Now put on the lid. It should fit tightly. Turn the heat to the lowest possible and let the rice cook; 15 minutes for white rice, 20 minutes for brown.
5 Turn off the heat, leave the pan for 5 minutes. When you look inside, the rice should be perfectly cooked, every grain separate and no water left.
6 Season to taste after cooking, forking the salt and pepper very gently through the rice.

Mary Watts

50 g/2 oz long grain rice
(or 3 fl oz)
300 ml/½ pint cold water
(or 10 fl oz)
A pinch of salt

1 Put the ingredients into an 18-cm/7-inch soufflé-type dish. Cover the dish with a serving plate (which will be nice and hot by the time you need to eat).
2 Cook on full power: 8 minutes for white rice; 12 minutes for 'pre-fluffed' brown* rice. Stir brown rice once during cooking. (If you have

100 g/4 oz rice to cook, measure in 600 ml/1 pint boiling water and put 2 plates on top to cover the dish and warm up at the same time.)
3 Leave the dish, covered, to stand for 5 minutes – or while cooking the accompanying food. The rice will absorb the remaining water and stay hot. Fluff it up with a fork before serving.

* If your brown rice is the ordinary hard grain type a different procedure is necessary.

1 Use an 18-cm/7-inch soufflé-type dish or casserole but it must be at least 9 cm/3½ inches deep.
2 Cook on full power for 5 minutes. Then cook on Medium for 12 minutes. Let it stand for 10 minutes and then cook on Medium for 5 minutes more. Stir at once and serve. It will stand for 5 minutes before beginning to cool.

No time is saved and you may prefer to follow the conventional method. However, at least in the microwave it will not burn if you forget it!

Yvonne Hamlett
Haddenham, Buckinghamshire

GARLIC RICE

For 1 or 2. Delicious on its own, or with cold meat. Reheats well.

125 g/4 oz long grain white or brown rice
2 medium to small potatoes, quartered
2 cloves of garlic, finely chopped
50 g/2 oz butter
25 g/1 oz Parmesan or finely grated Cheddar cheese mixed with a little Parmesan
(Parmesan on its own is better)

1 Boil rice with potato. If using brown rice, cut potato into 2.5-cm/1-inch cubes and add to rice for 10

88

minutes before end of cooking time. (Brown rice normally takes 20 to 25 minutes to cook.)

2 At last minute, fry garlic in butter until just turning golden.

3 Season the rice and potato with a little salt and pepper and put them into a warm serving dish. Pour over the garlic and fork it in lightly. Sprinkle top with cheese and serve piping hot.

To reheat: melt 15 g/½ oz butter in a shallow pan (non-stick is ideal). Add the garlic rice and stir for 1 minute to break the lumps of rice. Then cover pan, reduce heat to lowest and let it all heat through. Takes 5 minutes for half the above quantity.

To reheat in the microwave: half quantity, covered, on full power for 2 minutes.

Mrs. R. Bright
Sutton, Surrey

STIR-FRIED RICE WITH PRAWNS OR HAM

For 2. This tasty dish is a meal by itself. It is cooked over quite high heat, constantly stirring with a large kitchen spoon and fork.

3 tablespoons oil
A clove of garlic, chopped
1 onion, sliced
75 to 100 g/3 to 4 oz cooked peeled prawns or diced ham
75 g/3 oz cooked rice (cold rice will do)
2 eggs, beaten
1½ tablespoons light soy sauce
½ tablespoon dark soy sauce
100 g/4 oz diced cooked mixed vegetables
Spring onion curls and cucumber wedges to garnish

1 In a wok or large frying pan, heat 2 tablespoons oil. Add the garlic and

cook until slightly brown, then add the onion and cook for 2 minutes, stirring.

2 Add the prawns and allow them 2 minutes to heat through, then mix in the rice. Stir all the time.

3 Push the rice to one side of the wok or pan, add an extra tablespoon of oil and pour in the beaten eggs.

4 Scramble the eggs slightly, then cover with the rice and leave for about 1 minute until the eggs are set.

5 Pour the light and dark soy sauces into the pan, add the mixed vegetables and stir well, breaking the egg into little pieces.

6 Serve at once, garnished with spring onion curls and wedges of cucumber.

Jennie Siew Lee Cook
York

TUNA RISOTTO
A substantial dish for 2, this is pleasant either hot or cold.

1 tablespoon oil
2 rashers of bacon, finely chopped
1 large onion, chopped
50 g/2 oz mushrooms, chopped – but not too small
100 g/4 oz white or brown rice, washed
450 ml/¾ pint hot chicken stock, a cube will do
A 397 g/14 oz can of tomatoes
170 g/6 oz frozen mixed vegetables
A 200 g/7 oz can of tuna, drained
Salt and pepper
Slices of tomato, and chopped parsley, to garnish

1 Heat oil and fry bacon and onion for 2 or 3 minutes. Then add mushrooms and fry until oil is absorbed.

2 Add rice and fry for 2 minutes, stirring from time to time.

3 Add hot stock, bring to the boil and allow to simmer for 15 minutes

(20 minutes for brown rice).

4 Roughly chop the tomatoes and add with their juice and the frozen mixed vegetables.

5 Break tuna into quite large pieces and mix in gently; add salt and pepper to taste. Cook for 5 minutes more until liquid is absorbed.

6 Serve at once, garnished with tomato slices and parsley.

Miss Lisa Lant
Hazelrigg, Newcastle upon Tyne

SAVOURY VEGETABLE RICE

For 1 or 2. Eaten hot it goes well with Pork Stir-Fry (page 68). Mixed with French Dressing (page 106), it can be served cold as a salad.

75 to 100 g/3 to 4 oz long grain
  brown or white rice
½ tablespoon oil
1 small onion, diced
25 g/1 oz cucumber or courgette,
  or green or red pepper, diced
75 to 100 g/3 to 4 oz peas or
  sweetcorn, cooked
25 g/1 oz sultanas or raisins
Salt and pepper

1 Cook the rice by the absorption method (page 88).

2 Heat the oil and fry the onion until soft but not brown. Add the cucumber, courgette or pepper and stir-fry for 2 minutes.

3 Stir in the rest of the ingredients and cook to reheat, seasoning to taste.

Dilwen Phillips
Gileston, South Glamorgan

STUFFED PEPPER

For 1.

1 medium green or red pepper
50 g/2 oz lean bacon rasher

A 10 ml dessertspoon of oil
50 g/2 oz cooked brown rice
A 15 ml tablespoon of frozen peas
  or sweetcorn, cooked
A 15 ml tablespoon of raisins
Salt and pepper

1 Slice the top off the pepper and remove the seeds and any white pith.

2 Put the pepper in a saucepan of boiling water and simmer for 10 minutes, or until it is tender. Drain and keep it warm.

3 Chop the bacon and fry in the oil until crisp. Add the rice, vegetables, raisins and seasoning to taste. Heat through, then spoon the mixture into the pepper. Serve.

Jill Myers
The British Diabetic Association,
London

 Microwave

1 Slice the top off the pepper, remove the seeds and any white pith. Stand the pepper in a small cereal bowl.

2 Put the bacon on a small plate, cover loosely with a piece of kitchen paper. Cook on full power for 1 to 2 minutes until crisp.

3 In a basin, mix together the rice, vegetables and raisins. Crumble in the bacon and spoon the mixture into the pepper.

4 Replace the pepper's lid, cover the dish with clear film and cook on full power for 4 to 5 minutes. Let it stand for 5 minutes before serving. The pepper softens during the standing time.

CURRIED NUT LOAF

Delicious and quite filling for 2, but nice hot or cold served with a green salad with French Dressing (page 106).

2 tablespoons oil
1 small onion, sliced

1 small green pepper, deseeded
and chopped
175 g/6 oz tomatoes, skinned (page
26) and finely chopped
175 g/6 oz hazelnuts or walnuts,
finely chopped
75 g/3 oz fresh wholemeal
breadcrumbs
1 clove of garlic, crushed
1 teaspoon dried mixed herbs
1 teaspoon curry powder
1 egg, beaten
Salt and pepper

1 Heat the oil in a pan and cook
the onion, pepper and tomato until
soft.
2 Mix together the nuts,
breadcrumbs, garlic, herbs and curry
powder. Stir in the tomato mixture
with the egg and seasoning and put
the mixture into a greased 450-g/1-lb
loaf tin.
3 Bake in a moderate oven, Gas 4,
350°F, 180°C, for 30 minutes until
golden brown.
4 Turn out and serve either hot or
cold.

The June Hulbert Cookbook

Microwave 〜〜〜〜〜〜

1 Put just 1 tablespoon of oil with
the onion and green pepper into a
mixing bowl. Heat on full power for
5 minutes until soft. Add the
tomato.
2 Stir in the nuts, breadcrumbs,
garlic, herbs and curry powder.
Season with a little salt and pepper.
Bind together with the egg.
3 Line the base of a 450-g/1-lb loaf
dish with a piece of greaseproof
paper. Tip the mixture into the dish
and smooth over the top. Cook on
full power for 8 to 10 minutes until
the centre is just firm to the touch.
Let it stand for 5 minutes before
turning out.
4 Serve hot or cold in slices with a
green salad.

SAVOURY SEMOLINA WITH PEANUTS

*The garnishes are very important for
this dish. It's nice also with grilled
tomatoes or fresh Tomato Sauce (page
175).*

150 ml/6 fl oz coarse semolina,
available from Indian grocers *
300 ml/12 fl oz boiling water
2 tablespoons cooking or salad oil
1 small onion, chopped
1 medium potato, diced small
1 teaspoon black mustard seeds
1 tablespoon peanuts
Salt and pepper
A pinch of cayenne pepper
Garnish with lemon wedges, 1
tablespoon lightly toasted
desiccated coconut and chopped
fresh coriander leaves
Natural yoghurt or Yoghurt
Chutney for serving (page 111)

** Ordinary semolina can be used but the
coarse variety gives a crumbly texture to
the finished dish.*

1 Measure both semolina and water
separately in a measuring jug.
2 Put one tablespoon of the oil in a
pan and fry semolina on a low heat
until golden brown. Stir continuously
in case it burns.
3 In a small frying pan, fry onion
and potato in the rest of the oil with
mustard seeds and peanuts until
lightly browned and potato is cooked.
Add to semolina.
4 Add water and cook on a very low
heat, stirring continuously for 4 to 5
minutes. Season with salt, pepper and
cayenne to taste.
5 Serve on a warmed dish with lemon
wedges (or sprinkled with juice),
sprinkled with toasted coconut and
chopped coriander leaves.

Mrs Jaswant Chopra
Childwall, Liverpool

TO COOK DRIED BEANS AND PEAS

These freeze well when cooked and it makes sense to cook a substantial amount, pack into bags of suitably sized portions and freeze for another day.

1 Soak overnight.
2 Discard soaking water and cook in plenty of fresh water in a roomy pan as they often froth up and over the top.
3 Bring to the boil and always boil hard for 10 minutes before reducing heat and simmering until tender. The hard boiling is essential to eliminate either toxic or indigestible factors.

Cooking times vary enormously from soya ($2\frac{1}{2}$ to 3 hours) and chick peas (2 hours) to black-eye beans (40 to 45 minutes) and haricot (45 to 50 minutes). It is best to keep an eye on the pan until you are accustomed to the cooking times so that the beans are cooked until just tender. When they are beginning to overcook they will burst out of their skins and the appearance will be spoilt.

Pressure cooking saves time but always follow procedure given in the manufacturer's handbook, because you cannot see if they are ready and possibly bursting from their skins and turning to mush.

For salads it is best to have French dressing ready, well flavoured with garlic and herbs, and put the hot drained beans and peas into it to marinate.

TIP
Do not cook white beans in the same pan with red or black ones as the colours will spoil the look of the white ones.

HOT HARICOT BEANS AND HAM
Serves 2

This quick lunch or supper dish is cooked and served in a frying pan. Useful for the ham derived from cooking a Ham Shank (page 67).

15 g/$\frac{1}{2}$ oz butter or margarine
1 tablespoon oil
75 g/3 oz courgettes, trimmed and sliced into rounds
75 g/3 oz cooked ham, diced
50 g/2 oz cooked haricot beans *

SAUCE
15 g/$\frac{1}{2}$ oz butter or margarine
1 tablespoon flour
150 ml/$\frac{1}{4}$ pint ham stock – chicken or vegetable stock will do
1 tablespoon chopped chives
25 g/1 oz grated cheese

* *See opposite for notes on cooking dried beans and peas.*

1 Heat the butter and oil in a frying pan and cook the courgettes for a short while. Stir often and do not over-cook them or they lose their crispness.
2 Stir in the diced ham and haricot beans and leave on a low heat while the sauce is prepared.
3 For the sauce, put the butter, flour and ham stock into a saucepan. Whisk well to disperse any lumps of flour. Stirring all the time, heat up the sauce until it boils, then add the chives.
4 Pour the sauce over the courgettes and scatter the grated cheese on top.
5 Place the frying pan under a hot grill until the cheese melts and browns slightly. Eat at once.

Grace Mulligan

1 Put the butter or margarine (the oil is not needed) with the courgettes into a small shallow heatproof dish – about 600 ml/1 pint size. Cover with clear film and cook on full power for 2 minutes. Stir in the ham and haricot beans.

2 For the sauce, put the butter in a 600-ml/1-pint jug and heat on full power for 30 seconds. Stir in the flour and blend in the stock. Heat on full power for 1 minute. Stir in the chives and heat for 30 seconds.

3 Pour sauce over the courgettes and scatter the grated cheese on top. Put under a hot grill until the cheese melts, bubbles and begins to brown.

POTATO AND BEAN CASSEROLE

A substantial dish for 2, best eaten hot as a main course. Green salad goes well with it. Reheats easily.

15 g/½ oz butter, or a little oil
A 213-g/7½-oz can of red kidney
  beans
225 g/8 oz potatoes
Salt and pepper
50 g/2 oz mature Cheddar cheese,
  grated
1 egg
300 ml/½ pint milk, hot but not
  boiling

TOPPING
15 g/½ oz butter
1 large tablespoon sesame seeds
1 large tablespoon sunflower
  seeds
1 tablespoon soy sauce

1 Preheat oven to moderate, Gas 4, 350°F, 180°C.
2 Use butter or oil to grease a 900-ml/1½-pint ovenproof dish lightly.
3 Drain beans and rinse them with cold water.

4 Scrub the potatoes and slice them thinly.
5 Arrange half of the potatoes in the dish, season with salt and pepper. Spread half of the cheese over the potatoes and cover with the beans. Season again and cover with remaining potatoes.
6 Beat egg into hot milk and pour this over the potatoes and beans. Top with the remaining cheese.
7 Bake in preheated oven for about 1 hour, or until potatoes are tender.
8 Meanwhile prepare the topping. Melt butter in a saucepan and fry sesame and sunflower seeds for 2 minutes, or until golden. Add soy sauce and cook for 1 minute more. Leave to cool.
9 About 15 minutes before the casserole is cooked, sprinkle with the topping.

To reheat: cover with foil and give it 15 to 20 minutes in a moderate oven, Gas 3, 325°F, 160°C.

Grace Mulligan

LENTIL AND COTTAGE CHEESE CROQUETTES

Makes about 10.

75 g/3 oz red lentils
300 ml/½ pint water
About 4 spring onions
50 g/2 oz cottage cheese
25 to 50 g/1 to 2 oz wholemeal
  breadcrumbs
1 teaspoon dried thyme
½ teaspoon lemon juice, optional
Pepper and salt
25 g/1 oz sesame seeds for coating
A little oil for frying

1 Wash and pick over lentils for sticks and stones.
2 Cook lentils in the water. Bring to the boil, cover pan and simmer for 12 to 15 minutes, stirring occasionally,

94

until lentils are a soft paste and little water remains.

3 Strain if necessary and mash with a fork.

4 Chop spring onions finely and combine with the other ingredients except sesame seeds. Leave mixture in a cool place to firm up, about 30 minutes.

5 Make sausage shapes and roll them in sesame seeds.

6 Heat oil and fry lightly until golden brown.

Or, put on a greased baking tray and bake at the top of a moderate oven, Gas 4, 350°F, 180°C, for 25 to 30 minutes.

7 Serve with fresh vegetables.

Janet Horsley
Headingley, Yorkshire

minutes to dry them out. Remove from the heat and mash the peas with the garlic, cumin, basil, turmeric, half the beaten egg and the seasoning.

4 When the mixture is cool enough to handle, shape it into four little patties. It is easier to do this if you wet your hands first.

5 Dip the patties into the remaining beaten egg (if there is not quite enough egg, add a few teaspoons of milk).

6 Toss the patties in the dry oatmeal or bran and leave them in the refrigerator for at least 20 minutes to allow them to firm up a little.

7 Melt the butter and fry the patties until they are crisp and heated through.

Grace Mulligan

SPLIT PEA PATTIES

Serves 2. Nice with Tangy Tomato Sauce (see right). Remember to start the night before!

100 g/4 oz green or golden split peas
A small clove of garlic, crushed (optional)
½ teaspoon ground cumin
½ teaspoon dried basil
A pinch of ground turmeric
1 egg, beaten
Salt and pepper
Oatmeal or bran for coating
50 g/2 oz butter for frying

1 Soak the split peas overnight in cold water.

2 Drain, cover in fresh cold water and simmer for about 30 to 35 minutes or until soft.

3 Drain the peas thoroughly or the mixture may be difficult to shape. If necessary, return them to the pan and stir over a moderate heat for a few

TANGY TOMATO SAUCE

Good eaten hot with grills, or as a pizza topping. Keeps well in the refrigerator for 2 weeks. A liquidiser or food processor is useful. Makes about 450 ml/¾ pint.

1 tablespoon oil
1 large onion, finely chopped
A 400 g/14 oz can of tomatoes
3 tablespoons brown sugar
1 tablespoon Worcestershire sauce
2 teaspoons lemon juice
1 teaspoon dry mustard
Salt and black pepper
4 tablespoons malt vinegar
2 tablespoons water

1 Heat the oil and fry the onion for a few minutes until soft.

2 Liquidise the tomatoes and add them, with all the other ingredients, to the onions.

3 Bring to the boil and cook gently for 3 minutes, seasoning to taste.

Grace Mulligan

1 Put the oil and onion into a
1.1-litre/2-pint basin. Heat on full
power for 4 minutes.
2 Stir in all the remaining
ingredients. Heat, uncovered, on full
power for 6 to 7 minutes.

MACARONI AND TUNA LAYER

For 2.

100 g/4 oz wholewheat
  macaroni
25 g/1 oz low-fat spread
25 g/1 oz wholemeal flour
300 ml/½ pint skimmed milk
Salt and pepper
An 85 g/3½ oz can of tuna fish in
  brine, drained
25 g/1 oz reduced-fat Cheddar
  cheese, grated
Chopped parsley to garnish
  (optional)

1 Cook the macaroni in boiling
water for 10 to 15 minutes.
2 Meanwhile, melt the low-fat spread
in a saucepan and add the flour. Cook
for 1 minute, then gradually stir in
milk. Bring to the boil and cook
gently for a further 3 minutes. Season
to taste.
3 Drain the macaroni and mix it with
the sauce.
4 Pour half of the macaroni into an
ovenproof dish and sprinkle the tuna
fish over it. Cover with the remaining
macaroni mixture.
5 Sprinkle the grated cheese on top
and bake in a moderately hot oven,
Gas 6, 400°F, 200°C, for about 10
minutes. Garnish with chopped
parsley, or serve with green
vegetables.

Jill Myers
The British Diabetic Association,
London

PASTA AND VEGETABLE CASSEROLE

Enough for 2 but easy to make for 1.
Delicious!

1 tablespoon oil
1 onion, roughly chopped
Half a green and half a red
  pepper, diced (or 1 whole green
  pepper)
1 courgette, trimmed and sliced
175 g/6 oz wholemeal pasta
  shapes
125 g/4 oz mushrooms, sliced
A 400 g/14 oz can of ready-
  chopped tomatoes, or 4 fresh
  tomatoes
A pinch of dried mixed herbs, or
  1 tablespoon chopped fresh
  herbs
Pepper and salt
Chopped parsley to garnish

1 Heat oil and fry onion gently with
pepper and courgette for 3 to 5
minutes until onion softens.
2 Meanwhile put pasta on to cook in
boiling water until tender but not
soft.
3 Mix mushrooms into other
vegetables and cook for 2 minutes.
4 Add tomatoes and herbs, bring to
the boil, then simmer without the lid
for 5 minutes. Season to taste with
pepper and a little salt.
5 Drain pasta, mix it into vegetables
and serve sprinkled with chopped
parsley.

For a change, serve sprinkled with
grated cheese.

Mrs Debbie Munton
Llanedeyrn, Cardiff

1 Put the pasta into a 1.7-litre/3-pint
casserole. Cover with boiling salted
water and add 1 tablespoon oil. Stir
well. Cover and cook on full power

for 6 minutes. Stir, then drain.
2 Put the onion, peppers and 1
tablespoon oil into a 1.3-litre/2½–
pint basin. Heat on full power for 3
minutes. Add the courgettes and
mushrooms and cook on full power
for 2 minutes.
3 Stir the tomatoes and herbs into
the vegetables and season lightly.
Cook on full power for 2 to 3
minutes.
4 Stir in the drained pasta and heat
on full power for 1 minute. Serve
sprinkled with chopped parsley, or
sometimes with grated cheese.

OMELETTES

*An omelette makes a quick and
nourishing meal; try some of these
different fillings. For 1.*

BASIC RECIPE
2 eggs
2 teaspoons water
Salt and pepper
A tiny piece of butter
2 teaspoons oil

1 Lightly beat together the eggs,
water and seasoning with a fork; do
not use a whisk.
2 Heat the butter and oil in a small
frying pan about 15 cm/6 inches
across. Make sure the bottom and
sides are thoroughly coated with fat.
3 Pour the eggs into the hot pan and,
after a few seconds, pull the cooked
edges in towards the centre and let
the uncooked egg run out and fill the
space.
4 Cook the omelette until set
underneath and slightly golden but
still moist on top.
5 Pile the chosen filling on to one
half of the omelette, and fold the
other half over to enclose the filling.
6 Serve at once with vegetables or a
salad.

Suggested fillings:

CHICKEN AND BACON

50 g/2 oz cooked chicken, diced
1 cooked rasher of bacon, diced
1 teaspoon chopped parsley
Butter

Warm the ingredients through
thoroughly in a little butter.

HAM AND MUSHROOM

50 g/2 oz cooked ham, diced
50 g/2 oz mushrooms, wiped and
    sliced
Butter
1 teaspoon chopped parsley

Toss the ham and mushrooms in a
little butter over moderate heat until
mushrooms are cooked and ham is
hot. Stir in parsley.

COURGETTES

50 g/2 oz courgettes, trimmed
    and diced
Butter
A pinch of mixed herbs

Cook the courgettes briefly in a little
butter. Sprinkle in the herbs.

TOMATO

A little butter
1 tomato, skinned (page 26) and
    diced
1 teaspoon chopped chives
25 g/1 oz grated cheese

Melt the butter in a small pan, add
the tomato and chives and warm them
through. Spread them over half the
omelette and cover with the grated
cheese. When the omelette is folded,
there will be enough heat in the eggs
to melt the cheese.

Grace Mulligan

SAVOURY STUFFED OMELETTE

Serves 1. Delicious!

1½ tablespoons oil
½ small onion, sliced
100 g/4 oz cooked shelled
　prawns
½ red or green chilli, deseeded
　and finely chopped
A few sprigs of fresh parsley,
　chopped
50 g/2 oz beansprouts
1 teaspoon light soy sauce
Salt and pepper
1 tablespoon water
2 eggs
Sliced cucumber, spring onion
　curls or parsley to garnish

1 Heat 1 tablespoon of the oil in a
small frying pan and cook the onion,
prawns, chilli, parsley and
beansprouts for a few minutes,
until hot but not browned.
2 Add the soy sauce and salt and
pepper to taste.
3 Remove the filling from the pan,
set aside and keep warm.
4 Heat the ½ tablespoon of oil in
the pan. Beat the eggs together and
add 1 tablespoon water, salt and
pepper.
5 Pour the egg mixture into the pan
and cook quickly until the omelette
has set. As it cooks, use a fork to pull
aside the set mixture and let the
runny mixture flow underneath.

6 Place the filling on one half of the
omelette and fold over the other half.
Turn omelette on to a warmed plate.
7 Serve at once, garnished with sliced
cucumber, spring onion curls or
parsley.

Jennie Siew Lee Cook
York

CHEESY EGGS WITH SPINACH

For 2.

2 eggs
450 g/ 1 lb fresh spinach
Buttered wholemeal toast for
　serving

SAUCE
15 g/½ oz butter
1 tablespoon flour
300 ml/½ pint chicken stock
75 g/3 oz strong-flavoured cheese,
　grated

1 Cover the eggs with cold water,
bring them to the boil, then reduce
the heat and boil gently for 10
minutes. Put them in cold water and
shell them.
2 Put the spinach on to cook for 5
minutes. Then drain, chop small and
drain it again.
3 Put the spinach into a shallow
heatproof dish.
4 Meanwhile, in a small saucepan
melt the butter, add the flour and

cook for 1 minute.
5 Gradually pour in the chicken stock, stirring all the time, and bring up to the boil. Remove from the heat and stir in 50 g/2 oz of the cheese.
6 Cut the eggs in half and arrange them, yolks down, on the spinach. Pour over the cheese sauce and sprinkle with the remaining cheese.
7 Put the dish under a very hot grill to brown the top.
8 Serve with buttered wholemeal toast.

Grace Mulligan

1 Hard-boil eggs as above.
2 Wash the spinach well, drain and put it in a mixing bowl. Cover with clear film and cook on full power for 5 minutes. Drain well, then chop. Drain again, squeezing out as much water as possible.
3 Put the spinach in a shallow 18-cm/7-inch dish.
4 Put the butter in a 600-ml/1-pint jug and heat on full power for 30 seconds. Stir in the flour and gradually blend in the stock. Heat on full power for 1½ minutes, then stir in 50 g/2 oz of the cheese. Heat on full power for a further 30 seconds.
5 Finish as steps 6 and 7 above and serve with buttered toast.

EGG AND LEEK NESTS

For 2, but it's easy to halve the ingredients for 1 person.

225 g/8 oz young leeks
A knob of butter
Salt and pepper
2 eggs
2 tablespoons milk
A shake of paprika

1 Top and tail the leeks and remove any very coarse green tops. Cut in

half lengthways and wash under a running tap to remove any grit. Then slice them.
2 Cook the leeks gently in the butter over a medium heat, stirring all the time. Season lightly and keep hot.
3 Scramble the beaten eggs with the milk and take off the heat when just set. Season with salt and pepper.
4 Arrange the shredded leeks on two hot plates, making a nest.
5 Spoon the eggs into the nests, dust lightly with paprika and serve at once.

Grace Mulligan

1 Prepare the leeks as above, then slice into strips about 7 mm/¼ inch wide.
2 Put the leeks in a basin with the butter. Heat on full power for 4 to 5 minutes, stirring once.
3 In a jug, mix together the eggs and milk. Heat on full power for 1¼ to 1½ minutes, stirring once. The eggs should be creamy.
4 Arrange the leeks on two hot serving plates, making a nest. Season lightly. Spoon the eggs into the nest, dust lightly with paprika and serve at once.

SHRIMP EGG FU-YUNG

For 2. Cooked finely sliced pork, beef, chicken or turkey may all be substituted for the shrimps.

2 tablespoons oil
1 small onion, chopped
50 g/2 oz mushrooms, wiped and sliced
1 spring onion, chopped
50 g/2 oz cooked shelled shrimps
1 tablespoon light soy sauce
½ tablespoon dark soy sauce

A pinch of salt
½ teaspoon sugar
3 eggs

SAUCE
75 ml/2½ fl oz chicken stock
1 teaspoon light soy sauce
1 teaspoon cornflour mixed with 1
   tablespoon cold water
A pinch of salt

1 Heat one tablespoon of the oil in a
wok or large frying pan and cook the
onion, mushrooms and spring onion
for one minute. Stir in the shrimps,
soy sauces, salt and sugar. Mix well
and leave to cool.
2 Beat the eggs together and add the
cooled shrimp mixture to them.
3 Heat up one tablespoon oil in a
wok or frying pan and ladle in half
of the egg mixture.
4 Cook the eggs until the underside is
lightly browned, then turn over and
cook the other side. Set aside on a
hot plate and keep warm while the
remaining fu-yung mixture is cooked
in the same way. Turn this out on to
another hot plate.
5 For the sauce: put the chicken
stock, soya sauce, cornflour mixture
and salt into the wok and, stirring
continuously, heat until the sauce
thickens. Pour the sauce over the fu-
yung and serve with rice or boiled
potatoes.

Jennie Siew Lee Cook
York

CHEESE AND CAULI-
FLOWER SOUFFLÉ
For 2.

Half a small cauliflower
15 g/½ oz margarine or butter
15 g/½ oz flour
150 ml/¼ pint milk
50 g/2 oz grated cheese
2 eggs, separated
Pepper and salt

100

1 Preheat oven to moderately hot,
Gas 5, 375°F, 190°C.
2 Make cuts in cauliflower stem, so
that it will cook evenly throughout.
Steam it until nearly tender. Or, put
it in a saucepan with a good, tight-
fitting lid and 1.5 cm/½ inch of
water and simmer until nearly tender,
8 to 10 minutes.
3 Break cooked cauliflower into
florets, cutting the stem into bite-
sized pieces, and put in a 1-litre/1½-
pint greased soufflé dish or casserole.
4 Melt margarine or butter in a pan,
add flour and let it sizzle for 1
minute.
5 Mix in milk, stir as it thickens and
cook for 3 minutes.
6 Take pan off heat and beat in
cheese and egg yolks.
7 Whisk egg whites to a stiff froth
and gently fold into the sauce.
8 Pour sauce over cauliflower and
put it at once into the oven to cook
for 30 minutes. (As soufflés tend to
fall when cold air reaches them, try
not to open oven door during
cooking.) Serve immediately.

Judith Adshead
Porth Colmon, Gwynedd

GLAMORGAN
SAUSAGES
*For 1 or 2, to eat hot with a Tomato
Sauce (opposite) and potatoes, or cold
with a salad. Freeze well.*

75 g/3 oz mature Cheddar
   cheese, grated
75 g/3 oz fresh brown or white
   breadcrumbs
1 small onion, finely chopped
Half a large egg, beaten
½ teaspoon dried mixed herbs
½ teaspoon mustard powder
Salt and pepper

COATING
Half a large egg, beaten
50 g/2 oz fresh or dried
   breadcrumbs

Oil for frying

1 Mix together the first seven ingredients. Roll the mixture into six sausage shapes.
2 Dip each sausage in the beaten egg, then coat with the breadcrumbs.
3 Leave in a cool place for 30 minutes, then fry the sausages in hot oil for 6 to 8 minutes turning them frequently.
4 Drain on kitchen paper and serve hot.

Margaret Heywood
Todmorden, Yorkshire

QUICK TOMATO SAUCE

Goes nicely with Glamorgan Sausages (above).

1 teaspoon cornflour
1 tablespoon milk
A 220 g/8 oz can of tomatoes, drained and chopped small
1 dessertspoon tomato ketchup
A pinch of sugar
A pinch of basil, oregano or mixed herbs
Pepper and salt

1 Mix the cornflour into the milk.
2 Put all the ingredients together in a small pan over gentle heat and stir as it thickens and comes to the boil

Mary Watts

1 Put the cornflour into a 600-ml/1-pint jug. Mix to a smooth paste with the milk.
2 Stir in the remaining ingredients. Cook on full power for 4 to 5 minutes, stirring after half of the time.
3 Stir well then serve.

POTATO, HAM AND EGG PIE

Enough for 1, but it's easy to make more. A favourite way to serve potato.

1 tablespoon oil
1 onion, finely chopped
1 tablespoon flour
1 teaspoon made mustard
Salt and pepper
A dash of Worcestershire sauce
7 tablespoons milk
Butter or margarine for greasing
200 g/7 oz boiled potatoes, sliced
1 hard-boiled egg, sliced
75 g/3 oz cooked ham or bacon, chopped
40 to 50 g/1½ to 2 oz grated cheese (optional)

1 Heat the oil in a frying pan and cook the onion until soft.
2 Add the flour and cook for 1 minute, then stir in the mustard, seasoning, Worcestershire sauce and milk. Cook until the sauce thickens.
3 Arrange half the potato slices in a well-buttered oven dish. Cover with half the sauce, then arrange the sliced egg and chopped ham on top. Cover with the remaining sauce and potato slices.
4 Bake in a hot oven, Gas 8, 450°F, 250°C for 12 to 15 minutes or until the top is lightly browned.

Variation: sprinkle the top with grated cheese before baking.

1 Put oil and onion in a 600-ml/1-pint jug and cook on full power for 1 to 2 minutes to soften.
2 Stir in the flour, mustard, salt, pepper, Worcestershire sauce and milk. Cook, uncovered, on full power for 2 minutes or until the sauce thickens. Stir after 2 minutes.
3 Arrange the potato slices in a

buttered dish. Pour over it half the onion sauce, then arrange the egg and ham on top. Cover with remaining sauce and then the rest of the potatoes.

4 Cook, uncovered, on full power for 3 minutes.

5 Brown the top (adding grated cheese if you like it) under a hot grill.

Joan Tyers
Wingate, Co. Durham

POTATO SLICE

Serves 2. Simple, tasty and fits nicely in a 25-cm/10-inch frying pan.

2 medium potatoes, peeled
2 rashers bacon, chopped
1 onion, chopped
1 egg, beaten
2 tablespoons milk
Salt and pepper
25 g/1 oz fat

1 Grate the potatoes into a bowl and stir in the bacon, onion, egg, milk and seasoning.

2 Heat the fat in a frying pan, then press in the potato mixture.

4 Cook for 10 minutes, then turn it over and cook for a further 10 minutes.

Mrs S. E. Firth
Bradford, West Yorkshire

SAVOURY POTATO BAKE WITH FRANKFURTERS

Serves 2, but easy to make just for one. Very satisfying.

2 medium potatoes, peeled
1 small onion, roughly chopped
A knob of butter, and a little for greasing
100 g/4 oz Cheddar cheese, grated
1 egg, beaten

A 200 g/7 oz can of sweetcorn, drained
Black pepper
2 or 4 Frankfurters, depending on size
2 tomatoes, skinned (page 26) and sliced

1 Boil the potato and onion together in salted water until cooked, then drain and mash together. Add a knob of butter, half the cheese and the beaten egg. Stir in half of the sweetcorn and season with black pepper.

2 Spread the potato mixture in a buttered ovenproof dish, slice the Frankfurters and arrange them on top, then add the remaining sweetcorn and the tomatoes. Finally, sprinkle with the rest of the cheese.

3 Bake in a preheated moderately hot oven, Gas 6, 400°F, 200°C, for 20 to 25 minutes, or until the cheese is golden brown.

Miss G. J. Miles
Southend on Sea, Essex

 Microwave

1 Quarter the potatoes and put them with the onion into an 18-cm/7-inch soufflé-type dish. Sprinkle with 4 measured 15 ml tablespoons cold water. Cover with clear film and cook on full power for 6 minutes. Stand for 5 minutes.

2 Then drain and mash with the butter, half the cheese and the beaten egg. Stir in half the sweetcorn and season with freshly ground black pepper.

3 Slice the Frankfurters and arrange them over the potato. Sprinkle with the remaining sweetcorn and arrange the tomato slices on top. Finally sprinkle with the remaining cheese.

4 Heat on full power for 6 to 8 minutes.

5 Then brown the top under a preheated grill.

HOT VEGETABLE PANCAKES

Serves 2; very filling and satisfying.

225 g/8 oz parsnips, scrubbed
  and sliced
325 g/12 oz mixed raw vegetables
  e.g. carrots, leeks, cauliflower,
  peas, whatever you have
15 g/½ oz butter
Milk
4 cooked wholemeal pancakes
  (page 139)
75 g/3 oz matured Cheddar cheese,
  grated

1 Cook the parsnips in boiling salted
water until tender.
2 In another pan, bring carrots (if
using) to the boil, add the other
chosen vegetables and cook until
tender but not soft.
3 Drain the parsnips and mash them
up with the butter and a little milk.
Add the cooked vegetables to this.
4 Place a quarter of the vegetable
mixture on each pancake and roll
them up. Place them in a lightly
buttered ovenproof dish and cover
with the grated cheese.
5 Either put the dish under a hot grill
until the cheese melts or, heat in a
moderate oven, Gas 4, 350°F,
180°C, for 10 to 15 minutes.

Grace Mulligan

VEGETABLES WITH CHEESE

*A substantial dish on its own for 2.
Reheats well; can also be served with
baked jacket potatoes to accompany
grilled chops or cold meats. This recipe
won Mrs Webster a place in the semi-
finals of a microwave cooking
competition organised by Sharp. The
conventional method follows this
microwave version.*

2 medium leeks, well washed
2 medium courgettes, trimmed
  and sliced
225 g/8 oz broccoli
Two 15 ml tablespoons water
100 g/¼ lb grated cheese
1 tomato, sliced
Microwave browning or paprika
  (optional)

1 Cut the leeks into 1-cm/½-inch
pieces and put them in a shallow 18-
cm/7-inch flan dish. Arrange the
courgettes on top of the leeks.
2 Trim the broccoli stalks and divide
into 4 equal portions. Arrange these
on top of the courgettes so that the

stalks are pointing towards the edge of the dish. Sprinkle over the water and cover the dish completely with clear film. Cook on full power for 6 minutes.

3 Loosen the film and drain off any excess water. Remove film completely, then sprinkle over the cheese. Arrange the tomato slices on top of the cheese. Cook uncovered, for a further 2 minutes on full power.

If you wish you can sprinkle the cheese with a little microwave browning or paprika to give the cheese a 'brown' appearance. However, the dish is so colourful that this is not really necessary.

Mrs Jean Webster
Lea, Lancashire

CONVENTIONAL METHOD

1 Cut leeks into 1-cm/$\frac{1}{2}$-inch slices and cook them in a close-fitting pan until almost tender.

2 At the same time, cook the broccoli and courgettes separately so that they are still crunchy and keep their good green colours. Do not let them go soft and floppy.

3 Arrange leeks in a heatproof dish, then make a layer of courgettes and finally the broccoli, with the stems to the outer edge of the dish.

4 Over this spread the cheese and decorate with tomato slices.

5 Put the dish into a hot oven, Gas 6, 400°F, 200°C for 20 minutes. The cheese melts into the vegetables but it still looks attractive and there is no need for paprika – or microwave browning!

Chapter 7

Salads and Vegetables

SALAD DRESSING

An old recipe quite worth the trouble as it will keep for several weeks in the refrigerator. Makes 300 ml/½ pint.

2 eggs, lightly beaten
75 g/3 oz sugar
1 level teaspoon dry mustard
150 ml/½ pint milk
75 ml/3 fl oz vinegar
1 level teaspoon salt
15 g/½ oz margarine

1 Put all ingredients in a double saucepan or a basin, set over a pan of simmering water. Let it slowly come to the boil, stirring about every 5 minutes, for 30 minutes. If it should curdle, whisk with an egg-beater.
2 Once mixture has boiled, take pan off heat and allow to cool a little before bottling.

Mary Hunter
Addingham, Yorkshire

FRENCH DRESSING

3 tablespoons salad oil
1 tablespoon cider or wine
  vinegar
A squeeze of lemon juice
1 teaspoon sugar (try Barbados)
¼ teaspoon salt
A knife end of mustard
Freshly grated black pepper

1 Combine all ingredients in a screwtop jar and shake up well immediately before using.

Mary Watts

SOY SAUCE DRESSING

Makes about 150 ml/¼ pint. Keeps in the refrigerator for 6 or 7 days. Goes well with Rice Salad (page 108); or try it with a salad of beansprouts, bamboo shoots and fresh mushrooms.

5 tablespoons olive oil
2 tablespoons soy sauce

1 tablespoon lemon juice
A large clove of garlic, crushed
½ teaspoon peeled and chopped,
  or grated fresh root ginger
Salt and pepper

1 Combine all ingredients together in a screwtop jar and shake up well before using.

Grace Mulligan

TOMATO DRESSING

Makes about 150 ml/¼ pint. Very nice served with Green Split Pea Salad (page 109). Eat within 3 to 4 days before the garlic goes stale.

150 ml/¼ pint canned tomato
  juice
½ level teaspoon sugar
A clove of garlic, crushed
1 tablespoon chopped chives
1 tablespoon olive oil, or good
  salad oil
2 teaspoons lemon juice
Pepper and salt

1 In a small pan, mix the tomato juice and sugar. Bring it to the boil and boil for 1 or 2 minutes. Allow to cool.
2 Mix all the other ingredients into the cooled tomato juice, adding pepper and a little salt. Put all into a screwtop jar and shake well before serving.

Grace Mulligan

 Microwave

1 Put the tomato juice and sugar into a 600-ml/1-pint jug. Heat on full power for 2 to 2½ minutes, until it is boiling, then allow to cool.
2 Mix all the other ingredients into the cooled tomato juice, adding pepper and a little salt. Pour all of it into a screwtop jar and shake well before serving.

COTTAGE CHEESE AND YOGHURT DRESSING

This low-fat dressing keeps for a week in the refrigerator. Especially nice with Savoury Stuffed Apples, Chicken and Grape Salad, Potato and Herring Salad and Pasta Salad – all in this chapter.

225 g/8 oz cottage cheese
150 ml/5 fl oz natural yoghurt
2 tablespoons salad dressing,
    salad cream or mayonnaise
1 tablespoon vinegar – cider or
    wine vinegar is best
1 tablespoon lemon juice

1 Sieve cottage cheese into a bowl.
2 Add rest of ingredients and beat well together.

To vary flavour: made mustard or horseradish sauce can be added, to taste.

Mrs Margaret Heywood
Todmorden, Yorkshire

SAVOURY STUFFED APPLES

For 2.

2 large, red, crisp apples
A little lemon juice
1 stick of celery (optional)
25 g/1 oz raisins, roughly chopped
25 g/1 oz stoned dates, chopped
25 g/1 oz chopped nuts or seeds,
    e.g. walnuts, cashews, sunflower
    seeds
Salad dressing to bind – Cottage
    Cheese and Yoghurt
    Dressing (above) is ideal
Lettuce leaves or cress for serving

1 Take a slice off the top of each apple.
2 Remove apple core and carefully

take out apple flesh to leave a firm shell.
3 Brush cut surfaces of apple with lemon juice.
4 Chop apple flesh and mix with the finely sliced celery, dried fruits and nuts. Bind them together with dressing.
5 Pile mixture into apple cases, put tops back on and serve on a bed of lettuce or cress.

Mrs Margaret Heywood
Todmorden, Yorkshire

POTATO AND HERRING SALAD

For 2.

225 g/8 oz cold cooked potato
1 pickled herring (page 43) or
    rollmop
2 spring onions or 1 small onion,
    finely chopped
Cottage Cheese and Yoghurt
    Dressing (left)
Lettuce leaves and brown bread
    for serving

1 Roughly chop the potato.
2 Snip the herring into bite-sized pieces.
3 Mix all together with onions and enough dressing to bind.
4 Serve on a bed of lettuce with brown bread.

Mrs Margaret Heywood
Todmorden, Yorkshire

TUNA SALAD

A tasty snack for 2.

1 small onion or 2 to 3 spring
    onions, finely chopped
15 g/½ oz butter or margarine or
    cooking oil (optional)
A 100 g/4 oz can of tuna, or half
    of a large can, drained
1 hard-boiled egg, roughly
    chopped

Salt and pepper
2 to 3 tablespoons salad cream,
   mayonnaise, or Cottage Cheese
   and Yoghurt Dressing (page
   107)
A squeeze of lemon juice
   (optional)
Lettuce leaves or cress for serving

1 If you do not like the taste of raw
onion, cook it in butter or oil or even
in the oil from the tuna can, until
soft but not browning.
2 Break up tuna in a bowl and stir in
onion, egg, seasoning to taste and
enough salad cream to bind mixture
together.
3 Serve with a squeeze of lemon juice
in lettuce leaves, or on a bed of cress,
or on toast.

Mrs Doris Wilkinson
Hull, Humberside

CHICKEN AND GRAPE SALAD
For 2.

1 cooked, skinned chicken joint,
   or about 150 g/6 oz cooked
   chicken
100 g/4 oz seedless grapes, roughly
   chopped or halved
4 to 5 tablespoons Cottage Cheese
   and Yoghurt Dressing (page
   107)
Curry powder or paste – about ½
   teaspoon – to taste
Lettuce leaves

1 Cut chicken into bite-sized pieces.
Add grapes.
2 Put dressing into a bowl and blend
in curry powder or paste, adding
more if you like to suit your taste.
3 Gently mix in chicken and grapes.
Serve on a bed of lettuce.

Mrs Margaret Heywood
Todmorden, Yorkshire

PASTA SALAD
*For 2. A crisp, green salad goes well
with this.*

50 g/2 oz wholemeal pasta
2 to 3 spring onions or 1 small
   onion, finely chopped
1 stick of celery, finely chopped
Pieces of red and green pepper,
   chopped
A small piece of cucumber, peeled
   and chopped
A few chopped nuts, if liked
Cottage Cheese and Yoghurt
   Dressing (page 107)

1 Cook pasta in boiling salted water
until just tender. Drain, rinse with
cold water and drain again
thoroughly.
2 When pasta is cold, put it into a
bowl with the rest of the salad
ingredients.
3 Add enough dressing to give a
creamy consistency. Wholewheat pasta
needs more dressing than the white-
flour variety.
4 Serve with a green salad.

Mrs Margaret Heywood
Todmorden, Yorkshire

RICE SALAD
*This makes a substantial and nutritious
dish. It looks attractive served in lettuce
leaves. For 1 or 2.*

75 g/3 oz round grain brown
   rice (nicest with round, but long
   grain rice can be used)
Half a red pepper, chopped
2 spring onions, finely chopped
25 g/1 oz raisins
25 g/1 oz salted peanuts
1 tablespoon chopped parsley
2 tablespoons Soy Sauce Dressing
   (page 106)
Pepper and salt

1 Cook the rice in simmering water
until just done. Drain through a sieve
and cool under running cold water.

Or cook it by the absorption method (page 88).
2 Mix all the ingredients together, seasoning to taste with pepper and salt.

Grace Mulligan

THREE BEAN SALAD

For 2. If you add the chicken, it makes a very good lunchtime snack.

75 g/3 oz red kidney beans, cooked weight
75 g/3 oz haricot beans, canned or home-cooked
2 tablespoons French Dressing (page 106)
75 g/3 oz fresh green beans
3 spring onions, sliced
1 tablespoon fresh parsley
50 to 75 g/2 or 3 oz cold cooked chicken (optional)
Salt and pepper

To cook the dried beans:

50 g/2 oz dry red kidney beans and 50 g/2 oz haricots will give 75 g/3 oz of each when cooked.

1 Remember to start the night before by soaking both red kidney and haricots in separate bowls of cold water.
2 Cook them separately in fresh cold water, bringing them to boil and then boiling hard for 10 minutes before reducing heat and simmering until tender, about 45 to 50 minutes in all. Take care not to let them crack open or go mushy. Using a pressure cooker halves the cooking time but it is hard to gauge how long to give before the beans burst.

For the salad

1 As soon as you have drained them, toss the hot beans into the French dressing. If using canned beans, drain and then rinse them under the cold tap. Toss in dressing.
2 String the green beans. Top and tail them and cut into 1-cm/½-inch pieces. Cook them in a little simmering water for 7 to 8 minutes or less so that they are cooked but still crisp. Drain well.
3 Now mix all the ingredients together, seasoning carefully with pepper and a little salt before serving.

Grace Mulligan

GREEN SPLIT PEA SALAD

For 1 or 2. The dressed peas keep for 2 days but keep the fresh salad ingredients ready to toss in at the last minute. Remember to start the night before.

75 g/ 3 oz green split peas
3 tablespoons Tomato Dressing (page 106)
Pepper and salt
2 spring onions, sliced
2 very firm red tomatoes, deseeded and chopped small
1 large crisp stick of celery, trimmed and sliced
Chopped parsley

1 Soak the peas in cold water overnight.
2 Drain peas and put in a saucepan; cover with fresh cold water and bring to the boil. Boil them hard for 10 minutes, then simmer until just done but not mushy, or the texture of the salad will be spoilt.
3 Drain the hot peas and mix with the dressing. Season well and leave until cold.
4 Gently toss in the other ingredients, saving the parsley to sprinkle on top.

Grace Mulligan

CORN RAITA

A pleasant accompaniment to some of the other recipes contributed to this book by Nimmi Singh: Sheekh Kebabs (page 82), Lamb Kofta Curry (page 81), Turkey Kebabs (page 64) and Potato Bhaji (page 116).

50 g/2 oz frozen sweetcorn
150 ml/¼ pint natural yoghurt
A pinch of salt
½ teaspoon cumin seed
Ground black pepper
A pinch of paprika

1 Cook the corn in boiling salted water until tender, then rinse it in cold water and drain thoroughly, patting it dry with a cloth or paper towel.
2 Add the corn to the yoghurt and season with salt.
3 Put the cumin seeds into a frying pan and cook (that is, dry-roast) over a moderate heat for about 1 minute. Crush the hot seeds with the end of a rolling pin.
4 Put the yoghurt and corn mixture into a bowl, grind a little black pepper over the top then scatter over the crushed cumin seeds and a little paprika.

Nirmal Singh
Nuneaton, Warwickshire

MINTY TOMATO SALAD

Enough for 2 as a starter with soft brown rolls or hot brown bread. Makes a good accompaniment to cold roast lamb.

225 g/8 oz tomatoes, skinned
   (page 26)
Salt and pepper
A pinch of sugar
3 or 4 teaspoons freshly chopped
   mint

DRESSING
3 tablespoons soured cream or
   natural yoghurt
¼ teaspoon grated lemon rind
1 tablespoon lemon juice
Lettuce leaves for serving
Sprigs of mint to garnish

1 Quarter the skinned tomatoes and remove the seeds. Sprinkle lightly with salt, pepper, sugar and a little chopped mint.
2 Put the soured cream or yoghurt into a bowl and mix in the lemon rind and juice and more chopped mint.
3 Arrange a few crisp lettuce leaves on 2 plates, lay the tomatoes on top and spoon the soured cream/yoghurt dressing over them. Garnish with sprigs of fresh mint.

The June Hulbert Cookbook

YOGHURT CHUTNEY or RAITA

This is a good, hot, spicy dressing. If you prefer to leave out the ginger or chilli, add more mint and freshly ground black pepper. Nice to eat with Chicken Fingers (page 57), Savoury Semolina and other Indian dishes, curries etc., see Index.

150 g/5 oz natural yoghurt
1.5-cm/½-inch cube of peeled fresh ginger
Half a fresh green chilli (optional)
1 tablespoon chopped fresh mint
Salt and pepper

1 Put yoghurt in a bowl.
2 Chop ginger, chilli and mint and mix into yoghurt with salt and pepper to taste.

Mrs Jaswant Chopra
Childwall, Liverpool

CABBAGE WITH SOURED CREAM SAUCE

For 2. A delicious way to serve the humble cabbage.

15 g/½ oz butter
1 teaspoon vinegar
1 tablespoon water
1 onion, finely chopped

175 g/6 oz white cabbage, shredded and washed

SAUCE
15 g/½ oz butter
15 g/½ oz flour
150 ml/¼ pint milk
Salt and pepper
3 tablespoons soured cream*

See page 74 for other recipes using soured cream

1 Melt the butter in a saucepan, pour in the vinegar and water and bring to the boil. Add the onion and cook for 2 minutes.
2 Put the cabbage into the pan, cover with a tight-fitting lid and cook for about 10 minutes until the cabbage is tender. If necessary, add a little water to prevent it sticking.
3 For the sauce, melt the butter in a small pan, add the flour and cook for 1 minute. Gradually pour in the milk, stirring all the time, and heat until the sauce boils. Simmer the sauce for 1 minute then add the seasoning and soured cream.
4 Pour the sauce over the cabbage, mix well together and serve at once.

Joan Tyers
Wingate, Co. Durham

 Microwave

1 Put the butter and onion into a 15-cm/6-inch soufflé dish and cook on full power for 1 minute.
2 Add the cabbage, vinegar and 2 tablespoons water. Cover the dish and cook on full power for 5 minutes. Then leave to stand, covered, while you make the sauce.
3 Put the butter into a jug and heat on full power for 30 to 40 seconds. Stir in the flour and gradually blend in the milk. Heat on full power for 2 minutes, stirring once.
4 When the sauce has boiled, stir in the soured cream and seasoning and heat on full power for a further 30

seconds if necessary.

5 Uncover the cabbage and stir in the sauce, mixing well so that the cabbage is completely coated in the sauce. Serve at once.

 Microwave

GLAZED CARROTS

Accompanying Mandarin Chicken (page 59) with this dish, Mrs Roberts won a place in a national microwave cooking competition conducted by Sharp.

225 g/8 oz baby carrots
1 teaspoon sugar
One 15 ml tablespoon water
A knob of butter
Chopped parsley to garnish

1 Scrub the carrots. Put them in a dish, add sugar and water, cover and cook on full power for 3 to 4 minutes.
2 Drain, add butter, stir and garnish with chopped parsley.

Mrs Ann Roberts
Tarporley, Cheshire

CONVENTIONAL METHOD

1 Scrub the carrots and put them into a pan with the sugar and 120 ml/4 fl oz water. Bring to the boil, cover pan and simmer (making sure the pan does not boil dry) for about 6 minutes or until they are tender, slightly crisp, but not soft.
2 Drain, add butter and stir.
3 Serve sprinkled with chopped parsley.

CELERY FRITTERS

The batter is enough for 6 sticks of celery, almost too much for 2 people! The fritters are so delicious, however, that after you have eaten as many as you can, turn to page 114 for a Deep Fried Mushroom recipe using the spare

batter. *Serve as a first course with a dip (see below) or with grilled meats such as chops or sausages.*

Sticks of celery
Boiling water

BATTER
50 g/2 oz plain flour – delicious with wholemeal
Salt and pepper
$\frac{1}{2}$ teaspoon baking powder
1 beaten egg
A scant 150 ml/$\frac{1}{4}$ pint milk
Oil or fat for deep-frying

1 Clean celery, remove strings and cut into 10-cm/4-inch lengths. Cover with boiling water and leave for 10 minutes. Then drain and wipe dry.
2 Meanwhile, mix batter. Put flour in a bowl with salt and pepper. Mix in baking powder, make a well in centre and drop in the egg. Gradually beat in enough milk to make a smooth thick consistency.
3 Heat oil until very hot but not smoking.
4 Dip celery fingers into batter and fry until golden and crisp.
5 Drain on kitchen paper and eat at once. They are crisp and delicious.

Mrs A. M. Taylor
Boyton, Suffolk

A DIP FOR CELERY FRITTERS

2 tablespoons good thick mayonnaise
2 tablespoons natural yoghurt
A 2.5-cm/1-inch piece of cucumber, chopped
1 tablespoon freshly chopped mint
1 tablespoon freshly chopped parsley
Salt and freshly ground black pepper

1 Measure all the ingredients into a bowl.

2 Mix lightly and season to taste.
3 Serve well chilled.

Debbie Woolhead
Boston Spa, West Yorkshire

STIR-FRIED CHINESE LEAVES

For 2 – easy to make just enough for 1. Nice with chicken and other roast or grilled meats. Must be eaten the moment it is cooked or the Chinese leaves go soggy.

225 g/½ lb Chinese leaves
1 tablespoon oil
1 small onion, chopped
1 small clove of garlic, chopped
½ teaspoon grated fresh ginger,* or
    a pinch of ground ginger
A pinch of salt
½ teaspoon vinegar
½ teaspoon sugar
1 dessertspoon soy sauce

* See Soy Sauce Dressing (page 106) for another recipe using fresh ginger. Ground ginger is nothing like as good as fresh in these recipes.

1 Prepare all the ingredients before you start to cook, removing tough stalks on Chinese leaves before cutting it into manageable pieces.
2 Put a large shallow pan or wok on to a high heat.
3 Put in the oil, onion, garlic and ginger and fry for 1 minute.
4 Quickly add the chopped Chinese leaves and salt. Toss it all continuously, keeping the heat high.
5 Add the vinegar, sugar and soy sauce.
6 Lower heat and keep turning the vegetables for only one minute more. By now the liquid should be reduced to almost none and the Chinese leaves will be piping hot, brilliant green and white but still crisp. Serve at once.

Grace Mulligan

 Microwave

The microwave is ideal for 'stir-frys', although really it is not frying in the true sense – it gives quick, crisp results.

1 Prepare all the ingredients before you start cooking. Remove any tough stalks from the Chinese leaves before cutting into 3.5 cm/1½ inch pieces.
2 Put the oil, garlic, ginger and onion into a large mixing bowl and heat on full power for 2 minutes.
3 Stir in the vinegar, soy sauce and sugar. Add the Chinese leaves, tossing them well so that they are coated in the sauce. Cover the dish with clear film and cook on full power for 3 minutes, stirring after 2 minutes and at the end of cooking.
4 Season with a little salt and serve immediately. The leaves will be a brilliant green and white with a crisp texture.

COURGETTES WITH TOMATOES

This versatile dish may be served cold as a starter, a salad with hot and cold meats, eaten hot as an accompanying vegetable, or tossed in freshly cooked pasta shapes. For 1 or 2 or more.

1 tablespoon oil
1 small onion, sliced
A clove of garlic, crushed
50 ml/2 fl oz dry white wine or
    dry cider
Salt and pepper
275 g/10 oz courgettes, wiped
225 g/8 oz tomatoes, skinned (page 26)
Chopped fresh parsley or chervil

1 Heat the oil in a saucepan and cook the onion until soft but not coloured. Add the garlic, wine and seasoning.
2 Top and tail the courgettes and cut into slices. Quarter the tomatoes and

113

remove the seeds.
3 Add the courgettes and tomatoes to the saucepan and cook slowly for 10 minutes without a lid, or longer if you prefer the courgettes softer.
4 Sprinkle with chopped parsley.

The June Hulbert Cookbook

1 Put the oil, onion and garlic into an 18-cm/7-inch soufflé-type dish. Heat on full power for 3 minutes.
2 Top and tail the courgettes and cut into slices. Cut the tomatoes into quarters and remove the seeds.
3 Stir the wine and courgettes into the onion. Cover with clear film and cook on full power for 2 minutes. Then add tomatoes and cook 2 minutes more.
4 Season with salt and pepper and sprinkle with parsley.

DEEP-FRIED MUSHROOMS

A delicious way to use up batter made for Celery Fritters (page 112). Alternatively, make these and use up the batter on the Celery Fritters! For 2 or more.

About 50 g/2 oz garlic and herb soft cream cheese
100 g/4 oz button mushrooms

1 Remove the stalks from the mushrooms. Sandwich two mushrooms together with a little cream cheese and secure with a cocktail stick. Repeat with remaining mushrooms.
2 Dip each pair of mushrooms into the leftover batter and deep-fry until golden brown and crisp.
3 Drain well, remove cocktail sticks and serve at once.

Debbie Woolhead
Boston Spa, West Yorkshire

CASSEROLED POTATOES WITH ONION AND GARLIC

For 2.

225 g/½ lb potatoes, peeled and thinly sliced
1 small shallot or onion, sliced
A clove of garlic, crushed (optional)
1 teaspoon chopped parsley
Salt and pepper (optional)
150 ml/¼ pint milk or single cream
25 g/1 oz butter
Salt and pepper to taste

1 Arrange half the potatoes in an ovenproof dish, cover with shallot, garlic and parsley. Season with salt and pepper.
2 Place the remaining potatoes neatly on the top and pour over the milk or cream. Season again, dot with butter and put the dish on a baking tray.
3 Bake in the centre of a moderate oven, Gas 4, 350°F, 180°C, for 1 hour.

Dilwen Phillips
Gileston, South Glamorgan

For this only half of the milk or cream is used – four 15 ml tablespoons. A little paprika is added for colour.

1 Arrange half the potato slices in a 12.5-cm/5-inch soufflé-type or casserole dish. Cover with the shallot, garlic and parsley. Season with salt and pepper.
2 Arrange the remaining potatoes overlapping neatly on the top. Pour over the 4 tablespoons milk or cream and dot with butter. Sprinkle the top with a little paprika and cover the dish with clear film.

3 Cook on full power for 5 to 6 minutes then let it stand for 5 minutes. The potatoes should be tender when pierced with a knife.

CHEESE-BAKED POTATOES

For 2. Delicious on their own or with cold meat.

2 medium potatoes
1 tablespoon milk
15 g/½ oz butter
1 egg, lightly beaten
Pepper and salt
50 g/2 oz grated Cheddar cheese
1 tablespoon chopped parsley, if liked

1 Scrub potatoes and bake them near top of a moderate oven, Gas 4, 350°C, 180°C, until soft to the touch, about 1¼ hours. Alternatively, they will cook in 1 hour in a moderately hot oven, Gas 6, 400°F, 200°C. To save

more time, push a skewer right through the potatoes. The heat is conducted through the skewer so that the potato begins to cook from inside as well as the outside.
2 Wasting no time, cut each hot potato in half and scoop the flesh out into a basin.
3 Mash potato with milk and butter adding egg, pepper and a very little salt, the cheese and parsley.
4 Spoon the hot mixture back into the potato shells and either return them to the oven for 15 minutes or put them under the grill to brown.

Mrs S. Dislay
Newquay, Cornwall

The first way will make the skins more crisp.

1 Scrub the potatoes and dry on kitchen paper. Prick all over with a fork. Place the potatoes on a piece of

kitchen paper in the microwave, cook on full power for 7 to 8 minutes. Some microwave manufacturers recommend turning the potato over after half the cooking time.
2 Allow the potatoes to stand for 5 minutes, then cut them in half and carefully scoop out the potato, taking care not to tear the skin.
3 Mash the potato with the milk, butter, egg and season lightly with salt and pepper. Stir in the cheese and parsley.
4 Spoon the mixture back into the potato shells.
5 *Either* – place on a baking tray and cook in a conventional oven for 15 minutes at Gas 6, 400°F, 200°C, until crisp and brown.
Or – reheat on full power for 2 minutes then, if desired, brown under a hot grill for 2 to 3 minutes.

POTATO PUFFS

These are especially nice with bacon and peas.

225 g/8 oz firm cold boiled
   potatoes
A knob of butter
1 egg, separated
Pepper and a little salt
1 teaspoon flour, white or
   wholemeal
Oil or fat for frying (good with
   sunflower oil)

1 Mash the potatoes with a knob of butter, the egg yolk, seasoning and a little flour to make a firm mixture.
2 Beat egg white until stiff and mix it gently into potato mixture.
3 Heat fat or oil – you will need it 1 cm/$\frac{1}{2}$ inch deep in pan to ensure the potatoes do puff. Fry spoonfuls of the mixture until golden brown on both sides.

Mrs A. Hughes
Bethesda, Gwynedd

116

POTATO BHAJI

These spicy potatoes are delicious by themselves or served with a meat dish and rice or chappatis. For 2.

2 to 3 tablespoons oil
$\frac{1}{2}$ teaspoon cumin seeds
225 g/8 oz potatoes, peeled and cut
   into bite-sized pieces
$\frac{1}{2}$ teaspoon turmeric powder
$\frac{1}{4}$ teaspoon chilli powder
$\frac{1}{2}$ teaspoon coriander powder
$\frac{1}{4}$ teaspoon salt
Water
Chopped coriander or parsley
   leaves to garnish

1 Heat the oil in a shallow pan, add the cumin seeds and cook for about half a minute.
2 Add the potatoes and stir them around until they are well coated with oil. Add all the remaining spices and salt and mix well so that the spices coat the potato pieces.
3 Add about four tablespoons of water, cover the pan and cook very slowly until the potatoes are tender. Shake the pan occasionally to prevent sticking.
4 Remove the potatoes from the pan and put into a warmed serving dish. Sprinkle with the chopped coriander leaves or parsley.

Nirmal Singh
Nuneaton, Warwickshire

 Microwave

1 Heat the oil in an 18 cm/7 inch shallow casserole on full power for 1 minute.
2 Add all the spices and heat for half a minute.
3 Add the potatoes, mix well to coat and stir in 2 to 3 tablespoons of water. Cover the dish and cook on full power for 5 minutes, stirring half way through.
4 Allow to stand covered for 2

minutes, then stir in salt to taste and serve.

Nirmal Singh
Nuneaton, Warwickshire

MASHED POTATO

1 For 1: cook one 150 g/6 oz potato in its jacket on full power for 5 to 6 minutes.
For 2: cook two 150 g/6 oz potatoes in their jackets on full power for 7 to 9 minutes.
2 Let the potatoes stand for 2 to 3 minutes then scoop the flesh out of the skin and mash with butter, milk, salt and pepper to taste.

Yvonne Hamlett
Haddenham, Buckinghamshire

QUICK STIR-FRIED VEGETABLES WITH OYSTER SAUCE

Enough for 2, but easy to do for 1. A delicious way to cook green vegetables as a change from boiling or steaming. Cabbage, spring greens, Chinese leaves, celery, crisp lettuce and watercress are suitable. Must be served the moment it is cooked, so it is a last-minute job.

325 g/12 oz leafy vegetable of your choice
2 tablespoons oil
1 clove of garlic, chopped
1 tablespoon oyster sauce
Salt, pepper and a pinch of sugar

1 Prepare the vegetable, washing it thoroughly, and cut or shred it into bite-sized pieces. If it has thick stems separate these from the rest as they take longer to cook.
2 Heat the oil in a wok or large frying pan and quickly fry the garlic until lightly brown.
3 Add the stem pieces and cook for 3 to 4 minutes, tossing constantly over quite a high heat.

4 Add the rest of the vegetable and stir-fry only until its colour begins to change to a more brilliant green.
5 Add the oyster sauce, a little salt, pepper and sugar; stir and cook for 1 or 2 minutes more. Serve at once.

Jennie Siew Lee Cook
York

CHAPPATIS

The quantity of flour you need will depend on how many chappatis you want to make: 100 g/4 oz flour would make about 8 to 10, sufficient for 2 people with curries and other Indian dishes.

If you cannot get chappati flour it is possible to use finely ground strong wholewheat flour. Put the flour into a measure and then you can reckon that the amount of water needed will be approximately one third of that amount – but it does depend on the nature of the flour, the heat of your kitchen and the extent of your experience!

Chappati flour
Water
Melted butter

1 Put the flour in a bowl and mix in sufficient water to give a dough which is the consistency of putty. Knead it well for 5 minutes, then cover and put it aside for half an hour.
2 Take a small piece of dough about the size of a golf ball, knead it and then roll it out on a floured surface to a round about as thick as a 10p piece. Prepare the rest of the dough in the same way and keep them all covered as you begin the cooking.
3 Heat a griddle or frying pan and heat the grill until it is very hot.
4 Put one piece of the rolled-out dough on to the griddle or frying pan and reduce the heat to medium.
5 Cook for a few seconds until the top begins to look dry. Then turn it

117

over and cook until brown spots appear on the underneath.

6 Put the chappati under the grill with the undercooked side uppermost. It will start to blow up like a balloon and brown spots will appear on this side as well.

7 Put the chappati into a tea towel and brush the top lightly with melted butter or margarine.

8 Cook the rest of the chappatis in the same way, stacking them buttered sides together in the tea towel.

9 Wrap the tea towel in foil and keep warm until needed.

It does take a time or two to get your hand in at chappati-making. When you are skilled, you will find you can cook one in 30 seconds.

Nirmal Singh
Nuneaton, Warwickshire

SAVOURY PUDDING

A well-flavoured variation on Yorkshire Pudding, especially good with roast pork. Rather a lot for 2 people to eat all at once, but can be reheated carefully in the grill pan or by microwave, although the latter spoils the crispness. Mrs Maxfield simply adds sage and onion as she mixes the batter. You may prefer to cook the onion a bit more, as given below.

100 g/4 oz plain flour, either white or an even mixture of white and wholemeal
1 level teaspoon dried sage or 2 teaspoons chopped fresh sage
Salt
1 egg
300 ml/½ pint milk and water mixed
1 medium onion, finely chopped
A little dripping

1 Preheat oven to moderately hot, Gas 6, 400°F, 200°C.
2 Mix flour, sage and salt in a bowl and make a well in the centre.
3 Drop in egg and gradually beat in the milk and water to form a batter the consistency of pouring cream. Beat well.
4 Put dripping from the tin in which meat is roasting into a small roasting tin. Add onion and cook in oven for 10 minutes.
5 Then pour in the batter and cook at the top of the oven for 30 minutes.

Mrs A. Maxfield
Worksop, Nottingham

Chapter 8
Pies and Pasties Savoury and Sweet

QUICK EGG, BACON AND MUSHROOM PIE

If you like short cuts in the kitchen this recipe will appeal to you. Surprisingly, the pastry forms a golden crust all around the savoury filling and it seems like a crunchy omelette. If you use a large jug for beating the eggs, all the other ingredients can be mixed in it too. It's best served hot and fresh from the oven with a crisp green salad. Does not freeze well. Makes one 15-cm/6-inch pie.

75 g/3 oz bacon, finely chopped
75 g/3 oz mushrooms, sliced
2 eggs
120 ml/4 fl oz milk
100 g/4 oz shortcrust pastry mix, either white or wholemeal
1 tablespoon chopped parsley
25 g/1 oz grated cheese

1 Preheat oven to moderately hot, Gas 6, 400°F, 200°C, and put in a baking tray.
2 Fry bacon lightly, then toss mushrooms into the pan and fry them for 2 or 3 minutes.
3 Beat eggs and pour in the milk.
4 Mix all the ingredients together using all but 2 tablespoons of the cheese.
5 Pour the mixture into a greased flan dish, sprinkle over the reserved cheese, stand the dish on the hot baking tray and bake for 30 minutes. When cooked you will find that the pastry has formed nicely around the soft filling.

Mrs E. Jowett
Victoria, Australia

CHEESE AND LEEK FLAN
(*Fflan caws a cenyn*)

Serves 2, but very generously. There is enough to eat hot, then keep 2 portions to eat cold or freeze for another day. Another recipe from Lucy Barton-Greenwood, 14, who took second place in the 1987 Junior Cook of the Year competition. This was her starter (see page 179 for the other dishes in her menu).

PASTRY
100 g/4 oz wholemeal flour
1 teaspoon baking powder
25 g/1 oz lard
25 g/1 oz butter
4 teaspoons cold water

FILLING
1 large leek
25 g/1 oz butter
A pinch of nutmeg
A pinch of cayenne pepper
Salt
3 eggs
50 ml/2 fl oz milk
2 tablespoons soured cream
175 g/6 oz grated Cheddar cheese

1 Preheat oven to moderately hot, Gas 6, 400°F, 200°C.
2 Start with the pastry. Put flour and baking powder into a bowl and rub in the lard and butter. Add sufficient water to give a soft dough.
3 Roll out the pastry and line an 18-cm/7-inch flan tin.
4 Wash and slice leek in 1 cm/½ inch slices.
5 Melt butter and cook leek slowly until tender. Add nutmeg, cayenne and a little salt.
6 Whisk eggs, milk, soured cream and a little salt together.
7 Sprinkle half of the grated cheese over bottom of flan. Spread the leek on top and cover with remaining cheese. Pour over egg mixture.
8 Bake for 20 minutes until the top is golden.

Lucy Barton-Greenwood
Radyr, Cardiff

A little paprika is used to colour the dish.
This cooks successfully on Low but if you have a 2-power microwave cooker then do not try it – the result is not satisfactory and the flan should be baked conventionally.

1 Make the pastry, as in step 1.
2 Roll out the pastry and line a 18-cm/7-inch ceramic flan dish. Cover the pastry with a piece of kitchen paper – pressing it down lightly. Cook on full power for 2 to 3 minutes. The pastry should have lost its wet and shiny look and now be dry.
3 Wash and slice the leek into 1-cm/½-inch slices. Put them in a small basin with the butter. Cook on full power for 3 to 4 minutes, stirring once. Stir in the nutmeg, cayenne and a little salt.
4 Whisk together the eggs, milk, soured cream and a little salt.
5 Sprinkle the base of the flan case with half of the cheese. Spread the leeks over the top. Cover with the remaining cheese, then pour over the egg mixture. Sprinkle a little paprika on the top for colour.
6 Cook on Low for 10 to 12 minutes until the surface is firm to the touch.

FISH PIE IN PUFF PASTRY

Start this recipe in good time so that the fish and mushroom filling can cool before it is put into the pastry. This pie freezes well. For 2.

125 g/4 oz fillet of white fish, any variety
125 g/4 oz smoked white fish – Finnan haddock or other smoked fillets are suitable
150 ml/¼ pint milk
60 g/1½ oz butter
Freshly ground black pepper
1 small onion, finely chopped
50 g/2 oz mushrooms, wiped and chopped
15 g/½ oz plain flour
1 to 2 tablespoons frozen sweetcorn
1 tablespoon chopped fresh parsley
Half a 370 g/14 oz packet of frozen puff pastry*

* For another recipe using frozen puff pastry see Apple and Mincemeat Parcel (page 126).

1 Preheat the oven to moderate, Gas 4, 350°F, 180°C.
2 Skin the fish by placing the fillet skin side down on a board and sliding a very sharp knife under the flesh just above the skin. This is done by just slicing the knife in at the tail end of the fillet. Then, holding the tail piece firmly to the board with the other hand, work the knife along until flesh is separated and skin remains on the board.
3 Put fish into a shallow ovenproof dish in which it neatly fits, just cover with milk, dot with 15 g/½ oz of the butter and grind on some black pepper.
4 Cover dish and cook for 15 minutes in the preheated oven. Then strain liquid into a measuring jug and, when the fish is cool, flake it in quite large pieces, carefully removing bones.
5 Meanwhile melt another 15 g/½ oz butter and fry onion until transparent. Then add mushrooms, raise heat and cook them for 2 or 3 minutes, stirring so that onion does not go brown.
6 Now for the sauce. Melt remaining 15 g/½ oz butter in a small pan, stir in the flour and cook it for 1 minute.
7 Gradually stir in all but a tablespoon of the milk strained from the fish. Stir over a low heat as it thickens. The consistency should be slightly thicker than for pouring. Simmer for 2 minutes.

121

8 Mix in the fish, onion and mushrooms, sweetcorn and nearly all of the parsley. Remove from heat and allow to cool.

9 When you are ready to cook the pie, preheat the oven to moderately hot, Gas 6, 400°F, 200°C.

10 Cut the pastry into 2 even pieces and roll out thinly, taking care to mend any holes.

11 Place a piece of pastry on to a damp baking sheet and spoon the fish mixture along the middle.

12 Dampen the edges of the pastry with water, cover with the remaining piece of pastry and press the edges to seal.

13 Crimp the edges with a fork and trim to make them tidy. Make parallel slashes across the top, but do not cut right through the pastry. Brush over with the remaining fishy milk.

14 Bake near the top of the oven for 30 minutes or until the pastry is well risen and golden.

15 Serve sprinkled with the remaining chopped parsley.

To reheat a single piece of pie wrap it in foil and put it in a warm oven, Gas 3, 325°F, 160°C for 15 minutes, then remove the foil and heat for a further few minutes to crisp up the pastry.

Mary Hunter
Addingham, West Yorkshire

SARDINE PASTIES

Makes 2: nice hot or cold; serve with a fresh Tomato Sauce (page 175).

SHORTCRUST PASTRY
100 g/4 oz plain flour, white or
    wholemeal
A pinch of salt
50 g/2 oz margarine and lard or
    butter, mixed
2 to 3 teaspoons water
A little milk

FILLING
A 120 g/4½ oz can of sardines
1 onion, finely chopped
1 medium potato, peeled and
    diced small
Salt and pepper
1 heaped teaspoon parsley, finely
    chopped
A pinch of mixed herbs
1 dessertspoon water

1 First make the pastry: mix flour and salt and rub in fat. Add water and mix to a dough, then let it rest in refrigerator for half an hour, especially if using wholemeal flour.

2 Cut pastry in half and roll out each piece to a circle 18 cm/7 inches across.

3 Preheat oven to moderately hot, Gas 6, 400°F, 200°C.

4 Now for the filling: drain oil from sardines and mash them with a fork, adding onion, potato, seasoning, parsley and herbs.

5 Mix in enough water just to moisten the filling.

6 Spoon half of the filling on to each piece of pastry.

7 Moisten edges of pastry, fold over to pasty shape, press edges together to seal and brush top with a little milk.

8 Bake near top of preheated oven for 15 minutes, then reduce heat to Gas 4, 350°F, 180°C, for 15 to 20 minutes more to cook filling through.

Mrs Anne Walton
Frome, Somerset

HAM AND LEEK FLAN

Makes 3 good helpings. Nice hot or cold. Freezes successfully. A good way to use meat from a Ham Shank (page 67).

SHORTCRUST PASTRY
125 g/4 oz plain white or
    wholewheat flour or a mixture
A pinch of salt
25 g/1 oz hard margarine

122

25 g/1 oz lard
2 to 3 teaspoons cold water

FILLING
15 g/½ oz ham fat or lard
1 small onion, finely chopped
1 small whole leek, washed and
  finely sliced
50 g/2 oz cooked ham, diced
Ground black pepper
1 egg
About 300 ml/½ pint milk
25 g/1 oz grated cheese

*Use an 18-cm/7-inch loose-bottomed
flan tin or a ring set on a small baking
sheet.*

1 Mix flour and salt in a bowl, rub
in the fats and then add enough cold
water to make a dough. Put it in a
cool place to rest for half an hour,
especially if using wholemeal flour.
2 Roll out the pastry on a floured
surface and line the flan tin. Put
aside while the filling is prepared.
3 Preheat oven to moderately hot,
Gas 6, 400°F, 200°C, and put a
baking tray on the top shelf to
preheat also.
4 Melt the ham fat or lard in a small
frying pan and gently cook the onion
and leek until soft. Set aside to cool,
then spread this mixture over the base
of the pastry case.
5 Arrange the diced ham on top of
the leeks and season generously with
ground black pepper.
6 Beat together the egg and milk and
pour this into the pastry case, then
sprinkle the grated cheese on top.
7 Put the flan on to the hot baking
tray in the oven – this ensures that
the bottom of the pastry cooks
properly. Bake for 20 minutes, then
reduce the heat to Gas 4, 350°F,
180°C, and cook for a further 20
minutes.

Grace Mulligan

CHICKEN AND MUSHROOM PIE
2 generous helpings.

SHORTCRUST PASTRY
75 g/3 oz flour, wholemeal or
  white
A pinch of salt
40 g/1½ oz lard and margarine,
  mixed
1 to 2 teaspoons cold water
A little milk or beaten egg, to
  glaze

FILLING
15 g/½ oz butter
1 small onion, chopped
175 g/6 oz cooked chicken, diced
1 Frankfurter sausage, cut into
  slices
75 g/3 oz mushrooms, wiped and
  sliced

ALL-IN-ONE SAUCE
150 ml/¼ pint milk
40 g/1½ oz butter or margarine
40 g/1½ oz plain flour
150 ml/¼ pint chicken stock
1 teaspoon lemon juice
1 tablespoon chopped fresh
  parsley

1 Make the pastry. Mix flour and salt
in a bowl and rub in the fats. Mix to
a firm dough with the water – if
using wholemeal flour, it may require
a little more. Leave it in a cool place.
2 In a small frying pan, melt
15 g/½ oz butter and cook the onion
very gently until soft.
3 Meanwhile, prepare the sauce in
another pan. Put in the milk, butter
and flour and whisk the mixture until
the flour is all dispersed. Using a
wooden spoon, stir the 'all-in-one'
sauce over a moderate heat and, when
it has thickened, gradually add the
stock. Keep stirring and add the
lemon juice and parsley.
4 Remove sauce from heat and mix
in the onion, chicken and the
Frankfurter sausage.

123

5 Set a pie funnel in the middle of a deep pie dish and pour the chicken mixture all round it. Cover with the sliced mushrooms. Leave until cold.
6 Roll out the pastry to about 1.5 cm/½ inch wider than needed to cover the pie. Cut off a 1.5-cm/½-inch strip round the outer edge. Moisten the rim of the pie with water, then press the strip of pastry down on this rim.
7 Moisten the top of the strip with cold water and cover with the remaining pastry. Seal very well round the outer edge. Trim off any overlapping pastry and use a fork or a spoon handle to flute the outer rim. Press the pastry gently over the pie funnel to make a small hole to allow the steam to escape.
8 Roll out the pastry trimmings and make some leaves.
9 Paint the top of the pie with a little milk or beaten egg. Arrange the pastry leaves on top and brush again.
10 Put the pie dish on a baking tray and cook near the top of a preheated, moderately hot oven, Gas 6, 400°F, 200°C, for 20 minutes, when the pastry will be crisp and golden. Eat hot.

Grace Mulligan

SAUSAGEMEAT FLAN

Will cut into six slices. Nice hot or cold. Slices of this flan will freeze very satisfactorily.

SHORTCRUST PASTRY
100 g/4 oz flour, wholemeal or white
A pinch of salt
25 g/1 oz lard
25 g/1 oz margarine
2 brimming teaspoons water

FILLING
1 dessert apple, peeled, cored and chopped
450 g/1 lb sausagemeat

1 large egg
1 teaspoon of mixed herbs
Freshly ground black pepper

Use either a 20-cm/8-inch flan tin with a loose base or a 20-cm/8-inch flan ring set on a baking sheet, or an 18-cm/7-inch square sandwich tin.

1 Mix flour and salt in a bowl, rub in the fats and mix to a firm dough with water. Wholemeal flour may require a little more water.
2 Roll out the pastry and line the flan tin. Then put it in a cool place until needed.
3 Preheat oven to moderately hot, Gas 5, 375°F, 190°C and put in a baking tray to heat up.
4 In a large bowl, mix together all the filling ingredients so that the herbs and pepper are well distributed. Press the mixture into the pastry case and level it off.
5 Put the flan on to the hot baking tray and cook near the top of the oven for 30 minutes.

Grace Mulligan

FRIED CURRY PUFFS

Makes 4. Good to eat hot or cold and suitable also for picnics and packed lunches. When fried they are very rich, but they can also be baked.

FILLING
2 to 3 teaspoons curry powder
2 tablespoons water
3 tablespoons oil
1 small onion, chopped
175 g/6 oz minced beef
1 large potato, diced small
Water

PASTRY
225 g/8 oz flour, white or wholemeal
A pinch of salt
50 g/2 oz margarine
50 g/2 oz lard

124

1 egg, lightly beaten
Oil for deep-frying
Sprigs of parsley

1 Mix the curry powder and water to make a paste.
3 Heat the oil in a pan and fry the curry paste for a minute or two until it becomes fragrant.
3 Add the onion, minced beef and potato and mix well together to coat with the curry.
4 Add about 5 tablespoons cold water, cover with a lid and cook until the potatoes are soft. Leave the filling to cool.
5 Now mix the pastry. Mix the flour and salt in a bowl and rub in margarine and lard until the mixture resembles breadcrumbs. Mix in the egg and sufficient water to bring the dough together.
6 Divide the dough into four and roll out each piece to a circle about 15 cm/6 inches across.
7 Place a quarter of the filling on each circle of pastry, dampen the edge and fold over like a pasty. Seal the edges well and flute them.
8 Deep-fry the pasties in hot oil and until golden brown, then drain well and serve garnished with sprigs of parsley.

Alternatively, bake in a moderately hot oven, Gas 6, 400°F, 200°C, for 20 minutes.

Jennie Siew Lee Cook
York

PIZZA FOR TWO
Serve this hot or cold with a green salad.

SCONE BASE
75 g/3 oz wholemeal self-raising flour*
25 g/1 oz porridge meal or rolled oats
½ teaspoon dried mixed herbs
Freshly ground pepper

50 g/2 oz polyunsaturated margarine
50 g/2 oz cottage cheese
3 tablespoons natural low-fat yoghurt

FILLING AND TOPPING
2 tablespoons tomato pickle or red tomato chutney
1 teaspoon dried mixed herbs
75 g/3 oz cottage cheese, either plain or with added sweetcorn and peppers
A 120 g/4½ oz can of sardines in oil, drained
2 tomatoes

* *If you cannot buy wholemeal self-raising flour, sift in 1 level teaspoon baking powder.*

1 Preheat oven to hot, Gas 7, 425°F, 220°C.
2 Mix flour, oats, herbs and pepper.
3 Rub in margarine.
4 Lightly mix in cheese and use enough yoghurt to make a soft dough.
5 Roll out about 1 cm/½ inch thick into a circle about 18-cm/7-inches across, and lift on to a greased baking tray. Work up a little raised edge to the dough to contain filling.
It will make a nice crusty edge when baked.
6 Now for the filling. Spread pickle over scone base, sprinkle with herbs and cover with cottage cheese.
7 For the topping, split sardines in half lengthways and arrange them cut side down like the spokes of a wheel. Cut tomatoes into enough slices to fit in the gaps between sardines. Brush over with oil from sardine can.
8 Bake for 35 minutes, just above the middle of the oven.

Mrs Powell
Enfield, Middlesex

APPLE AND MINCEMEAT PARCEL

Serves 2. Delicious with a spoonful of yoghurt or cream.

110 g/4 oz frozen puff pastry*
3 tablespoons mincemeat
1 cooking apple, peeled, cored and
   cut into thin slices
Caster sugar

* For other recipes using bought, frozen puff pastry see Fish Pie in Puff Pastry (page 121).

1 Preheat oven to hot, Gas 7, 425°F, 220°C.
2 Cut the pastry in half and roll out one piece to an oblong 10 to 12 cm/4 to 5 inches long.
3 Spread the mincemeat over the pastry, but leave a clear border around the edges. Cover the mincemeat with the apple slices.
4 Roll out the other piece of pastry to cover the base and, keeping a 2-cm/¾-inch border all round, make cuts across the centre 2 cm/¾ inch apart. Dampen edge of the base piece, then carefully place the top piece over the apple slices and seal the edges well.
5 Brush with water and sprinkle with a little caster sugar. Lift the parcel on to a baking tray.
6 Bake in the preheated oven for 20 to 25 minutes when it will be crisp and golden.

Joan Tyers
Wingate, Co. Durham

MARMALADE FLAN

This flan can be made with any type of thick-cut orange marmalade – preferably Seville. It freezes well either whole or in portions.

SHORTCRUST PASTRY
125 g/4 oz flour

126

A pinch of salt
15 g/1 oz butter
15 g/1 oz lard
1 tablespoon cold water

FILLING
25 g/1 oz sugar
25 g/1 oz margarine
1 egg, beaten
225 g/8 oz marmalade

1 Mix flour and salt and rub in the butter and lard. Mix to a firm dough with water. Leave the dough to rest for 15 minutes.
2 Roll out the pastry, and use it to line an 18-cm/7-inch flan ring.
3 Now for the filling. Cream together the sugar and margarine, then gradually stir in the beaten egg.
4 Mix in the marmalade. The mixture will curdle and look messy at this stage, but it looks fine when it is cooked.
5 Pour the filling into the pastry case and bake in the centre of a preheated moderate oven, Gas 4, 350°F, 180°C for 35 minutes.
6 Leave to cool then cut into slices and serve with cream, custard or yoghurt.

Miss Kathleen Cliff
King's Heath, Birmingham

PECAN PIE

Expensive but delicious! Makes 6 good helpings but it is good both hot and cold and can be frozen in portions for up to 3 months. A less extravagant pie can be made substituting walnuts, but it is not quite so good. Serve hot or cold with ice-cream or whipped cream.

PASTRY
50 g/2 oz plain flour, white or
   wholemeal
A pinch of salt
25 g/1 oz margarine
About 2 teaspoons water

FILLING

1 egg
25 g/1 oz butter
75 ml/2½ fl oz dark corn syrup or
  maple syrup*
25 g/1 oz muscovado sugar
½ teaspoon vanilla essence or
  flavouring
A pinch of salt
50 g/2 oz shelled pecan nuts

* *Golden syrup can be used but will produce a heavier texture.*

1 Preheat oven to moderately hot, Gas 6, 400°F, 200°C.
2 Mix flour and salt and rub in margarine. Mix to a firm dough with water.
3 Roll out to fit a 15-cm/6-inch flan dish or ring set on a baking tray (2.5 cm/1 inch deep is about right for this pie).
4 Now for the filling. Beat the egg lightly but not to a frothy state.
5 Melt butter and mix into it all the remaining ingredients and then the egg.
6 Pour mixture into pastry case.
7 Bake for 15 minutes in preheated oven, then reduce to moderate, Gas 4, 350°F, 180°C, for 20 minutes more, when pie should be firm around edges and soft in centre.

Mary Hunter
Addingham, West Yorkshire

ALMOND MINCE PIES

Makes 12. These are popular all year round and the almond topping makes a pleasant change from the usual pastry crust. Serve by themselves or with ice-cream. They freeze well. Just defrost them and warm through in a moderate oven, Gas 3, 325°F, 160°C.

PASTRY

50 g/2 oz margarine
110 g/4 oz plain flour, white,
  wholemeal or a mixture
2 to 3 teaspoons cold water

FILLING AND TOPPING

12 teaspoons mincemeat
50 g/2 oz margarine
40 g/1½ oz caster sugar
1 egg
50 g/2 oz ground almonds
Icing sugar for dusting

1 Rub the margarine into the flour and add enough cold water to make a firm dough. Let it rest for 20 minutes before rolling out, especially if using wholemeal flour.
2 Roll the pastry out on a floured board and cut out 12 rounds using a fluted biscuit cutter. Grease 12 tartlet tins and line with the pastry rounds.

3 Preheat oven to moderately hot, Gas 6, 400°F, 200°C.

4 Put a teaspoonful of mincemeat in each tart case.

5 To make the topping, cream the margarine and sugar together, beat in the egg and ground almonds. If the mixture is too dry, add a small spoonful of milk to slacken it.

6 Spread the almond topping over the mincemeat and bake for 15 or 20 minutes.

7 Let the pies cool slightly before removing to a wire rack.

8 Dust with icing sugar when cold.

Grace Mulligan

APRICOT AND COCONUT TARTS

Makes 10 tarts. They freeze well and taste just as nice when thawed as when freshly baked.

PASTRY
50 g/2 oz plain white or wholemeal flour
50 g/2 oz self-raising white flour
A pinch of salt
25 g/1 oz hard margarine
25 g/1 oz lard
2 to 3 teaspoons cold water

FILLING
25 g/1 oz dried apricots
Apricot jam
40 g/1½ oz soft margarine
40 g/1½ oz caster sugar
40 g/1½ oz desiccated coconut
1 small egg, beaten

1 Mix the two types of flour together, add the salt and rub in the margarine and lard until the mixture resembles breadcrumbs. Add sufficient cold water to bring the pastry together. Chill for 15 minutes in the refrigerator, especially if using wholemeal flour.

2 Cut the apricots into small pieces and pour some boiling water over them. Leave them to soak for 10 minutes, then drain.

3 Roll out the pastry and line bun tins.

4 Place a teaspoonful of apricot jam in each pastry case and then prepare the filling.

5 Cream together the margarine and sugar, stir in the coconut, drained apricots and enough beaten egg to bind.

6 Put the filling over the apricot jam, smooth the top and bake in a preheated moderate oven, Gas 4, 350°F, 180°C, for about 15 minutes.

Mrs L. Johnson
York

MEGAN'S TREACLE ROLL

When making pies, utilize the small leftover pieces of pastry by making this rich, fattening and delicious dish.

Pastry
Golden syrup
Milk

1 Roll out the pastry into a square.

2 Spread golden syrup quite thickly on to the pastry, roll up quickly and loosely seal the edges.

3 Place the roll in a small milk pudding or pie dish and cover with milk until only the top of the pastry is visible.

4 Put the dish into the top part of a warm oven, Gas 3, 325°F, 160°C for about 1 hour.

During the cooking the milk will become a thick, golden sauce. The milk may curdle if the oven is too hot.

Megan Mallinson
Fixby, Huddersfield

Chapter 9

Puddings

OLD-FASHIONED MILK PUDDINGS

Despite the fact that nearly all milk puddings are available in cans these days, they do not have the same authentic flavour as home-made ones. Milk puddings are delicious by themselves or served with all kinds of stewed fruits, or just a spoonful of jam.

SEMOLINA – PEARL TAPIOCA – GROUND RICE

The old way of cooking semolina was to bring it to a boil and simmer for 3 to 4 minutes, then pour the mixture into a pie dish and finish the cooking in the oven for a very long time. I think it is easier to make it on the top of the cooker. The following method can be used for both tapioca and ground rice.

300 ml/½ pint milk*
25 g/1 oz semolina, pearl tapioca or ground rice
25 g/1 oz sugar

* *If you wish to make a pudding with 600 ml/1 pint milk then increase the semolina etc. and the sugar to 40 g/1½ oz each.*

1 In a small pan, heat the milk and sprinkle on the semolina (or tapioca or ground rice).
2 Stirring continuously, bring the mixture up to the boil, then simmer gently for 3 to 4 minutes.
3 Stir in the sugar. Pour the mixture into a jug or bowl, stand it in a pan of gently simmering water and continue cooking for a further 20 to 30 minutes or until the mixture is thick. Stir with a wooden spoon from time to time. (Tapioca especially needs stirring or it sinks to the bottom and glues together.)

TO MAKE A BAKED PUDDING

After adding the sugar, stir in a beaten egg, then pour the mixture into an ovenproof dish and bake in a moderate oven, Gas 4, 350°F, 180°C, for 15 to 20 minutes or until the pudding has set. It is best to use the quantities based on 600 ml/1 pint milk for this or the egg sets it too hard.

Grace Mulligan

BAKED RICE PUDDING

Too much for 2 people to eat all at once but as the oven has to be on for such a long time it makes sense to cook a substantial pudding. It is good to eat warm or cold, on its own or with stewed fruit, especially prunes and apricots. Also try Quick Peach Condé, see next recipe.

You can use any type of milk for this recipe but the richer the milk the creamier the pudding. Gold Top milk (from Channel Islands breeds of cow) is the best one, but a good substitute is Silver Top (ordinary pasteurised) or homogenised milk with a heaped tablespoon of dried milk mixed into it. Stir it around well to ensure that the milk powder dissolves.

40 g/1½ oz round pudding rice, well washed
600 ml/1 pint milk
40 g/1½ oz granulated sugar
15 g/½ butter

1 Put all the ingredients in a buttered pie dish and leave overnight.
2 Bake the pudding uncovered in a cool oven, Gas 2, 300°F, 150°C for about 2 hours. Stir often during the first hour until the rice begins to thicken and the skin forms. When it begins to turn golden, gently slide a knife in at the edge of the dish to stir the pudding without disturbing the lovely brown skin – the part that many people like the best.

Grace Mulligan

Rice pudding cooked in the microwave is every bit as creamy as that cooked in the conventional oven. However it will not have a skin on top – the part some people particularly like! You can transfer the pudding to the oven for 20 minutes to brown the surface if desired.

1 Put the milk into a deep 2¼-litre/4-pint casserole. You need a very large dish to allow the milk to boil up – if you use too small a dish, the milk will boil over and on to the turntable. Cook on full power for 3 minutes.
2 Stir in the rice, sugar and butter. Cook on Low for 1 hour, stirring twice.

For a 2-power microwave cooker: Cook on Defrost for 50 to 60 minutes, stirring twice.

The rice should have absorbed all the milk and become creamy.

To reheat leftover rice pudding, put the rice pudding into the serving dish, heat on full power for 1 minute, then stir.

QUICK PEACH CONDÉ
For 2.

2 peach halves
150 ml/¼ pint cold rice pudding*
2 tablespoons raspberry jam

* *See opposite for home-made rice pudding recipes.*

1 Put the peach halves into two ramekin dishes.
2 Top with the rice pudding and level out evenly.
3 Warm the raspberry jam gently in a small pan, then pour over the top of the rice pudding.
4 Chill well before serving.

Debbie Woolhead
Boston Spa, West Yorkshire

BOILED RICE AND RAISIN MILK PUDDING
Easy to make half-quantity.

40 g/1½ oz round pudding rice
600 ml/1 pint milk
40 g/1½ oz granulated sugar
25 g/1 oz raisins

1 To burst the rice, wash it first, drain and then barely cover with cold water. Bring it to the boil and boil gently until the water has all evaporated. Shake the pan occasionally to prevent it sticking.
2 Add the milk and simmer until soft and creamy, about 15 to 20 minutes.
3 Add the sugar and raisins, reheat and serve.

Grace Mulligan

ZARDA OR SWEET SAFFRON RICE
A rich and aromatic sweet. Serves 2, but it's easy to make more.
When cooking rice, it is easier to measure it by the cupful (than by weight), then use the same cup to measure the water. Any size cup will do but for two people a teacup is ideal.

1 cup basmati rice
A few drops of orange colouring
50 g/2 oz sugar
75 ml/3 fl oz water
50 g/2 oz ghee or clarified butter, or unsalted butter
2 to 3 cloves
2 to 3 green cardamoms
25 g/1 oz flaked almonds
25 g/1 oz pistachio nuts

25 g/1 oz sultanas
1 dessertspoon rose water or
Kevda water
A pinch of saffron
Lightly whipped cream for
serving

1 Wash the rice in several changes of cold water to remove the excess starch. Pick out any husks or grit.
2 Put the rice into a saucepan with 1½ cups of hot water and a few drops of orange food colouring. Bring to the boil and let it boil quite steadily without the lid until you can see the grains just below the surface. Then cover the pan lightly, reduce the heat to a gentle simmer and cook until all the water has been absorbed, about 20 minutes.
3 When the rice is cooked, spread it out on a large plate and leave it to cool.
4 Put the sugar and 75 ml/3 fl oz water into a saucepan and stir to dissolve the sugar over a gentle heat. Bring to the boil and cook for 1 minute.
5 In a large saucepan, melt the ghee or butter and cook the cloves and cardamom seeds for a few seconds. Add the rice and stir it gently so that the grains are coated.
6 Add the sugar syrup, nuts and sultanas to the rice.
7 Warm the rose water with the saffron and pour it over the rice. Cover the pan with a lid and cook over a very gentle heat until the liquid has been absorbed. Alternatively, turn the rice out into an ovenproof dish and put it into a cool oven, Gas 2, 300°F, 150°C, for about 20 minutes when the syrup will have dried out and the rice will be hot.
8 Serve hot with lightly whipped cream.

Nirmal Singh
Nuneaton, Warwickshire

SIMPLE CHRISTMAS PUDDING

50 g/2 oz self-raising
wholemeal or plain flour
50 g/2 oz shredded suet
50 g/2 oz fresh breadcrumbs,
wholemeal or white
100 g/4 oz mixed dried fruit
100 g/4 oz soft brown sugar
1 egg
90 ml/3 fl oz milk
1 tablespoon black treacle
1 teaspoon mixed spice
½ teaspoon baking powder

1 Simply put everything into a large bowl, mix well and make a simple wish.
2 Put into a 600-ml/1-pint pudding basin or two smaller ones, cover with greaseproof paper and foil and steam in simmering water for 1½ hours.

Mrs Bernice Graham
Wirral, Merseyside

 Microwave

This pudding is not one to cook in advance to store like a traditional pud – but it is ideal to make at the last minute. It has good flavour and the texture of a steamed pudding.

For this method use wholemeal self-raising flour, 50g/2 oz grated butter instead of suet, wholemeal breadcrumbs and dark brown sugar. Leave out the baking powder.

Never leave the microwave cooker unattended when cooking or reheating Christmas puddings, especially if your recipe contains large quantities of spirits. Overcooking in the microwave means dehydration and, when the moisture has evaporated, the fats and sugar can become hot enough to ignite.

1 Simply put everything into a large bowl and mix well together. Wish carefully!

2 Put the mixture into a 600-ml/1-pint basin. Cover the top with clear film and cook on full power for 3 minutes, let it stand for 5 minutes and then cook on full power again for 2 minutes more.

Alternatively, 2 little puddings can be made in teacups: cover them with clear film and cook one at a time on full power for $1\frac{1}{2}$ minutes, allow to stand for 2 minutes then cook again on full power for 1 minute more.

To reheat leftover pudding: pack into a clean small basin, cover with clear film and heat on full power for 1 to $1\frac{1}{2}$ minutes.

To reheat portions of pudding: on a plate, covered with clear film, allow 20 to 30 seconds on full power for each portion.

BRANDY OR SHERRY SAUCE
Makes about 300 ml/$\frac{1}{2}$ pint.

15 g/$\frac{1}{2}$ oz cornflour
300 ml/$\frac{1}{2}$ pint milk
15 g/$\frac{1}{2}$ oz butter
1 level tablespoon caster sugar
1 to 2 tablespoons brandy or sherry

1 Mix cornflour to a smooth paste with a little of the cold milk.
2 Warm remaining milk, pour on to cornflour mixture and mix well.
3 Return to pan and cook, stirring, until sauce thickens and comes to the boil.
4 Simmer 2 minutes.
5 Remove from heat, stir in butter, sugar and brandy or sherry.

Mrs Margaret Heywood
Todmorden, Yorkshire

 Microwave 〰〰〰〰〰〰〰

1 In a 600-ml/1-pint jug, mix the cornflour to a paste with a little of the cold milk. Blend in the remaining milk. Cook on full power for $1\frac{1}{2}$ minutes then stir.
2 Cook on full power for a further 30 to 60 seconds until thick.
3 Then stir in the butter, sugar and brandy or sherry.

CHRISTMAS MINCEMEAT ROLL
Light, rich and delicious!

75 g/3 oz self-raising flour
3 eggs
75 g/3 oz caster sugar
Icing sugar for dredging

FILLING
150 ml/$\frac{1}{4}$ pint double cream
2 tablespoons mincemeat
1 tablespoon brandy, rum or sherry

1 Preheat oven to moderately hot, Gas 6, 400°F, 200°C.
2 Line a Swiss roll tin 35 by 23 cm/14 by 9 inches with greased, greaseproof paper.
3 Sieve flour three times.
4 Put eggs and caster sugar into a basin over a pan of hot water and whisk well until really thick.
5 Fold in flour with a metal spoon.
6 Pour mixture into prepared tin and put straight into oven on the top shelf for about 10 minutes, until firm to the touch.
7 Meanwhile, sprinkle a sheet of greaseproof paper generously with icing sugar from a dredger or sifter.
8 Turn the hot cake upside down on to the sugared paper. Remove the lining paper, trim edges of cake and lay over it a clean sheet of greaseproof paper. Roll up and leave to cool.

133

9 Whip the cream, mix in gently the mincemeat and brandy, rum or sherry.

10 When cake is cold, gently unroll and remove both sheets of paper. Spread inside of cake with filling. Roll up.

11 Chill the cake and dust finally with icing sugar before serving. It can be decorated with a sprig of holly.

Mrs Stella Boldy
Sykehouse, North Humberside

APPLE PUDDING

Rudin Afal is the Welsh for this delicious soufflé, which must be eaten straight out of the oven. From Lucy Barton-Greenwood, 1987 Junior Cook of the Year. For 2.

450 g/1 lb cooking apples
Sugar to taste
15 g/½ oz butter
15 g/½ oz plain white flour
150 ml/¼ pint milk
15 g/½ oz sugar
Vanilla essence
1 large egg, separated

1 Preheat oven to moderately hot, Gas 6, 400°F, 200°C.

2 Peel, core and slice the apples. Stew them in a very little water until nearly tender but still crunchy. Sweeten to taste. Put them into a buttered 1-litre/1½-pint soufflé or pie dish.

3 Melt the butter and stir in flour. Cook for 1 minute as it sizzles. Then gradually stir in the milk and bring to the boil to make a smooth sauce.

4 Mix in sugar, vanilla and egg yolk.

5 Beat the egg white until stiff and fold it into the sauce. Pour it over the prepared apples.

6 Bake immediately for 12 minutes until well risen and golden brown.

Lucy Barton-Greenwood
Radyr, Cardiff

134

APPLE SAUCE PUDDING

For 1 or 2 to eat hot or cold. A good way to cook apples to retain their flavour.

3 good-sized cooking apples
Demerara sugar
15 g/½ oz sultanas
½ teaspoon finely grated lemon rind

1 Wash the apples and remove the cores, then place in a saucepan which just contains them standing upright. Pour in enough cold water to cover the bottom of the pan, about 5 mm/¼ inch. Put on the lid and cook gently for about 30 minutes or until the apples are soft.

2 Remove the apples from the pan and scoop out the pulp, discarding the skins. While still hot, stir in enough sugar to sweeten, then add the sultanas and lemon rind.

3 Serve hot with custard.

Mrs Susan Hersee
Hayling Island, Hampshire

 Microwave

1 Peel, core and slice the apples. Put them in a small casserole with the sugar. Cover and cook on full power for 6 minutes.

2 Mash the apples with a fork, stir in the sultanas and lemon rind and serve.

BAKED APPLES WITH MUESLI

A good pudding to make when cooking the main course in a moderately hot oven, Gas 5, 375°F, 190°C. For 2.

2 large Bramley apples
25 g/1 oz raisins
2 heaped teaspoons golden syrup

250 ml/8 fl oz liquid (you can use apple juice, cider or water)
2 large tablespoons muesli (see page 16 for a recipe)

1 Wipe the apples and remove the cores. Using a sharp knife, score around the centre of the apples, just cutting the skin.
2 Stand the apples upright in a small ovenproof dish and fill the centres with the raisins. Spoon golden syrup over each apple and pour the liquid into the dish.
3 Bake uncovered in a moderately hot oven, Gas 5, 375°F, 190°C, for about 40 minutes or until the apples are soft. About 15 minutes before they are ready, put the muesli on to a baking sheet and cook in the oven until it is lightly browned.
4 Serve the apples and juice in individual bowls with the muesli scattered over the top.

Grace Mulligan

1 Prepare the apples following steps 1 and 2 above, but pour only 120 ml/4 fl oz of the liquid into the microwave dish.
2 Cook uncovered on full power for 5 to 6 minutes. Some apples may take up to 7 minutes to cook. Allow to stand for 5 minutes before serving. The apples will look quite green and shiny when they come out of the oven; however, during the standing time they will become dull and soft.
3 Sprinkle the muesli on to a baking tray and grill carefully under a hot grill for 2 to 3 minutes until lightly browned. Shake the tray every minute to prevent the muesli burning.
4 Serve as above.

SAVOURY BAKED APPLE

This delicious pudding can be cooked on top of the stove or put in the oven if you have it on. Serve hot. For 1.

Butter
1 cooking apple, peeled, cored and sliced
1 tablespoon brown sugar
1 tablespoon water
25 g/1 oz seedless raisins
50 g/2 oz Cheddar cheese, grated

1 Arrange the apple slices in a shallow, buttered, ovenproof dish. Sprinkle the sugar, water and raisins over the top and cover with a lid or some foil. Bake in a moderately hot oven, Gas 5, 375°F, 190°C, for about 25 minutes or until the apple is tender.

Alternatively, put the apple, sugar, water and raisins in a pan and cook gently until tender but not mushy. Then put it all into a heatproof dish.

2 Cover the apple with the cheese and put the dish under a hot grill until the cheese has melted.

Joan Tyers
Wingate, Co. Durham

1 Arrange the apple slices in a shallow 12-cm/5-inch round ovenproof dish. Sprinkle the sugar and raisins over the top and cover with a piece of clear film. Cook on full power for 2 minutes.
2 Remove the clear film and cover the apple with the cheese. Grill until the cheese has melted.

BANANA FRITTERS

Pineapple rings, apple slices or rounds of sweet potato may be used. For 2.

50 g/2 oz plain white flour
1 tablespoon rice flour
½ teaspoon baking powder
A pinch of salt
60 ml/2 fl oz milk
1 to 2 tablespoons water
Oil for deep frying
2 bananas, skinned and cut in half lengthways *
Golden syrup for serving

* *To keep sliced bananas from going brown, see below.*

1 Sieve the flour, rice flour, baking powder and salt into a bowl. Make a well in the centre; pour in the milk.
2 Stir to make a smooth batter, gradually adding the water if necessary to achieve a coating consistency. (If any lumps develop, use a whisk to disperse them.)
3 Heat the oil until hot, then dip the banana halves in the batter and fry them until golden brown.
4 Drain the fritters on kitchen paper.
5 Serve on hot plates with a little golden syrup dribbled over them.

Jennie Siew Lee Cook
York

TO KEEP SLICED BANANAS FROM GOING BROWN

Put unpeeled bananas in cold water for 5 to 10 minutes. They may then be peeled, sliced and left for some time without going brown.

Miss M. Owen
Elworth, Cheshire

In our test, with firm bananas, there was only slight discolouration after 4 hours. It was 8 hours before they were brown and soft. Very ripe bananas and a warm kitchen could give less good results. This useful tip was given to Farmhouse Kitchen in 1977 and has appeared in our books ever since.

Mary Watts

CHERRY SPONGE PUDDING

This recipe is known to Mrs Jackson's family as 'Queen Mum's Hat'! Can be eaten warm or cold. For 2.

2 trifle sponge cakes
1 to 2 tablespoons sherry or rum
A 220 g/7½ oz can of black cherries, drained and stoned
75 ml/2½ fl oz stiffly whipped cream
1 egg white
50 g/2 oz caster sugar

1 Place the sponge cakes on a heatproof plate and sprinkle with the sherry or rum.
2 Arrange the cherries on top then cover with the stiffly whipped cream. Put the dish in the refrigerator for one hour.
3 Whisk the egg white until stiff then gradually whisk in the sugar. Spread this meringue mixture over the cream to cover it completely.
4 Bake in a preheated moderately hot oven, Gas 6, 400°F, 200°C, for 5 minutes until the meringue is slightly brown.

Mrs Joan Jackson
Swinton, Manchester

OATY RHUBARB CRUMBLE

For 1 or 2. Nice hot or cold. Mrs Knight makes this without sugar, which is useful for diabetics. You may prefer to use the small amounts of sugar given below, or try it without and simply sprinkle with sugar or sweetener on serving. The topping is delicious.

225 g/8 oz rhubarb, cut into 2.5-cm/1-inch pieces
Two 15 ml tablespoons soft brown sugar
Juice of 1 orange
25 g/1 oz margarine
25 g/1 oz wholemeal flour

25 g/1 oz rolled oats
25 g/1 oz bran flakes, crushed
slightly

1 Preheat oven to moderately hot,
Gas 5, 375°F, 190°C.
2 Put the rhubarb into an ovenproof
dish, sprinkle with 1 tablespoon of
the sugar, and pour orange juice over
the top.
3 Rub margarine into flour until the
mixture resembles breadcrumbs, then
lightly mix in the rolled oats, crushed
bran flakes and remaining sugar.
4 Sprinkle the crumble topping over
the rhubarb and bake for 30 to 40
minutes. Serve with custard or
cream.

Mrs Knight
Belvedere, Kent

1 Put the rhubarb into a 12.5-cm/5-
inch soufflé-type dish or small
casserole. Sprinkle with 1 tablespoon
sugar and pour over the orange juice.
2 Rub the margarine into the flour
until the mixture resembles fine
breadcrumbs. Mix in the remaining
sugar, oats and bran flakes.
3 Spread the crumble over the
rhubarb and cook on full power for
7 minutes. Let it stand for 5 minutes
before serving.

OATY APPLE CRUNCH

*Nice hot or cold. Makes 2 helpings.
Serve with fresh cream, custard,
yoghurt or top of the milk. This crumble
topping can be used over any fruits.*

25 g/1 oz butter
25 g/1 oz demerara sugar
25 g/1 oz wholemeal flour
25 g/1 oz rolled oats
1 large eating apple
1 tablespoon lemon juice

A generous pinch of cinnamon
25 g/1 oz sultanas

1 Preheat oven to moderately hot,
Gas 5, 375°F, 190°C.
2 Melt butter and mix into it the
sugar, flour and oats.
3 Peel, core and slice the apple thinly
into a small ovenproof dish. Sprinkle
with lemon juice, cinnamon and
sultanas.
3 Cover with crumble mixture,
pressing down lightly.
5 Bake in preheated oven for 20 to 25
minutes until apple is tender.

Mrs Patrick
Motherwell, Scotland

*The crumble topping used for this
delicious pudding is ideal for
microwave cooking. If you are fond of
coconut, add 1 tablespoon along with
the oats.*

1 Rub the butter into the flour until
it is like fresh breadcrumbs, mix in
the sugar and oats.
2 Peel, core and slice the apple into a
450 ml/¾ pint casserole. Sprinkle
with lemon juice, cinnamon and
sultanas.
3 Cover with the crumble mixture,
pressing down lightly. Cook on full
power for 5 minutes. Let it stand for
5 minutes before serving.

STEAMED PUDDING

Makes 2 small puddings.

50 g/2 oz margarine
50 g/2 oz caster sugar
50 g/2 oz self-raising flour
1 size 4 egg
1 to 2 tablespoons water

SOME TOPPINGS:
Lemon curd, golden syrup or jam,
apple sauce or fruit purées

137

Cream, top-of-the-milk or custard for serving

1 Combine all the ingredients and beat until smooth. The mixture should drop off the spoon to the count of 3. This can be quickly done in a food processor.
2 Divide the mixture between two greased cups and cover them with greaseproof paper and foil.
3 Steam the puddings for 45 minutes. If you have no steamer, put a bread and butter plate upside down in a suitable saucepan, stand the cups on it and pour in 2.5 cm/1 inch of boiling water. Put on the lid and let the puddings steam for 45 minutes, taking care not to let the water go off the boil, nor to let the pan boil dry.
4 Turn the puddings out on to hot plates and pour the topping over.

This is where the microwave cooker really excels.

1 Proceed up to step 2 above.
2 Put the mixture in two greased cups, cover loosely with clear film and cook on full power for 2 minutes.
3 Leave to stand for 1 minute. During the standing time warm the chosen topping for one minute on full power.
4 Turn out the puddings and pour topping over.

Joan Tyers
Wingate, Co. Durham

138

WHOLEMEAL PANCAKES

When making pancakes, it is much easier to make at least a dozen at one time and keep the rest either in the refrigerator for a few days, or store them in the freezer. It is not necessary to pack the pancakes with a sheet of paper or film between each one. It is quite safe to thaw and refreeze these pancakes. Makes about 12.

125 g/4 oz fine plain wholemeal
   flour
1 egg
360 ml/12 fl oz semi-skimmed
   milk, or whole milk and water
   mixed
A pinch of salt
Oil

1 Put all the ingredients, except the oil, into a liquidiser or food processor and mix until the batter is smooth. Pour the batter into a large jug.
2 Put a little oil into a small heavy-based frying pan (about 15 cm/6 inch in size). Heat it up and tilt the pan until the inside is well coated, then pour off any excess oil.
3 Pour a little batter into the hot pan and tip the pan from side to side so that the base is covered. Do be careful not to pour in too much batter or the pancakes will be too thick.
4 Cook the pancake until the surface looks dry (about 1 minute) then flip it over and cook the other side for about 30 seconds.
5 Tip the pancake out, if necessary add a little more oil and cook the remaining pancakes in the same way. It is a good idea to stir the batter in between cooking each pancake.

Instead of using oil to grease the frying pan, you can tie up a piece of beef suet in a circle of muslin or fine cloth and use this to rub over the frying pan.

Grace Mulligan

SWEET PANCAKES

A variety of fillings and an orange sauce in which to heat the pancakes. (See previous recipe for Grace Mulligan's pancakes.)

Wholemeal Pancakes as in
   previous recipe

FILLINGS
Stewed apples and raisins
Canned fruit pie fillings
Mincemeat
Banana halves warmed in the
   Orange Sauce (below)

Warm the filling before putting it into the pancakes.

ORANGE SAUCE
75 ml/3 fl oz orange juice
10 g/¼ oz butter
10 g/¼ oz brown sugar
1 tablespoon cream

1 Put the orange juice, butter, sugar and cream into a frying pan and heat it gently.
2 Place the pancakes in, one at a time, and warm them through, then fill the pancakes with your chosen filling and if any sauce is left, pour it over the pancakes.

Dilwen Phillips
Gileston, South Glamorgan

Pancakes are not very suitable for microwave cooking, but to reheat 4 cold pancakes in the cold sauce will take 1 to 1½ minutes on full power.

BUTTERSCOTCH CUSTARD

This is very quick, easy and delicious. When turned out it seems a bit spotty; however, the sprinkling of nutmeg hides this effectively. For 1.

139

Butterscotch Custard continued
1 large egg
1 teaspoon dark soft brown sugar
120 ml/4 fl oz milk
A grating of nutmeg (optional)

1 Whisk egg and sugar into milk.
2 Pour the mixture into a small, buttered, heatproof dish or cup and cover the top – foil will do.
3 Put the dish on to a saucer placed inside a small saucepan. Pour in just enough boiling water to come to the rim of the saucer. Put the lid on the saucepan and let the water only just simmer for 15 minutes.
4 Leave the custard inside the closed pan until it is cool.
5 Turn it out to serve and sprinkle with nutmeg, or more dark brown sugar, or both, just before you eat it.

Grace Mulligan

1 Whisk the egg and sugar into the milk.
2 Pour the mixture into a small ramekin dish or teacup. Cook on Low for 3 to 5 minutes until just set.

For 2-power microwave cookers: Use Defrost setting for 5 to 7 minutes.

3 Leave the custard to cool, then turn out and serve sprinkled with nutmeg, or a little dark brown sugar, or both.

QUICK FRUIT PUDDINGS

For 1 or more, this is lovely made with soft fruits but is perfectly suitable for stewed fruit, or any fruit you like.

Soft fruit, blackcurrants, blackberries, raspberries etc.
Sugar
Double cream
Natural yoghurt
Demerara sugar

1 Cook the fruit with some sugar and a very little water, just to soften, then put it into a small heatproof dish.
2 Whisk equal amounts of cream and yoghurt and spread it over the fruit.
3 Sprinkle with demerara sugar and put the dish immediately under a very hot grill until the sugar melts slightly.
4 Serve immediately, or chill the pudding for a few hours.

Dilwen Phillips
Gileston, South Glamorgan

GRAPES WITH MUSCOVADO SUGAR AND SOURED CREAM

An unusual, simple and delicious dessert to make in any quantities. Apart from the time it takes to de-pip the grapes, this is a delightful sweet for a dinner party. Of course, you could use seedless grapes.

Large white grapes of the muscatel type
Dark muscovado sugar
Soured cream,* chilled

* *See Smoked Mackerel and Lemon Dip (page 28) for another recipe to use up the soured cream.*

1 Cut each grape in half and take out the pips. This can be done 2 or 3 hours in advance. Leave the prepared grapes in a bowl in a cool place until you are ready to eat the sweet course.
2 Sprinkle with sugar and smother with soured cream.
3 Serve at once while the sugar is still crunchy.

Jane Temperley
London

GOOSEBERRY FOOL

For 1 or 2. No need to top and tail the gooseberries as these bits go when the fruit is sieved.

225 g/8 oz fresh or frozen
  gooseberries
2 tablespoons water
50 g/2 oz granulated sugar
150 ml/¼ pint thick custard or
  whipped cream

1 Cook the gooseberries gently with
the water and sugar for about 15
minutes until soft and pulpy.
2 Sieve the fruit and leave it to cool.
3 Stir the custard or cream into the
purée and pour into individual
glasses. Chill for several hours.

Mrs Butler
Sheffield

1 Put the fresh gooseberries and
water into an 18-cm/7-inch round
dish. Cover and cook on full power
for 3 to 5 minutes. (If you are using
frozen fruit, omit the water. Cook the
frozen gooseberries for 6 to 7 minutes
on full power, stirring once.) Leave to
stand for 5 minutes. Then sieve the
fruit and leave to cool.
2 Stir the custard or cream into the
purée and pour into individual
glasses. Chill for several hours before
serving.

ORANGES AND NECTARINES IN CARAMEL SAUCE

*The caramel sauce and orange segments
may be prepared in advance, but do not
cut up the nectarines more than a few
hours before serving or they may
discolour. Makes 2 helpings.*

3 oranges
50 g/2 oz granulated sugar
1 teaspoon lemon juice
2 nectarines
1 to 2 tablespoons Grand Marnier
  or Cointreau

1 Squeeze the juice from one orange,
strain it into a measuring jug, and if
necessary add cold water to make 60
ml/2 fl oz of liquid. Set aside while
you prepare the caramel.
2 Put the sugar, lemon juice and 4
tablespoons of cold water into a
saucepan and stir over gentle heat.
Once the sugar has dissolved, increase
the heat and let the liquid boil
fiercely until it turns a brown caramel
colour. Pour the prepared orange juice
into the saucepan – be careful to
cover your hand as it will bubble up
and spit. Stir over the heat until all
the caramel has dissolved. Leave
sauce to cool.
3 Peel the oranges and cut into
segments, making sure all the pith
and membrane are removed. Wash
the nectarines and cut into segments.
4 Mix the nectarine and orange
segments together in a serving bowl
and pour over them the caramel
sauce. Stir in the liqueur and chill
slightly before serving.

Angela Henderson
Fleet, Hampshire

FRESH PEACHES WITH RASPBERRY SAUCE

*For 2. This makes a light and
refreshing finish to a meal, quick and
easy to prepare, especially if the sauce
is made beforehand. The peaches should
not be peeled and prepared more than a
few hours before serving or they may
discolour. The raspberry sauce may be
frozen.*

175 g/6 oz fresh or frozen
  raspberries
A few drops of lemon juice
Icing sugar to taste
3 ripe peaches
Whipped cream or natural
  yoghurt to serve separately
  (optional)

141

1 Purée the raspberries and pass them through a fine nylon sieve to remove all the pips. Add the lemon juice and sufficient icing sugar to sweeten.

2 To peel the peaches, plunge them into boiling water for about 15 seconds, then remove and place immediately in cold water. The skins should now be easy to peel away.

3 Cut the peaches into segments and add them to the raspberry purée. Ensure that all the segments are well coated with the sauce.

4 Serve slightly chilled in sundae dishes and hand the whipped cream or yoghurt separately.

Angela Henderson
Fleet, Hampshire

STRAWBERRIES AND KIWI FRUIT IN A CREAM-FILLED SPONGE

This 'roulade' was the dessert prepared by Simon Dunn, aged 14, when he won third place in the 1987 Junior Cook of the Year competition. For a less extravagant occasion, or when strawberries are out of season, replace them with diced fresh orange which goes perfectly with Grand Marnier.

3 eggs, separated
50 g/2 oz caster sugar, plus a little more
A few drops of vanilla essence
2 tablespoons white flour, sifted
100 g/4 oz strawberries
1 kiwi fruit
Icing sugar
1 tablespoon Grand Marnier
75 ml/2½ fl oz double cream

1 Oil a 27 by 18-cm/11 by 7-inch Swiss roll tin and line it with oiled greaseproof paper or non-stick silicone paper.

142

2 Preheat oven to moderate, Gas 5, 350°F, 180°C.

3 Whisk the egg whites until they are stiff but not dry.

4 Beat the egg yolks with 500 g/2 oz of the caster sugar until very thick and pale yellow.

5 Add vanilla and carefully fold in flour and whisked egg whites.

6 Spread the mixture evenly in the prepared tin and bake for about 12 minutes or until the sponge is firm.

7 Remove from the oven, and turn the cake out upside-down on to a sheet of greaseproof paper which has been lightly dusted with caster sugar. Peel off the baking paper and leave the cake to cool.

8 Prepare the fruits, keeping 2 or 3 small strawberries and 2 or 3 thin slices of kiwi fruit for decorating later. Roughly chop the rest and put it in a bowl with 1 tablespoon icing sugar and the Grand Marnier. Leave to soften for 20 minutes, turning fruit gently from time to time.

9 Beat the cream until it is thick.

10 Drain Grand Marnier from fruit and whisk it into the cream, along with a little sieved icing sugar to taste.

11 Fold the fruit and cream together and spread it over the cake. Roll it up and lift carefully on to a pretty plate.

12 Sieve a little extra caster sugar over the cake and decorate with the reserved fruit. Serve within 2 hours.

Simon Dunn
Bickley, Kent

BANANA ALASKA

This is a good recipe to make when the oven has been on for other cooking as it requires only a few minutes at a high temperature. For 1; easy to make more.

1 trifle sponge
1 tablespoon sherry
1 large egg white
25 g/1 oz caster sugar

1 individual block of ice cream –
  store in the freezer until
  needed
1 small banana *

* *To prevent sliced banana from going
brown, see page 136.*

1 Cut the trifle sponge in half
horizontally and lay the pieces side by
side on a heatproof plate.
2 Dribble the sherry over the
sponges.
3 Whisk the egg white until very
stiff, then gradually whisk in the
sugar until the meringue is firm and
glossy.
4 Take the ice cream out of the
freezer and lay it on top of the
sponge.
5 Quickly peel and slice the banana
horizontally and cut each piece to fit
neatly on top of the ice cream.
6 Spread or pipe the meringue neatly
over the ice cream and the banana,
making absolutely sure the ice cream
and banana are completely covered.
7 Place near the top of a preheated
hot oven, Gas 7, 425°F, 220°C, for
about 3 to 4 minutes until the
meringue is slightly brown. Serve at
once.

Grace Mulligan

ICE CREAM CHRISTMAS PUD

*It is worthwhile making up the whole
quantity, then dividing the mixture
between a variety of small basins or old
teacups. Once frozen, the puddings can
be released from their containers by
dipping momentarily into hot water.
Then refreeze them on a tray and in
polythene bags for storage. The full
quantity fits a 1-litre/1½-pint pudding
basin. Easy to make less.*

A 495 ml/17½ fl oz carton of
  vanilla ice cream *
75 g/3 oz each of raisins, sultanas
  and currants

2 tablespoons sherry or brandy
40 g/1½ oz broken walnuts
50 g/2 oz glacé cherries, red, green
  and yellow

* *Use chocolate ice cream if you want
the pud to look dark.*

1 Overnight soak the raisins, sultanas,
and currants in the sherry or brandy.
2 Turn out the ice cream to soften
very slightly. Chop the walnuts and
cherries.
3 Mix everything together very
swiftly. Pack into pudding basins or
teacups.
4 To serve, allow to soften slightly
and turn out into a deep dish and top
with a sprig of holly.

Grace Mulligan

COFFEE ICE CREAM
For 2. Very nice with brandy snaps.

75 ml/2½ fl oz double cream
1 egg, separated
1 tablespoon instant coffee,
  dissolved in 1 teaspoon boiling
  water
25 g/1 oz icing sugar
1 tablespoon Tia Maria (optional)
Chopped walnuts or hazelnuts to
  decorate, if desired

1 Whip the cream until stiff, then
stir in the egg yolk and dissolved
coffee.
2 In a separate bowl, whip the egg
white until stiff, then gradually whisk
in the sieved icing sugar.
3 Fold the egg white into the coffee-
cream mixture and add the liqueur, if
desired.
4 Pour into 2 ramekin dishes, cover
with clear film and freeze. Decorate
just before serving.

Angela Henderson
Fleet, Hampshire

CHOCOLATE MOUSSE

A really light and delicious sweet to which you could add a dessertspoon of Brandy or Cointreau for a treat. For 1.

25 g/1 oz plain chocolate
1 egg, separated

1 Melt the chocolate in a bowl set over a pan of hot water.
2 Remove the bowl from the heat and mix in the egg yolk.
3 Whisk the egg white until stiff, then fold it into the chocolate mixture.
4 Pour into a dish and chill for about one hour.

Caroline Hyde
Maltby, Rotherham

CHOCOLATE MOULDS

Makes 2.

1 packet miniature chocolate
  Swiss rolls
1 teaspoon gelatine
25 g/1 oz plain chocolate
120 ml/4 fl oz milk
1 egg yolk
25 g/1 oz caster sugar
¼ teaspoon instant coffee
  powder
1 teaspoon cocoa powder
1 teaspoon ground arrowroot
75 ml/2½ fl oz double cream

1 Cut the Swiss rolls into round slices and carefully line the inside of two cups or small bowls with the slices (dishes with sloping sides are easiest). Make sure the Swiss roll pieces are well pushed together so that there are no gaps.
2 Now prepare the filling: put 2 tablespoons of cold water into a small saucepan and sprinkle over the gelatine. Put to one side.
3 Break up the chocolate, put it into another saucepan with the milk and heat gently until the chocolate melts.
4 Beat together the egg yolk, sugar, coffee powder, cocoa and arrowroot, then gently stir in the warmed chocolate and milk. Mix well, pour into a clean saucepan and heat slowly without boiling until the liquid thickens slightly. It is ready when the custard will coat the back of a spoon.
5 Gently warm the gelatine over a low heat until it is clear and runny. Do not let it boil. Then pour it on to the chocolate custard. Strain the custard into a clean bowl and allow to cool. (To speed up the cooling, stand the bowl in a basin of cold water.)
6 When the mixture is cold and just starting to set, lightly whip the cream and fold it into the custard.
7 Pour into the prepared mould and leave in the refrigerator for several hours until completely set and well chilled.
8 When serving turn the moulds upside down on to the serving plates. Give them a shake to help them out.

Angela Henderson
Fleet, Hampshire

CHOCOLATE BRANDY CAKE

A very rich and exotic pudding for a special dinner, or to serve in small slices with coffee afterwards. It can be made a couple of days before it is needed and also freezes well.

100 g/4 oz butter
100 g/4 oz good-quality dessert
  chocolate
1 egg
40 g/1½ oz caster sugar
100 g/4 oz digestive biscuits,
  coarsely crushed
25 g/1 oz walnuts, chopped
25 g/1 oz glacé cherries, chopped

1 tablespoon brandy or sherry
Walnut halves and glacé cherries
  to decorate

1 Put the butter and chocolate into a
bowl set over a pan of hot water and
leave until both have melted.
2 Beat the egg and sugar together
until light and fluffy, then stir in the
melted chocolate and butter.
3 Fold in the biscuits, nuts and
cherries and lastly add the brandy or
sherry.
4 Spread the mixture into a loose-
bottomed 18-cm/7-inch round cake
tin (or you could use an 18-cm/7-inch
square tin lined with non-stick paper)
and press on the walnuts and cherries.
Put into the refrigerator to set and
keep it there until you serve it.

Mary Hunter
Addingham, Yorkshire

MANDARIN SURPRISE

*For 2, twice! Use 2 small, shallow
margarine or yoghurt tubs as moulds,
each of which will make 2 adequate
helpings. You also need a liquidiser.
Tangerines, clementines, satsumas can
also be used for this dish – but choose
large fruits.*

MANDARIN FILLING
100 g/4 oz large fresh mandarin
  oranges plus 2 more for
  decorating

1 small cooking apple
1 tablespoon lemon juice
50 g/2 oz caster sugar
Orange food colouring
1 egg white

ICE CREAM
25 g/1 oz meringue shells
150 ml/¼ pint double cream
25 g/1 oz caster sugar

1 Chill the moulds you plan to use in
the freezer or refrigerator ice-making
compartment.
2 Peel the 100 g/4 oz mandarins and
keep half of the rind. Using a sharp
knife, remove the white pith from the
rind, then put this scraped rind into
a saucepan. Divide the mandarins into
segments, removing pith, and add
them to the pan.
3 Peel, core and slice the apple, add
it to the mandarins in the pan,
along with lemon juice and
25 g/1 oz of the sugar. Cook over a
low heat until the fruit is soft and
pulpy. Allow to cool slightly.
4 Pour mixture into a liquidiser with
1 or 2 drops of orange food
colouring, switch on until mixture
is smooth. Allow to cool.
5 Put the egg white in a clean,
grease-free bowl and whisk until stiff
but not dry. Whisk in 25 g/1 oz caster
sugar and the mandarin purée.
6 Now prepare the ice cream. Crush
the meringue shells. Whisk cream
until it just holds its shape, then fold
  the meringue and sugar into
  the cream.

7 Place this mixture in the iced moulds. Using the back of a spoon, smooth the cream up the sides of the moulds to make a hollow in the centre.
8 Fill the hollows with mandarin mixture.
9 Cover with foil and freeze for at least 3 hours.
10 To serve, dip the mould in hand-hot water for a few seconds. Place a chilled plate on top, invert and shake. Decorate with fresh mandarin segments.

Grace Mulligan

PEACH MOUSSE

A very light pudding for 1 or 2.

4 peach halves from a can of
　peaches in natural juice
1 egg, separated
Two 15 ml tablespoons low-fat
　natural yoghurt
Half a sachet of powdered
　gelatine

1 Put the peach halves, egg yolk and yoghurt into a food processor or liquidiser and process until smooth.
2 Put 2 tablespoons cold water into a small saucepan; sprinkle over the gelatine. Leave it for a few minutes, then warm it over a gentle heat until it is runny and looks clear.
3 Add the gelatine to the peach purée. Then whisk the egg white until stiff but not dry, and fold it into the purée.
4 Pour the mousse into a bowl or sundae dishes and leave in the refrigerator until set.
5 Decorate the mousse with a few sliced peaches.

Jill Myers
The British Diabetic Association,
London

RASPBERRY CLOUD

For 2.

1 orange
Half a lemon
2 trifle sponges
1 tablespoon Cointreau
15 g/$\frac{1}{2}$ caster sugar
120 ml/4 fl oz double cream
125 g/4 oz frozen or fresh
　raspberries

1 Grate rind from half of the orange and the half lemon. Squeeze juice.
2 Cut up sponges and divide between two sundae glasses or dishes.
3 Put half of the rind and half of the juice on top of sponges.
4 Put remaining rind, juice and liqueur into a bowl. Stir in sugar and cream.
5 Whisk until it forms a soft peak. Fold in raspberries.
6 Pile mixture into the dishes and chill in refrigerator for at least 3 hours before serving.

Judith Adshead
Porth Colman, Gwynedd

APPLE SOUFFLÉ CHEESECAKE

This cheesecake freezes well (before decorating). Cut individual slices and open-freeze them before wrapping to store. Allow 2 hours to thaw at rooom temperature.

BISCUIT BASE
50 g/2 oz butter
75 g/3 oz ginger biscuits, crushed

FILLING
225 g/8 oz cooking apples, peeled,
　cored and sliced
5 tablespoons cold water
2 teaspoons gelatine

100 g/4 oz cottage cheese, sieved
75 ml/2 fl oz soured cream*
75 g/3 oz caster sugar
1 egg, separated
A drop of green vegetable
  colouring (optional)
Apple slices, lemon juice and
  whipped cream (optional) to
  decorate

** See Grapes with Muscovado sugar
page 140 for another recipe using soured
cream*

1 Melt the butter in a pan, then
pour it over the biscuit crumbs and
mix well together. Press this mixture
into the base of a loose-bottomed
flat tin, about 15 cm/6 inches
across.
2 Now for the filling. Cook the
apples with 3 tablespoons of cold
water until they are tender, then sieve
or blend them to a purée. Set aside to
cool.
3 Put 2 tablespoons water into
a small pan and sprinkle over
the gelatine. Leave it to soak for
5 minutes then, without letting
it boil, melt the gelatine over a
gentle heat until it is clear and
runny.
4 Mix together the apple purée,
gelatine, cottage cheese, soured cream,
sugar and egg yolk. This can quickly
be done in a food processor. If you
want to colour the filling a little, add
one or two drops of green food
colouring, but take great care not to
put in too much.
5 Whisk the egg white until
stiff then fold it into the apple
mixture.
6 Pour the filling into the biscuit case
and leave in the refrigerator for
several hours until set.
7 Decorate the top at the last minute
with slices of apple dipped in lemon
juice and also with whipped cream if
you like it, but the cake is already
very rich.

Mrs Jean McKean,
Lifford, Co. Donegal

 Microwave

CUSTARD SAUCE

*It's simple to make custard in a
microwave cooker. Here's enough for 2.*

300 ml/½ pint milk
1 slightly rounded dessertspoon
  custard powder
1 dessertspoon of sugar
A spoonful of cream, for a special
  occasion

1 In a 600 ml/1 pint jug blend the
custard powder, sugar and a little of
the milk to a paste. Stir in the rest
of the milk.
2 Heat, uncovered, on full power for
2 to 2½ minutes, stirring once after 1½
minutes.
3 Stir the custard before serving and
mix in the cream.

CONVENTIONAL METHOD
1 Pour the milk into a small pan and
whisk in the custard powder and
sugar.
2 Stirring continuously, heat the
mixture until it boils and thickens.
Remove from the heat and stir in the
cream.

Grace Mulligan

CRYSTALLISED LEAVES, FLOWERS, PETALS

**Violets, Primroses, Mint Leaves,
Geranium Petals**

All the above flowers and leaves can
be painted with beaten egg white,
dipped in caster sugar to preserve
their colour and flavour, and used to
decorate food. Make sure they are
dry, free from dew or rain drops.

1 Brush flowers and leaves clean.

2 Beat egg white until frothy.
3 Using a fine camel paint brush, coat each leaf back and front with egg white and while still wet dip in caster sugar. Shake off surplus sugar and leave to dry and crisp.

FROSTED FRUITS
The above method also applies to fruit like grapes, damsons, cherries.

1 Dip them in egg white in little bundles of two or three.
2 Drop them in a plastic bag with a little caster sugar, shake a little and then lay out carefully to dry.

TO DECORATE GLASS BOWLS AND TUMBLERS FOR PARTY DRINKS
1 Colour some caster sugar by rubbing a few drops of food colouring into dry sugar using the same movement as you would for rubbing fat into flour. Put the sugar into a flat dish about 5-cm/$\frac{1}{4}$-inch deep.
2 Whip egg white as usual and dip inverted bowl into the egg white, then into the coloured sugar.
3 Leave to dry. Be careful to keep colours very pale.

Grace Mulligan

Chapter 10
Breads, Scones and Bakes

A NOTE ON 'EASY' YEASTS

The bread dough recipes in this chapter are all made using the 'Easy' dried yeasts which come in sachets called 'Easy Blend', 'Easy Bake', etc. It is wise to read the labels carefully to be certain which type it is.

1 The main feature is that you do not have to ferment these yeasts in water before starting. You mix them directly with the dry ingredients. In some cases if you do not mix them in dry they will not work.
2 The next feature is that some packets have a label such as 'Fast Action'. These contain a variety of improvers, sometimes Vitamin C (ascorbic acid) and with these it is not necessary to leave the bread to rise more than once.

It is important to note this detail because in some of the 'Easy'-labelled sachets, the contents are simply yeast granules in a pulverised form and, apart from being suitable to mix in with dry ingredients, this type works just like fresh yeast and the older forms of dried yeast, and the dough will mostly require two risings.

WHITE BREAD

Makes two 450-g/1-lb loaves or 12 medium-sized rolls or 18 dainty rolls. All freeze well.

675 g/1½ lb strong white bread flour
1 teaspoon salt
25 g/1 oz lard
1 sachet of 'easy blend' yeast *
450 ml/¼ pint warm water
Beaten egg and water to glaze (optional)

* *See above for a note about the 'easy' yeasts.*

150

1 Sieve the flour and salt into a warm bowl. Rub in lard and then stir in the dry yeast. Mix well.
2 Stir in the warm water with a wooden fork or spoon. When the dough has formed, use your hand to knead until it is soft and elastic. Finally turn out on to a slightly floured board and knead again for 5 minutes.
3 Return the dough to a clean greased bowl, cover and leave in a warm place to rise until doubled in size.
4 Knock back the dough by kneading the air out of it for a minute or two. Then cut it into two, knead briefly and shape to fit into the two, greased 450-g/1-lb tins.
5 Brush with the glaze if wanted.
6 Set loaves aside, covered loosely (a piece of oiled polythene is ideal) to prove until the dough rises to just above the top of the tins.
7 Preheat oven to hot, Gas 8, 450°F, 230°C, and bake for 30 to 40 minutes until brown and sounding hollow when removed from tin and tapped on the bottom. Cool on a wire rack.

BREAD ROLLS OR DINNER BUNS
Makes 12 to 18 rolls.

For a crusty top to the rolls, brush with a salt glaze: 5 ml/1 teaspoon salt dissolved in 30 ml/2 tablespoons water.

1 Use the above recipe for White Bread and proceed up to step **4**.
2 Divide the risen dough into 12 or 18 pieces. Knead each piece to form either round buns or fancy shapes.
3 Place buns, not too close together, on greased baking sheets. Brush with the glaze if wanted and cover lightly until puffed up again – about 15 minutes.

4 Preheat oven to hot, Gas 8, 450°F, 230°C, and bake for 10 to 15 minutes according to the size of rolls. Cool on a wire rack.

Grace Mulligan

WHOLEMEAL BREAD

Makes two 450 g/1 lb loaves. Easy to make, excellent results. Freezes well.

675 g/1½ lb wholemeal plain flour
2 teaspoons salt
25 g/1 oz lard
1 sachet of 'easy blend' or 'easy bake' yeast*
1 tablespoon soft brown sugar
450 ml/¾ pint warm water
5 ml/1 teaspoon salt dissolved in 30 ml/2 tablespoons water to glaze

* For a note on 'easy' yeasts, see opposite page.

For loaves with a lighter texture, use one third white flour to two thirds wholemeal. Wheatmeal flour also gives a good light result but does not have the flavour of wholemeal.

1 Mix flour and salt in a warm bowl and rub in lard. Stir in dry yeast.
2 Stir the sugar into the warm water and add to the dry ingredients.
3 Stir first of all, then knead in the bowl and then turn the dough out on to a lightly floured board. Knead briefly until smooth and elastic. If using a fast-action type of yeast you can leave out steps **4** and **5** and go straight to step **6**.
4 Return the dough to a clean, greased bowl. Cover lightly and leave to rise in a warm place until the dough has doubled in size.
5 Knock back the dough, by kneading the air out of it for a minute or two.
6 Cut dough into 2 pieces and shape them to fit the greased bread tins, making sure that there is a smooth surface on top. Brush with the glaze.

7 Cover the tins loosely (a piece of oiled polythene is useful) and prove for 15 minutes or until the dough rises just above the rim of the tins.
8 Preheat oven to hot, Gas 8, 450°F, 230°C, and bake the loaves for 10 minutes. Then reduce the heat to moderately hot, Gas 6, 400°F, 200°C, for a further 10 minutes. Turn out and cool on wire racks.

Grace Mulligan

MILK BREAD

This is an enriched dough. Both loaves and rolls keep and freeze well. Makes two 450 g/1 lb loaves or 12 medium-sized rolls or 16 smaller ones.

450 g/1 lb strong white flour
1 teaspoon salt
50 g/2 oz lard or butter
1 sachet 'easy blend' yeast*
300 ml/½ pint warm milk
1 large egg, beaten
A little extra milk

* See opposite page for a note about the 'easy' yeasts.

1 Sieve the flour and salt into a warm bowl. Rub in the fat. Add the dried yeast. Mix well.
2 Mix the warm milk and all but one teaspoon of the beaten egg into the dry ingredients.
3 Mix and knead to a soft elastic dough, about 5 to 6 minutes. If using a fast-action type of yeast you can leave out steps 4 and 5 and go straight on to step 6.
4 Return the dough to a clean greased bowl. Cover lightly and leave to rise in a warm place for about 30 minutes or until the dough is almost doubled in size.
5 Knock back the risen dough by kneading the air out of it for a minute or two.
6 Cut dough in 2. Knead and shape to fit 2 well-greased 450 g/1 lb loaf tins.

151

7 Mix the leftover egg and about one tablespoon milk and glaze the 2 loaves. Set aside to prove, that is, let the dough rise, for about 15 minutes until it reaches to just above the top of tins.

8 Bake in a hot oven, Gas 8, 450°F, 230°C, for about 30 minutes.

POPPY SEED PLAIT

Milk Bread dough as above
25 g/1 oz poppy seeds

1 Make up the milk bread recipe then, starting at step 6, cut the dough in half.

2 Using a lightly floured surface, roll out the dough into a long oblong. Take a sharp knife and make two long cuts in the dough, making 3 fairly even strips. Squeeze together one end, plait the 3 pieces and squeeze the other end.

3 Brush with the glaze, see step 7 above, and cover with poppy seeds.

4 Set the plait on a greased baking sheet. Cover lightly – a sheet of oiled polythene is ideal –and let it rise in a warm place for 10 to 15 minutes until puffy.

5 Preheat oven to hot, Gas 8, 450°F, 230°C, and bake for about 30 minutes until golden and crisp on top and underneath. Cool on a wire rack.

BRIDGE ROLLS OR BATCH ROLLS

1 Use the milk bread recipe up to step 6 above. Then divide the dough into 16 pieces.

2 Roll each piece into a fat cigar shape. Try not to use too much flour on the board while you do this or you will get a streaky finish.

3 Place the long rolls close together on a greased baking sheet. Brush with the egg and milk glaze. Set aside, covered loosely, to puff up.

4 Bake in a preheated hot oven, Gas 8, 450°F, 230°C, for about 15 minutes. The rolls will join up during baking giving soft sides when they are pulled apart. Cool on a wire rack.

Grace Mulligan

HOT CROSS BUNS

Makes 12 buns which will freeze well for up to 2 months. Using dried yeast with added Vitamin C, one rising only is necessary.

450 g/1 lb plain wholemeal flour
1 sachet 'easy bake' yeast *
1 level teaspoon salt
25 g/1 oz soft brown sugar
2 level teaspoons mixed spice
25 g/1 oz lard
25 g/1 oz currants
25 g/1 oz sultanas
1 medium egg, size 3 or 4
200 ml/7 fl oz warm milk and water, mixed

BATTER FOR CROSSES
50 g/2 oz plain white flour
60 ml/2 fl oz cold water

GLAZE
2 level tablespoons sugar
2 tablespoons water

* For a note on 'easy' yeasts, see page 150.

1 In a roomy bowl, mix flour, dry yeast, salt, sugar and spice. Rub in lard and then mix in the fruit.

2 Beat the egg in a measuring jug, then add to it enough of the warm milk and water to make about 250 ml/8 fl oz.

3 Stir the liquid into the dry ingredients. Stir and mix until the dough comes together as a soft mixture. You may need to add a little more warm water.

4 Turn the dough on to a lightly floured surface and knead for 6 to 7 minutes until smooth and pliable.

5 Leave the dough covered for about 5 minutes to rest.

6 Divide the dough into 75 g/3 oz pieces and shape into buns. Place on greased baking sheets.

7 Leave lightly covered in a warm place to rise. In 45 minutes to 1 hour they should have doubled in size.

8 Preheat oven to moderately hot, Gas 6, 400°F, 200°C.

9 For the crosses, mix together the flour and water to achieve a thick batter. Put this into a small icing bag with a thick writing nozzle in it. Pipe a neat cross gently on each bun.

10 Bake the buns for about 10 minutes when they will sound hollow when tapped underneath.

11 Meanwhile, prepare the glaze. In a small saucepan dissolve the sugar and water and then boil it for just 2 or 3 minutes. Brush the warm glaze on the hot buns as they come out of the oven. Cool on wire trays.

Grace Mulligan

HONEY AND MALT FRUIT LOAF

This loaf can be eaten plain, or in buttered slices. Delicious, easy, and quick!

225 g/8 oz self-raising fine wholemeal flour
2 large tablespoons powdered malt drink
100 g/4 oz mixed dried fruit
2 tablespoons of runny honey
240 ml/8 fl oz milk or semi-skimmed milk

1 Mix all the ingredients together very thoroughly.

2 Grease a 450-g/1-lb loaf tin and line the base with a piece of greaseproof paper.

3 Pour the mixture into the tin and bake in the centre of a moderate oven, Gas 4, 350°F, 180°C, for about 1 hour or until a skewer inserted into the centre of the loaf comes out clean.

Grace Mulligan

DUMPLING LOAF

Don't be put off by the name; this isn't at all heavy and is delicious by itself, or sliced and buttered. It freezes well. Cut it into slices and wrap individually in film, then put into the freezer.

100 g/4 oz margarine
175 g/6 oz sugar
150 ml/¼ pint water
1 teaspoon bicarbonate of soda
225 g/8 oz sultanas
2 eggs
225 g/8 oz self-raising white or wholemeal flour, or a mixture of each
1 teaspoon mixed spice

1 Put the margarine, sugar, water, bicarbonate of soda and sultanas into a saucepan. Heat up, then boil for 5 minutes. Leave to cool for 10 minutes.

2 Beat in the eggs, flour and spice. Turn the mixture into a greased and lined 1-kg/2-lb loaf tin.

3 Bake in a warm oven, Gas 3, 325°F, 160°C, for 1¼ hours. Leave in the tin for 5 minutes, then turn out on to a wire rack to cool.

Mrs Oswald
Dalwhinnie, Inverness-shire

SPICED CARROT TEABREAD

This rather unusual teabread is very tasty, sliced and spread with butter or cream cheese. It is moist and keeps well lightly wrapped in foil, or it can be frozen. Makes two 450 g/1 lb loaves.

100 g/4 oz margarine
100 g/4 oz soft brown sugar
2 eggs, beaten
Finely grated rind of 1 orange
225 g/8 oz plain flour
1 teaspoon bicarbonate of soda
1 teaspoon salt
1 teaspoon ground cinnamon
1 teaspoon ground nutmeg

175 g/6 oz carrots, peeled and
   grated
50 g/2 oz candied mixed peel, very
   finely chopped
4 tablespoons orange juice
2 tablespoons water

1 Grease two 450-g/1-lb loaf tins and
line the bases with greaseproof paper.
2 Cream together the margarine and
sugar, then beat in the eggs and
orange rind.
3 Sieve in the flour, bicarbonate of
soda, salt and spices and carefully mix
everything together.
4 Stir in the grated carrot, mixed
peel, orange juice and water.
5 Put the mixture into the loaf tins
and bake in the middle of a moderate
oven, Gas 4, 350°F, 180°C, for about
50 minutes or until they are firm to
the touch.
6 Leave in the tins for 5 minutes
then turn out on to a cooling rack.

Margaret Heywood
Todmorden, Yorkshire

SPICY APPLE LOAF

Makes 2 tasty, moist, small loaves.
Serve sliced and spread with butter,
margarine, or cream cheese. Freeze
well.

1 size 2 egg
4 tablespoons oil
150 g/6 oz white or brown sugar
150 g/6 oz flour
$\frac{1}{4}$ teaspoon bicarbonate of soda
$\frac{1}{2}$ teaspoon baking powder
$\frac{1}{2}$ teaspoon salt
1 teaspoon cinnamon
25 g/1 oz chopped nuts
50 g/2 oz sultanas
2 dessert apples (about 250 g/9 oz)
   peeled, cored and grated

1 Grease two 450-g/1-lb loaf tins and
line the bases with greaseproof paper.
2 Whisk the egg and oil together
until foamy, then whisk in the sugar.

154

3 Fold in the sieved flour,
bicarbonate of soda, baking powder,
salt and cinnamon.
4 Lastly, stir in the nuts, sultanas and
grated apples and ensure that
everything is well mixed.
5 Put the mixture into the prepared
tins and bake in the middle of a
moderate oven preheated to Gas 4,
350°F, 180°C, for about 50 minutes,
or until firm to the touch.

Margaret Heywood
Todmorden, Yorkshire

BRAN MUFFINS

Delicious served with a cup of mid-
morning coffee. Makes 12 to 14. Freeze
well.

50 g/2 oz All-Bran
150 ml/$\frac{1}{4}$ pint milk
50 g/2 oz soft margarine
50 g/2 oz soft brown sugar
3 tablespoons lemon curd
25 g/1 oz chopped nuts
1 egg, beaten
1 tablespoon baking powder
100 g/4 oz plain flour, white or
   wholemeal

1 Soak the All-Bran in the milk until
it is soft.
2 In another bowl, beat together the
margarine, sugar and lemon curd. Stir
in the nuts, beaten egg and the milk
and All-Bran.
3 Sift the baking powder into the
flour and fold in.
4 Set 14 paper bun cases in a bun
tray and spoon the mixture into the
cases.
5 Bake in a moderately hot oven, Gas
6, 400°F, 200°C, for about 15
minutes.

Grace Mulligan

In the microwave this mixture comes
out better as a loaf than as muffins.

Use 100 g/4 oz wholemeal self-raising flour and leave out the baking powder. Thick-cut marmalade, honey or ginger preserve can be used instead of lemon curd. Delicious sliced and buttered.

1 Line the base of a 450-g/1-lb loaf dish with a piece of greaseproof paper.
2 Put the All-Bran and milk into a bowl, heat on full power for 2 minutes then stir well and leave to cool for 5 minutes.
3 In another bowl, cream together the margarine, sugar and lemon curd. Stir in the nuts, egg and All-Bran mixture. Lastly fold in the flour.
4 Tip the mixture into the prepared dish, smooth over the top and cook on full power for 5 to 7 minutes. Shield the ends with small pieces of foil after 3 minutes, making sure the foil does not touch the sides of the cooker cavity. At the end of cooking the top may be sticky to the touch, but it should not have any uncooked batter on it. A cocktail stick inserted near the centre should come out clean when the loaf is cooked. Any stickiness should dry out while the loaf is standing.
5 Cool in the dish for 5 minutes, then turn on to a wire cooling rack.

COCONUT SCONES

These scones are delicious with butter or cream and black cherry jam. Easy to make half quantity, but they also freeze successfully. Makes about 12.

225 g/8 oz self-raising flour
½ teaspoon salt
50 g/2 oz lard or butter
50 g/2 oz caster sugar
50 g/2 oz desiccated coconut
About 150 ml/¼ pint milk

1 Preheat oven to hot, Gas 7, 425°F, 220°C.
2 Sieve the flour and salt into a bowl, then rub in the lard or butter until the mixture resembles fine breadcrumbs.
3 Stir in the sugar and coconut.
4 Pour in sufficient milk to make a stiff dough, then knead it lightly.
5 Roll out dough about 2 cm/¾ inch thick.
6 Cut out the scones using a 5-cm/2-inch cutter and re-roll the trimmings until all the dough is used up.
7 Put the scones on a greased baking sheet and cook towards the top of the preheated oven, for 10 to 15 minutes.
8 Cool on a wire rack.

Michelle Watkin
Thorngumbald, Hull

155

OATCAKES

Delicious hot or cold with butter and cheese or honey. Keep well in a tin for about 10 days; freeze well. Makes 10.

175 g/6 oz medium oatmeal,
   plus a little extra
A pinch of salt
A pinch of bicarbonate of soda
1 tablespoon melted butter
4 tablespoons hot water
A knob of suet or a *very* little lard
   to grease girdle

1 Mix 175 g/6 oz oatmeal with other ingredients to a workable dough.
2 Form a round lump, sprinkle with oatmeal and roll out almost paper thin.
3 Cut a large circle, using a dinner plate for guidance. Then cut this into triangles. You can get about 10 triangles.
4 Heat girdle and grease it. Cook oatcakes, turning carefully until they are crisp but not brown.

Grace Mulligan

TOM'S VANCOUVER CARROT CAKE

A lovely moist cake with a delicious topping. It freezes well with its topping and the nuts. Either freeze it in a piece, or in individual slices. These are best frozen on a tray, then transferred to a freezer box.

100 g/4 oz caster sugar
75 g/3 oz self-raising flour
A pinch of salt
½ teaspoon cinnamon
½ teaspoon bicarbonate of soda
60 ml/2 fl oz oil
1 egg
75 g/3 oz carrots, grated

TOPPING
100 g/4 oz cream cheese
50 g/2 oz butter

50 g/2 oz icing sugar
A few drops of vanilla essence
Chopped nuts

1 Grease an 18 cm/7 inch square cake tin and line the base with greaseproof paper.
2 Preheat the oven to moderate, Gas 4, 345°F, 180°C.
3 Sift the first five ingredients into a bowl, then beat in the oil and egg.
4 Mix in the grated carrots.
5 Put the mixture into the prepared tin and bake in the middle of the preheated oven, for 45 minutes or until firm.
6 Turn the cake out on to a wire rack to cool. When cold, slice it carefully through the middle ready for the filling and topping.
7 Cream together all the topping ingredients except the nuts. Divide the mixture and sandwich the two pieces of cake together with half of it. Spread the rest over the top and sprinkle with chopped nuts.

Tom Stephenson
Highgate, London

QUICK LEMON CAKE

Makes 2 very light cakes – one to eat, one to freeze for another day. For a change this cake can be made with orange rind and juice.

175 g/6 oz caster sugar
175 g/6 oz curd cheese or cottage
   cheese, sieved
Grated rind and juice of 1 lemon
2 beaten eggs
225 g/8 oz self-raising white flour,
   sieved
Milk

1 Preheat oven to moderate, Gas 3, 325°F, 160°C.
2 Mix together the caster sugar, curd cheese, lemon rind, lemon juice and beaten eggs.
3 Fold in the sieved flour and, if

156

necessary, add a little milk to make a dropping consistency.

4 Put the cake mixture into 2 greased and lined 250-g/1-lb loaf tins and bake in the middle of the oven for 40 to 45 minutes, until well-risen, firm to touch and golden brown.

4 When the cakes are cooked, leave them in the tins for 5 minutes then turn them on to a wire rack to cool.

Mrs Anne Walton
Frome, Somerset

GRANDMOTHER'S GINGER FRUIT CAKE

This recipe makes an 18-cm/7-inch cake, but it keeps well or can be cut into slices and frozen.

175 g/6 oz margarine
175 g/6 oz caster sugar
2 eggs, beaten
275 g/10 oz self-raising flour
2 teaspoons ground ginger
40 g/1½ oz glacé cherries, chopped
40 g/1½ oz sultanas
40 g/1½ oz raisins
100 g/4 oz crystallised ginger, chopped
Milk
1 to 2 tablespoons caster sugar

1 Cream together the margarine and sugar, then gradually stir in the beaten eggs.
2 Sieve together the flour and ground ginger and fold into the mixture.
3 Add the dried fruit and half of the crystallised ginger and pour in sufficient milk to make a dropping consistency.
4 Turn into a greased and lined 18-cm/7-inch cake tin and scatter the remaining crystallised ginger on top.
5 Sprinkle the top of the cake with caster sugar and bake in a moderate oven, Gas 4, 350°F, 180°C, for 1¾ hours.

Mrs Dawn Brown
Darlington, Co. Durham

HAROLD'S FRUIT CAKE

Simple and quick. Freezes well. Makes a 15-cm/6-inch sponge.

150 ml/¼ pint milk
100 g/4 oz dried mixed fruit
100 g/4 oz dark soft brown sugar
100 g/4 oz margarine
1 size 3 egg, beaten
150 g/5 oz wholemeal self-raising flour

1 Put the milk, dried fruit, sugar and margarine into a saucepan and boil for 5 minutes. Leave it to cool.
2 Stir the egg and flour into the saucepan.
3 Grease a 15-cm/6-inch sponge tin and line the base with a circle of greaseproof paper.
4 Pour the cake mixture into the prepared tin and level the top.
5 Preheat oven to moderately hot, Gas 5, 375°F, 190°C.
6 Bake in the centre of the oven for 25 minutes.
7 Leave in tin for 10 minutes and then turn out on to a wire rack to cool.

Mrs Winifred Bulstrode,
Waterlooville, Hampshire

 Microwave 〰〰〰〰〰〰〰

This comes out very moist and has a good dark colour if it is made with dark soft brown sugar.

1 Put the milk, dried fruit, sugar and margarine into a mixing bowl, heat on full power for 4 minutes then stir. Leave to cool.
2 Stir the egg and flour into the cooled fruit mixture.
3 Line the base of an 18-cm/7-inch round cake dish with a circle of greaseproof paper. Tip the cake mixture into the prepared dish and smooth over the top.

157

4 Cook on full power for 3½ to 4 minutes. Test the cake with a wooden cocktail stick. It should come out clean when the cake is cooked. If you need to add extra time, continue to cook on full power, checking every 10 to 20 seconds. Let it cool in the dish for 5 minutes before turning on to a cooling rack.

5 Preheat oven to moderate, Gas 3, 325°F, 160°C, bake for 1 hour, then reduce the temperature to cool, Gas 2, 300°F, 150°C and cook for a further 1 to 1½ hours. To test to see if it is cooked insert a fine skewer into the middle of the cake; if it comes out clean, the cake is ready.

Mrs F. E. Thompson
Crossgate Moor, Durham

SHERRY CAKE

This recipe uses quite a lot of sherry, but it makes the fruit very moist and gives the cake a special taste. It also keeps well and can be frozen in slices. Makes an 18-cm/7-inch square cake.

175 g/6 oz sultanas
175 g/6 oz raisins
100 g/4 oz currants
75 g/3 oz glacé cherries, chopped
75 g/3 oz mixed peel, chopped
150 ml/¼ pint sherry
175 g/6 oz butter or margarine
175 g/6 oz dark brown sugar
3 eggs
100 g/4 oz white or wholemeal
plain flour
100 g/4 oz white or wholemeal
self-raising flour
½ teaspoon mixed spice
A pinch of salt
25 g/1 oz ground almonds

1 Put the dried fruits, glacé cherries and mixed peel into a bowl and pour over the sherry. Leave overnight covered with a damp cloth.
2 Next day, cream together the butter or margarine and sugar until light and fluffy, then gradually stir in the eggs.
3 Sieve the flours, mixed spice and salt and mix with ground almonds, then fold into the cake mixture.
4 Lastly, stir in the fruit and any sherry that remains at the bottom of the bowl and turn into a lined 18-cm/7-inch square cake tin.

1 Put the dried fruits, glacé cherries and mixed peel into a bowl and pour over the sherry. Cover with clear film and heat on full power for 5 minutes. Leave to stand until cold, stirring from time to time. Alternatively leave the mixture overnight to absorb the sherry.
2 Use margarine rather than butter and cream it with the sugar until light and fluffy, then gradually stir in the eggs, beating well after each addition.
3 Fold in the flour, mixed spices, almonds and salt. Lastly stir in the fruit and any remaining sherry.
4 Line the base of a 20-cm/8-inch round cake dish with a circle of greaseproof paper. Tip the cake mixture into the prepared dish, smooth over the top and cook on Low for 18 to 20 minutes. To test if the cake is cooked, insert a fine skewer into the centre of the cake. If it is cooked it will come out clean. The top of the cake will have lost its glossy appearance and look dry and it should pull away from the sides easily if it is properly cooked. If the cake needs extra time continue cooking on Low, checking every 30 to 60 seconds.

For a 2-power microwave cooker: Cook on Defrost for 25 to 30 minutes, testing as above.

PLAIN SPONGE

The quantity of mixture will make one small sponge cake, four currant buns AND two small steamed puddings. They all freeze well. Also see the Chocolate Sponge recipe for the same idea.

BASIC ALL-IN-ONE MIXTURE

175 g/6 oz soft margarine
175 g/6 oz caster sugar
175 g/6 oz self-raising flour
1 teaspoon baking powder
3 eggs
2 to 3 drops vanilla flavouring

Put all the ingredients into a large bowl and mix well together. Alternatively, use a food processor.

1 Grease a small (18-cm/7-inch) round sandwich tin and line the base with a circle of greaseproof paper.
2 Three-quarters fill the tin with the cake mixture and level off the surface.
3 Bake in a moderate oven, Gas 4, 350°F, 180°C, for 20 to 25 minutes or until the cake is firm and just shrinking away from the sides of the tin.
4 Turn it out on to a wire rack. When cold, decorate the top with either of the following toppings:

CRUNCHY LEMON TOPPING

1 tablespoon lemon juice
1 tablespoon granulated sugar

Quickly stir together the juice and the sugar and spread this over the top of the cake. The idea is to spread it over before the sugar melts to achieve a crunchy surface.

RASPBERRY AND COCONUT TOPPING

1 tablespoon raspberry jam
1 dessertspoon coarse desiccated coconut

Spread the jam over the top of the cake and scatter the coconut on top.

STEAMED PUDDINGS

1 Grease two small cups and put a little lemon curd or plum jam into each.
2 Half-fill the cups with the sponge mixture, then cover each cup with foil and steam for 45 minutes until firm to the touch. (It is a good idea to cook something else in the simmering water under the steamer e.g. rice, or pasta.) If you haven't got a steamer, stand the cups on an upturned saucer (or on 2 jam-pot lids) in a saucepan with a well-fitting lid. Pour in boiling water to come halfway up the sides of the cups, put on the lid and keep the water simmering for 45 minutes until firm to the touch.
3 Leave for a few moments before turning out.

CURRANT BUNS

1 Stir 1 tablespoon of currants into the remaining sponge mixture.
2 Set 4 paper bun cases in a metal bun tray and half-fill them with the bun mixture.
3 Bake in a moderate oven, Gas 4, 350°F, 180°C, for 15 to 20 minutes or until the buns are risen and firm to the touch.

Grace Mulligan

 Microwave

The 2 steamed puddings cook perfectly.

1 Put a little lemon curd or plum jam into 2 small tea cups and half fill them with sponge mixture.
2 Cover with clear film and cook both together on full power for 2 to 3 minutes. Allow to stand for a minute before turning out.

One pudding cooks in 1 to 1½ minutes.

159

CHOCOLATE SPONGE

This recipe quantity will make one small sponge cake, four cherry or walnut buns AND two small steamed puddings. They all freeze well. Also see Plain Sponge for the same idea.

BASIC ALL-IN-ONE MIXTURE

175 g/6 oz soft margarine
175 g/6 oz caster sugar
175 g/6 oz self-raising flour
1 level tablespoon cocoa
2 tablespoons warm water
1½ teaspoons baking powder
3 eggs

Mix all the ingredients together in a large bowl or in a food processor.

SPONGE CAKE

1 Grease a small (18-cm/7-inch) round sandwich tin and line the base with a circle of greaseproof paper.
2 Three-quarters fill the tin with the cake mixture and level off the surface.
3 Bake in a moderate oven, Gas 4, 350°F, 170°C, for about 20 to 25 minutes, or until the cake is firm and just shrinking away from the sides of the tin.
4 Turn it out on to a wire rack. When cold, decorate with one of Debbie's toppings suggested below:

CHOCOLATE FUDGE TOPPING

40 g/1½ oz butter
25 g/1 oz cocoa
2 tablespoons milk
100 g/4 oz icing sugar, sieved

1 Melt the butter in a small pan, add the cocoa and cook for a minute.
2 Remove from the heat and stir in the milk and icing sugar. Beat well until smooth then leave it, stirring from time to time until it thickens to a spreading consistency. Spread thickly and evenly over the top of the cake.

160

GINGER TOPPING

50 g/2 oz crystallised ginger, chopped
50 g/2 oz icing sugar, sieved
About 2 teaspoons water

1 Scatter the ginger on top of the cake.
2 Measure the icing sugar into a bowl and work in sufficient water to give a smooth glacé icing.
3 Spoon into a small polythene bag, snip off the corner of the bag with a pair of scissors and drizzle the icing over the ginger. Allow to set.

STEAMED PUDDINGS

1 Grease two small cups and put a little marmalade or apricot jam into each.
2 Half-fill the cups with sponge mixture, then cover each cup with foil and steam for 45 minutes until firm to the touch. (It is a good idea to cook something else in the simmering water under the steamer e.g. rice or pasta.) If you haven't got a steamer stand the cups on an upturned saucer (or even on 2 jam-pot lids) in a saucepan with a well-fitting lid. Pour in boiling water to come halfway up the sides of the cups, put on the lid and keep the water simmering for 45 minutes until the puddings are firm to the touch. Leave to stand for a few moments before turning out.

CHERRY BUNS

1 Chop up 4 glacé cherries or 2 or 3 walnuts quite small and stir them into the remaining sponge mixture.
2 Set 4 paper bun cases in a metal bun tray and half-fill them with the mixture.
3 Bake in a moderate oven, Gas 4, 350°F, 180°C, for 15 to 20 minutes or until the buns are risen and firm to the touch.

Grace Mulligan and
Debbie Woolhead

The 2 steamed puddings cook perfectly.

1 Put a little marmalade or apricot jam into 2 small teacups and half-fill them with the sponge mixture.
2 Cover with clear film and cook both together on full power for 2 to 3 minutes. Allow to stand for a minute before turning out.

One pudding cooks in 1 to 1½ minutes.

WHOLEMEAL CHOCOLATE CAKE

A moist cake, not too sweet, with a nutty feel given by the wholemeal flour. Freezes well with or without icing.

120 ml/4 fl oz boiling water
25 g/1 oz cocoa
175 g/6 oz caster sugar
60 ml/2 fl oz oil
A pinch of salt
60 ml/2 fl oz milk – sour milk can be used
1 egg, beaten lightly
½ teaspoon vanilla essence
175 g/6 oz wholemeal flour
1 teaspoon baking powder

1 Put the boiling water, cocoa, sugar, oil and salt into a bowl; mix well and leave until cool.
2 Stir in the milk, egg and vanilla.
3 Mix the flour and baking powder together, then fold into the cake.
4 Pour the mixture into a greased and lined round cake tin about 18 cm/7 inches in diameter, or an 18-cm/7-inch square tin.
5 Bake the cake in the middle of a warm oven, Gas 3, 325°F, 160°C, for about 45 minutes or until a fine skewer inserted into the centre of the cake comes out clean.

6 Leave the cake in the tin for 15 minutes, then turn out on to a cooling rack.
7 When the cake is cool either dust the top with icing sugar, or cover the top and sides with chocolate butter icing.

CHOCOLATE BUTTER ICING

50 g/2 oz butter or margarine or a mixture, softened
75 g/3 oz icing sugar
1 dessertspoon cocoa powder

Beat butter or margarine until soft, sift in the icing sugar and cocoa and mix to a paste. Spread over the top and sides of the cake and put it in a cool place to firm up.

Olive Robin
Abbeytown, Carlisle

 Microwave

Yvonne Hamlett, who did all the microwave conversions for this book, says this is one of the nicest microwave cakes she has made and has now used it as a base for a gâteau filled with fresh fruit and cream.

For this you should use self-raising wholemeal flour to obtain the best results and leave out the baking powder.

1 Put the boiling water, cocoa, sugar, oil and salt into a mixing bowl, and beat well so that the mixture is smooth like batter. Leave to cool.
2 Stir in the milk, eggs and vanilla flavouring. Fold in the flour.
3 Line the base of 20-cm/8-inch round cake dish with a circle of greaseproof paper. Tip the cake mixture into the dish and smooth over the top.
4 Cook on full power for 4 to 4½ minutes. When the cake is cooked, it should just pull away from the sides of the dish; the top may look a little

161

wet but there should be no raw batter. A wooden cocktail stick inserted into the centre should come out clean.

5 Let it cool in the dish for 5 minutes then turn on to a wire cooling rack.

Decorate with a dusting of icing sugar or with Chocolate Butter Icing, (above).

WHOLEMEAL GINGERBREAD

This bakes best in a 18-cm/7-inch square tin. It improves with keeping in a tin for 2 days before eating. Freezes well in the piece or cut into individual slices.

100 g/4 oz block margarine
100 g/4 oz black treacle
100 g/4 oz golden syrup
50 g/2 oz Demerara sugar
125 ml/$\frac{1}{4}$ pint milk
225 g/8 oz wholemeal flour
2 teaspoons ground ginger
2 level teaspoons mixed spice
2 level teaspoons bicarbonate of
   soda
1 beaten egg

1 In a large saucepan, warm together margarine, treacle, syrup, and sugar until the fat has melted.
2 Stir in the milk and allow to cool.
3 Mix the dry ingredients, sieving the spices and bicarbonate of soda to break up any lumps.
4 Add the beaten egg to the cooled syrup mixture and pour it into the bowl of dry ingredients. Mix well.
5 Grease an 18-cm/7-inch square tin and line the bottom with greaseproof paper. Pour in the gingerbread mixture.
6 Bake in a cool oven, Gas 2, 300°F, 150°C, for 1 to 1$\frac{1}{4}$ hours or until well risen and firm to the touch.
7 Cool on a wire rack.

Grace Mulligan

 Microwave

Gingerbreads cook well in the microwave – but you must have the correct size of dish. If the dish is too small, the mixture will either erupt out of the dish like a volcano or cook very unevenly.

Microwave gingerbreads tend to be slightly less deep, as they cook better in a shallow, wider dish than is used when baking conventionally.
They keep well – and the flavour, as always, improves if they are wrapped in foil and stored for 2 to 3 days before cutting.
The above ingredients give too much mixture, so halve them as follows:

50 g/2 oz margarine
50 g/2 oz black treacle
50 g/2 oz golden syrup
25 g/1 oz Demerara sugar
4 tablespoons milk
1 egg, beaten
100 g/4 oz wholemeal flour
1 teaspoon ground ginger
1 teaspoon mixed spice
1 teaspoon bicarbonate of soda

1 Put the margarine, treacle, syrup and sugar into a mixing bowl. Heat on full power for 3 minutes, then stir in the milk and leave to cool.
2 Add the beaten egg to the cooled syrup mixture. Then fold in the dry ingredients.
3 Line the base of a 20-cm/8-inch round cake dish with a circle of greaseproof paper. Pour the cake mixture into the prepared dish and smooth over the top.
4 Cook on full power for 4$\frac{1}{2}$ to 5 minutes. The top might look a little shiny, but the sides should pull away from the dish easily and a wooden cocktail stick inserted in the centre should come out clean.
5 Let the cake cool in the dish for 5 minutes then turn it on to a cooling rack.

6 When cold, wrap in foil and store for 2 to 3 days before slicing.

YOGHURT CAKE

A very easy cake to make because nearly all the ingredients are measured in the 150 ml/5 fl oz carton in which the yoghurt comes. Makes a moist 18-cm/7-inch cake, not rich; freezes well.

1 carton (150 ml/5 fl oz) of
   orange or mandarin yoghurt
1 carton of oil
1 carton of caster sugar
3 cartons of self-raising flour
3 eggs
Finely grated rind of 1 orange
   (optional)
1 pinch of salt

1 Preheat oven to moderately hot, Gas 5, 375°F, 190°C.
2 Stir all the ingredients together and put the mixture into a greased 18-cm/7-inch cake tin, or a 900-g/2-lb loaf tin, or two 450-g/1-lb loaf tins. It is wise to line the bottom with greaseproof paper.
3 Bake the cake in the centre of the preheated oven for about 45 minutes, or until firm to the touch.

4 Leave cake in tin for about 15 minutes, then turn it out on to a wire rack to cool.

Mrs Doreen Wright
Forthampton, Gloucestershire

AUSTRALIAN CAKES

Delicious. Like cookies, they are crisp on the outside and soft inside.

75 g/3 oz margarine
75 g/3 oz caster sugar
1 egg
75 g/3 oz self-raising flour, sieved
½ teaspoon baking powder
Cornflakes, crushed slightly

1 Preheat oven to moderately hot, Gas 6, 400°F, 200°C.
2 Cream together the margarine and caster sugar, then stir in the egg.
3 Fold in the sieved flour and baking powder.
4 Take teaspoonfuls of the mixture and roll them in the crushed cornflakes.
5 Space them well apart on a greased baking sheet and bake in preheated oven for 15 minutes.
6 Transfer to a wire rack and allow to cool.

Mrs Hunter
Hessle, N. Humberside

163

CHERRY AND ALMOND SLICE

Can be made in an electric mixer or processor. Freezes well.

125 g/5 oz soft margarine
125 g/5 oz caster sugar
3 eggs
125 g/5 oz self-raising flour
50 g/2 oz ground almonds
75 g/3 oz chopped glacé cherries
A few drops of almond essence
A sprinkle of caster sugar to
    finish

1 Cream margarine and sugar until
light and fluffy.
2 Mix in eggs one at a time
alternately with flour.
3 Mix in almonds, cherries and
essence.
4 Grease a Swiss roll tin and line it
with greased and floured paper.
Spread mixture evenly in tin.
5 Preheat the oven to moderately hot,
Gas 5, 375°F, 190°C, and bake in the
middle for 30 minutes.
6 Carefully remove cake from tin as
soon as it is baked and sprinkle with
caster sugar. Cut into slices when
cold.

Anne Wallace
Stewarton, Ayrshire

LUCY CAKE

*This nicely fits an 18-cm/7-inch square
shallow tin. If you double the quantities
it fits a small Swiss roll tin. Keeps well
for a week.*

50 g/2 oz block margarine
25 g/1 oz caster sugar
1 egg yolk
85 g/3½ oz self-raising flour
Jam, raspberry or apricot are both
    nice

TOPPING
1 egg white
50 g/2 oz caster sugar
25 g/1 oz desiccated coconut

1 Grease the tin.
2 Preheat oven to moderately hot,
Gas 5, 375°F, 190°C.
3 Cream together the margarine and
sugar until light and fluffy, then stir
in the egg yolk and fold in the flour.
4 Press this mixture into the tin and
spread some jam over the top of it.
5 Whisk the egg white until stiff,
then gradually whisk in the sugar.
Fold in the coconut.
6 Spread the meringue mixture on
top of the jam and bake the cake in
the middle of the oven for 35 to 40
minutes.
7 Cut the cake into portions in the
tin while it is still warm.

Mrs Joyce Beresford
Bolton, Lancashire

QUICK HONEY SQUARES

*Very easy to make; very bad for the
figure.*

225 g/8 oz Marie biscuits (or
    any plain sweet biscuit)
75 g/3 oz butter or margarine
3 tablespoons set honey
3 tablespoons crunchy peanut
    butter

1 Crush the biscuits in a food
processor or put them in a strong
plastic bag and crush with a rolling
pin.
2 In a medium-sized pan, melt the
butter and the honey very gently,
then stir in the peanut butter.
3 Mix in the biscuit crumbs and stir
very well together.
4 Press into a greased 18-cm/7-inch
square tin. Level off the top and
allow to cool. Then cut into small
squares.

Grace Mulligan

WALNUT FLAT CAKE

Easy to mix – all in one saucepan.

1 tablespoon golden syrup or
   black treacle
50 g/2 oz margarine
100 g /4 oz brown sugar
100 g/4 oz self-raising flour
50 g/2 oz broken walnuts, roughly
   chopped
1 egg, beaten

1 Preheat oven to moderate, Gas 4,
350°F, 180°C. Grease and line a 15 to
18 cm/6 to 7 inch square tin with
greaseproof paper.
2 Put the syrup or treacle, margarine
and sugar into a saucepan and stir
until the margarine melts.
3 Let it cool slightly, then stir in the
flour and walnuts.
4 Mix in the beaten egg then put the
mixture into the prepared tin.
5 Bake in the middle of the oven, for
25 to 30 minutes.
6 Leave the cake in the tin until
completely cold, then cut it into
squares.

Mrs M. Boon
Stockton, Cleveland

ANZACS

*These large crisp biscuits are well-
known all over Australia. They will
keep very well in an airtight container.
You will get about 24 biscuits. Easy to
mix – all in one large saucepan.*

150 g/5 oz butter or margarine
1 tablespoon golden syrup
2 tablespoons water
1 teaspoon bicarbonate of soda
100 g/4 oz plain flour
75 g/3 oz porridge oats
50 g/2 oz desiccated coconut
100 g/4 oz caster sugar

1 Melt the butter gently with the
syrup in a large saucepan. Remove
from heat.
2 Stir in the water and bicarbonate of
soda, then all the remaining
ingredients.
3 Put teaspoonfuls of the mixture on
to greased baking sheets. Leave plenty
of room between the biscuits as they
spread as they cook.
4 Bake in a cool oven, Gas 3, 325°F,
160°C, for about 20 minutes until just
golden brown.
5 Leave the biscuits on the baking
sheets for a few minutes to harden up
slightly, then put them on a wire rack
to cool.

Mrs Eunice Heath
Thirsk, North Yorkshire

BRAN BISCUITS

*Yields about 30 light crisp biscuits
which are very 'more-ish'. Keep well in
an airtight container for at least 2
weeks.*

100 g/4 oz butter or block
   margarine
75 g/3 oz caster sugar
1 egg, beaten
Grated rind of 1 orange
50 g/2 oz bran
100 g/4 oz plain flour

1 Preheat oven to moderate, Gas 4,
350°F, 180°C.
2 Cream together the butter or
margarine and sugar until light and
fluffy.
3 Stir in the egg, orange rind, bran
and flour.
4 Form into a ball and roll out on a
well-floured board. Cut out the
biscuits with a 5-cm/2-inch cutter and
place them on a well-greased baking
tray.
5 Bake for about 25 minutes.

Variation: add a few chopped
walnuts or raisins to the recipe at
step 2.

Sylvia McBeth
Coventry, Warwickshire

165

CUMBERLAND SHORTBREAD

Keeps for weeks in an airtight container.

150 g/5 oz butter
25 g/1 oz margarine
75 g/3 oz caster sugar
200 g/7 oz plain flour
25 g/1 oz self-raising flour
A pinch of salt
Extra caster sugar

1 Cream together the butter, margarine and sugar. Work in the flour and salt then put the mixture into an ungreased 20-cm/8-inch tin and prick all over.
2 Bake at the top of a cool oven, Gas 2, 300°F, 150°C, for 45 minutes or until golden brown.
3 Remove from the oven and, while still warm, mark the shortbread into portions and sprinkle with caster sugar.
4 When cold, remove from the tin and cut up. Store in an airtight container.

Mrs E. M. Brunt
Keepers Corner, Surrey

MUESLI BARS

Makes 6 pieces. Keep well in an airtight tin. (See page 16 for a home-made muesli mix.)

3 tablespoons golden syrup
75 g/3 oz margarine
50 g/2 oz rolled porridge oats
50 g/2 oz plain peanuts, roughly chopped
100 g/4 oz muesli

1 In a large pan, melt the syrup and margarine, then stir in the rest of the ingredients.
2 Line the base of an 18-cm/7-inch square tin with non-stick paper and pour in the mixture.
3 Level it off and bake at Gas 4, 350°F, 180°C for about 20 minutes.
4 Mark into bars while still warm and leave to cool in the tin.

Grace Mulligan

Chapter 11

Preserves
and Chutneys

plus Home-made Sweets

TESTING JAMS AND JELLIES FOR SETTING POINT

1 Volume test If you know the expected yield of your fruit – e.g. the recipe says you will get, say 2.5 kg/5 lb of jam, then measure out that amount in water. Take a 450 g/1 lb jam jar (not a 325g/12 oz jar), fill it 5 times and pour this into your pan. Use a wooden spoon handle, stand it upright in the water and mark this level with a pencil. Keep the spoon handy. Then, when you are testing for a set, draw pan off heat, wait until bubbling subsides and stand spoon in the jam. When the volume has returned to the level of the pencil mark, the jam is ready to pot.

2 Cold plate test Have some plates cooling in the refrigerator, and take a teaspoon of jam and drop it on a cold plate. Wait a minute and, if it wrinkles when pushed, the jam is ready. If not, go on boiling a little longer.

3 Flake test Dip a clean wooden spoon in boiling jam. Allow the cooling jam to drop from the spoon. If the drops run together and form a flake or curtain it is ready to pot.

4 Temperature test Use a sugar thermometer. It is important to dip the thermometer in hot water immediately before using it in the jam. Submerge the bulb fully in the boiling jam, but do not let it touch bottom of pan. When the thermometer registers 220°F or 106°C the jam is ready to pot.

TIPS FOR MAKING PRESERVES IN THE MICROWAVE

It is best to make small batches to avoid the mixture boiling over.
Use the biggest bowl that will fit into your microwave cooker: 4 to 5-litre/7 to 8-pint size. Pyrex bowls are ideal. If you have a large plastic dome from a roasting dish this is ideal *providing* it is made from a plastic called Polysulphane. Check the manufacturer's instructions, as some plastics will not withstand the high temperatures of boiling sugar mixtures.

There is no need to turn the oven off each time you stir – as soon as the door is opened the oven switches off, so you can set the time at the beginning rather than keep on resetting every 2 to 3 minutes.

Take care always to lift the dish using oven gloves, as the preserve will transfer its heat to the cooking container so it will be very hot.

Don't be tempted to leave the wooden spoon in the mixture – it will absorb the microwave energy and become too hot to handle.

Start checking the setting of jams etc. in the usual way after 8 to 10 minutes, then check every minute until the correct setting point is reached.

Yvonne Hamlett
Haddenham, Buckinghamshire

MATRIMONIAL JAM
Makes 1.8 to 2.2. kg/4 to 5 lb.

This recipe was given to us once before and was called High Dumpsie-Dearie Jam. Please let us know if you have ever been told any of the origins of these quaint old names.

450 g/1 lb plums
450 g/1 lb pears
450 g/1 lb cooking apples
Finely grated rind and juice of 1 lemon
1.3 kg/3 lb sugar

1 Cut the plums in half and remove the stones. Peel and core the pears and apples and cut into chunks.
2 Put all the fruit into a large

saucepan and add the lemon rind and lemon juice. Put on the lid.
3 Cook slowly until the fruit is soft.
4 Meanwhile put sugar and clean jam jars to warm in a very cool oven, Gas $\frac{1}{4}$, 225°F, 110°C.
5 Add the warm sugar and bring slowly up to the boil, stirring all the time. Boil the mixture until setting point is reached (see left).
6 While jam is hot, fill the warmed jars to the brim. Put on waxed paper discs, waxed side down. Either put the jam pot covers on at once or leave till jam is quite cold. Never put covers on while jam is between hot and cold or condensation could occur which might lead to mould forming on top of the jam.

Mrs Heather Wade
Leyburn, North Yorkshire

 Microwave

See opposite page for a few tips on making preserves by microwave.

225 g/8 oz plums
225g/8 oz pears
225 g/8 oz cooking apples
Finely grated rind and juice of
one lemon
750 g/1½ lb sugar

Jam in the microwave has to be made in fairly small quantities. These ingredients will be safe if your bowl is big enough and will yield two 450-g/1-lb jars plus enough for a ramekin or small jar.

1 Cut the plums in half and remove the stones. Peel and core the pears and apples and cut into chunks.
2 Put all the fruit, lemon rind and peel into a 5-litre/8-pint Pyrex mixing bowl. Heat on full power for 8 to 10 minutes until the fruit is soft.
3 Stir in the sugar, heat on full power for 3 to 5 minutes. Stir every minute until the sugar has dissolved.

4 Continue cooking on full power for 15 to 20 minutes, stirring every 3 to 5 minutes as the jam boils up. Start testing for correct setting point after 12 minutes. (See testing notes on opposite page).
5 Cool in the bowl for 10 minutes, then pot, seal and label as in step 6 above.

QUINCE JAM

Makes about 600 g/1¼ lb of quite tart jam which has good colour and consistency.

450 g/1 lb quinces
A good 150 ml/¼ pint water
450 g/1 lb sugar, warmed
Juice of half a lemon

1 Peel and core the quinces. Put the peel and cores into a saucepan with the water and simmer until soft and pulpy.
2 Sieve the mixture and discard the peel and cores.
3 Grate (or chop and mince) the quinces and put them into a saucepan with the purée. If necessary add a very little more water. Heat to boiling point, cover the pan and simmer until soft.
4 Add the sugar and lemon juice to the pan and heat slowly, uncovered, until the mixture boils.
5 Boil the jam steadily until setting point is reached, about 15 minutes. Then bottle in clean warm jam jars.
6 Put on waxed paper discs immediately, waxed side down. Put on jam jar covers either at once or when jam is quite cold. This is to avoid condensation which can lead to mould on top of jam.

John H. J. Slater
Fareham, Hampshire

See page 168 for a few tips on making preserves by microwave.

Yields about 675 g/1½ lb

1 Peel and core the quinces. Put the peel and cores into a large Pyrex mixing bowl (use the largest one that will fit in your microwave cooker). Heat uncovered on full power for 10 minutes.
2 Sieve the mixture, reserve the liquid, and discard the cores and peel.
3 Grate the quinces into the bowl. Add the watery purée. Heat on full power for 5 minutes.
4 Add the sugar and lemon juice, stirring well. Heat on full power for 5 minutes, stirring twice. The sugar should by now have melted.
5 Heat the mixture on full power for 8 to 10 minutes until boiling, then continue heating on full power, stirring every minute until setting point is reached. Once the mixture boils it will take about 5 to 9 minutes to reach setting point. (See page 168 for testing for setting notes.) Always use a wooden spoon for stirring and stir every minute or the mixture will boil over. Do not leave the wooden spoon in the jam as this will absorb the microwave energy and get too hot to handle. It will also prolong the cooking time.
6 Allow the jam to cool for 5 minutes, then pot it in warm jars. Put on waxed paper discs at once to seal the surface. Then either put on jam pot covers immediately or else wait until the jam is quite cold. This is to avoid condensation inside the covers which can turn to mould.

RASPBERRY JAM
Yields 2.25 kg/5 lb. Easy to make less.

1½ kg/3 lb freshly picked ripe raspberries
1½ kg/3 lb granulated sugar

1 Avoid over-ripe fruit or the jam may not set. Pick over the raspberries. Do not wash unless absolutely necessary. Put in a roomy pan with the lid on.
2 Put sugar to warm in a slow oven, Gas ¼, 225°F, 110°C' Put clean jars to warm at same time.
3 Simmer fruit gently until juice begins to run. Mash it down with a potato masher to speed the process.
4 Take lid off pan and continue cooking until the fruit is tender and the contents of the pan have reduced slightly.
5 Make a pectin test: remove pan from heat. Take out a teaspoonful of the juice into a glass and let it cool. Then add 3 teaspoons methylated spirits to the sample, swirl it around gently. If plenty of pectin is present, a clear jelly clot will form. If a medium amount of pectin is present, several small clots will form. If a poor amount of pectin is present, no real clot will be found. If a reasonable clot does not occur, cook fruit in pan a little longer to reduce liquid. *Do not on any account return the test sample to the pan.*
6 Now add the warmed sugar and stir over low heat until it is dissolved.
7 Raise the heat and bring to a full rolling boil until setting point is reached. (See page 168.)
8 Pot in warmed jars, put on waxed paper discs at once and either put on jam pot covers immediately, or wait until the jam is quite cold – never in between. This is to avoid condensation inside the cover which can lead to mould on the jam. Label and store in a cool dark place.

Grace Mulligan

See page 168 for a few tips on making preserves by microwave.

It is best to make small batches of the jam in the microwave, to prevent the mixture boiling over. The amounts given below are safe if you use a large enough bowl. Any soft fruit can be substituted for the raspberries.

450 g/1 lb raspberries, fresh or frozen*
450 g/1 lb sugar
Two 5 ml teaspoons lemon juice

* Put the frozen fruit into the bowl and heat on full power for 4 minutes, then mix in the sugar and continue as follows.

1 Put all the ingredients in a large Pyrex mixing bowl. Use the largest that will fit in your microwave cooker, a 4-litre/7-pint size is ideal.

Heat, uncovered, on full power for 5 minutes, stirring twice. The sugar should now have melted; if not, continue to heat on full power for a further 1 to 2 minutes.
2 Once the sugar has dissolved, heat the jam on full power for 10 to 16 minutes, stirring occasionally. Start testing for setting point after 8 minutes and every 2 minutes thereafter. (See page 168 for testing notes.)
3 Finish the jam as given in step 8 above.

RHUBARB MARMALADE

This recipe came originally to Mrs Hopkins from a Canadian cousin. It's easy to make more than the 2.25 kg/5 lb this yields. Although rhubarb does not have a high pectin content, the orange makes up for this and there are no problems at all if you use the 'sugar-with-pectin' now available in shops.

171

4 oranges
1.35 kg/3 lb rhubarb, washed and
 cut into 5-cm/2-inch pieces
1.35 kg/3 lb sugar, warmed
100 g/4 oz walnuts, roughly
 chopped

1 Squeeze the juice from the oranges
and put it into a large pan with the
rhubarb.
2 Scrape away and discard the pith
from some of the orange rind. Cut
rind into fine shreds. Cook these
in boiling water until tender, then
drain and add to the rhubarb.
3 Cook the rhubarb over a low heat
with a lid on the pan until the juice
starts to run out. Then mash it down
and cook until soft.
4 Meanwhile, put the sugar to warm
in a very cool oven, Gas $\frac{1}{4}$, 225°F,
110°C. Put clean jam jars to warm at
the same time.
5 Add the warmed sugar and stir
until dissolved. Add the walnuts.
6 Increase the heat to obtain a rolling
boil and boil until setting point is
reached. (See page 168 for notes
about testing for a set.)
7 Pot the hot marmalade into the
warmed jars and immediately put on
waxed paper discs to seal the surface.
Either put on jam pot covers at once
or else wait until it is quite cold –
never in-between. (Condensation can
occur and the marmalade could go
mouldy.) Label and store in a cool
dark place.

Mrs H. Hopkins
West Midlands

*See page 168 for a few tips on making
preserves by microwave.*

1 Use the largest Pyrex bowl that will
fit into your microwave cooker. If
your microwave has only a small
cavity, make half the quantity given.

172

2 Squeeze the juice from the oranges
and put it with the rhubarb into the
bowl.
3 Scrape away and discard the pith
from some of the orange rind and cut
it into fine shreds. Put these in a
basin with 150 ml/$\frac{1}{4}$ pint hot water.
Cook on full power for 5 minutes,
then let it stand for 5 minutes so that
they become tender. Drain and then
add to the rhubarb.
4 Cook the rhubarb on full power for
10 minutes, stirring twice. Tip in the
sugar and stir well. Continue cooking
on full power for 5 minutes, stirring
every minute until all the sugar has
dissolved. Then continue cooking on
full power for 8 to 10 minutes,
stirring every 2 to 3 minutes – or as
the mixture boils up to the top of the
dish. For half quantities, cook on full
power for 5 to 7 minutes. (See page
168 for some notes on testing for
setting.)
5 When the correct setting point is
reached, stir in the walnuts. Allow to
cool slightly so that the walnuts don't
all float to the top, then pot, cover
and label as in step 7 above.

A JAR OF
LEMON CURD
FOR ONE

*Makes one 225 g/8 oz jar. The addition
of custard powder helps to speed the
thickening process.*

1 egg
$\frac{1}{2}$ teaspoon custard powder
75 g/3 oz sugar
25 g/1 oz butter
Finely grated rind and juice
 of 1 lemon

1 Use a basin that will fit nicely over
a pan of simmering water. Do not let
basin touch the water.
2 Beat the egg with custard powder.
Then add sugar, butter, lemon rind
and juice.

3 Set basin over pan of simmering water and stir mixture from time to time until it thickens. It will take about 15 to 20 minutes.
4 Fill a small jar and leave it to cool.

Keep in refrigerator and use within 4 weeks.

Mrs M. Alderson
Leeds, Yorkshire

1 Use a 1.1-litre/2-pint basin. Melt the butter on full power for 10 seconds. Then whisk in all the other ingredients (except the custard powder).
2 Heat on full power for 30 seconds. Stir well. Continue to cook in 10-second bursts, whisking well, until the mixture thickens. In total the lemon curd will take 60 to 90 seconds.
3 Pour it into a small jar and leave to cool.
4 Keep refrigerated and use within 4 weeks.

ELDERBERRY AND APPLE JELLY

This jelly is delicious with meat or poultry and it makes a pleasant change from the cranberry sauce traditionally served with turkey. Can be made at any time of the year, using dried elderberries available at home-brewing shops. With these it is necessary to start the night before.

450 g/1 lb elderberries or
  225 g/$\frac{1}{2}$ lb dried elderberries
150 ml/$\frac{1}{4}$ pint vinegar
1 small onion, peeled and spiked
  with 6 cloves
2 large cooking apples, peeled,
  cored and sliced
Sugar or 'sugar-with-pectin'

1 With dried elderberries just cover with boiling water and leave overnight to plump up. Then strain them.

2 Put the elderberries, vinegar and onion into a pan and boil for 20 minutes then strain, keeping the juices.
3 Cook the apples with a very little water until soft.
4 Add the strained elderberry juice.
5 Measure the amount of purée you now have and add 450 g/1 lb sugar for each 600 ml/1 pint of purée.
6 Bring the mixture to the boil, stirring to help the sugar dissolve. Then keep it at a rolling boil until setting point is reached. Using 'sugar-with-pectin', this will take only 4 minutes. (See page 168 for notes on testing for setting.)
7 Pot the jelly into small warmed jars while very hot. Put on waxed paper discs at once and either put jam pot covers on straight away, or else leave until the jelly is quite cold.

Mrs Joyce Beresford
Bromley Cross, Bolton

'Sugar-with-pectin' is recommended for this method.

Plumping the dried elderberries by microwave was not found satisfactory; it is better if you soak them overnight as recommended in the recipe.

1 With dried elderberries, just cover with boiling water and leave overnight to plump up. Then strain them.
2 Put the elderberries, vinegar and onion into a 4-litre/7-pint mixing bowl, cover with clear film and cook on full power for 6 to 8 minutes. Then leave to stand while you cook the apple.
3 Put the apple and two 15 ml tablespoons water in a basin, cover with clear film and heat on full power for 5 minutes. Mash with a fork or a potato masher.
4 Strain the elderberry juice into the apple purée. Rinse out the large mixing bowl and measure the purée

173

into it. Add 450 g/1 lb 'sugar-with-pectin' for each 600 ml/1 pint purée.
5 Heat the mixture on full power for 5 to 6 minutes, stirring occasionally with a wooden spoon, to help the sugar dissolve. Once the sugar has dissolved, continue heating on full power for 4 to 5 minutes until setting point is reached.
6 Put the jelly immediately into small warm jars, cover the surface with waxed paper discs and put on the jam pot cover straight away.
7 Label and store in a cool dark place.

SWEET CHUTNEY

This recipe involves no cooking. Makes 1 kg/2½ lb —easy to make more.

225 g/½ lb cooking apples, peeled and grated
225 g/½ lb onions, finely chopped
225 g/½ lb dates, stoned and finely chopped
¼ teaspoon salt
¼ teaspoon freshly ground pepper
¼ teaspoon pickling spice
225 g/½ lb sultanas
225 g/½ lb light brown sugar
150 ml/¼ pint vinegar

1 Mix all the ingredients together and leave them for 48 hours.
2 If the chutney looks a bit dry, stir in some extra vinegar. Bottle the chutney in jars with vinegar-proof lids and store in a cool, dark place.

Mrs M. Robinson,
Hexham, Northumberland

RED TOMATO CHUTNEY

Yields 2½ to 3 kg/5 to 6 lb. Can be made with green tomatoes.

1 kg/2 lb red tomatoes
500 g/1 lb onions or shallots
500 g/1 lb cooking apples
375 g/12 oz sultanas
500 g/1 lb brown sugar
1 slightly rounded teaspoon ground cloves
1 teaspoon ground ginger
1 teaspoon dry mustard
½ teaspoon cayenne pepper
1 tablespoon salt
½ litre/1 pint vinegar

1 Skin tomatoes (see page 26) and cut them up.
2 Peel and chop onions finely.
3 Peel, core and chop apples finely.
4 Put all the ingredients into a large pan and cook slowly, stirring, until sugar has dissolved.
5 Turn heat down and let chutney

just simmer gently for about 1½ to 2 hours, stirring occasionally, until it is thick and smooth. Draw a wooden spoon through it. If the trail of the spoon holds without immediately filling with liquid the chutney is ready.

6 Meanwhile prepare clean jars with vinegar-proof lids. (Coffee jars with plastic lids are ideal.) Put jars to warm in a very slow oven, Gas ¼, 225°F, 110°C.

7 Pour hot chutney into jars and at once put on a waxed paper disc, waxed side down. Then leave until cold.

8 When jars of chutney are quite cold, put on the vinegar-proof lids. Label jars and store in a cool, dry, dark cupboard.

Always allow chutney to mature for at least three months as the flavour improves the longer it is kept.

Mrs A. I. McBain
Hull, N. Humberside

See page 168 for some notes on making preserves by microwave.

Only 450 ml/¾ pint vinegar is needed, otherwise the ingredients are as given above.

1 Prepare tomatoes, onion and apple, following steps 1 to 3 above.

2 Put onion and apple in a large 3-litre/5-pint casserole. Cook on full power for 5 to 7 minutes to soften the onion.

3 Mix in all the rest of the ingredients. Cook uncovered on full power for 15 minutes, stirring every 3 to 5 minutes.

4 When the mixture is thick, so that a spoon drawn through it leaves its mark without instantly filling with liquid, the chutney is done.

5 Pot it into warm jars, put on the waxed paper discs to seal the surface while it is still hot. Then leave to cool. Put on vinegar-proof lids for storage. Label and store in a cool dark place.

The flavour will mature if the chutney is kept for 2 to 3 months.

TOMATO SAUCE

Makes 1.2 litres/2 pints.

1.75 kg/4 lb ripe tomatoes, chopped
2 medium onions, chopped
1 clove of garlic, crushed
¼ teaspoon cayenne pepper
225 g/½ lb white sugar
225 g/½ lb muscovado sugar
25 g/1 oz salt
15 g/½ oz whole cloves
175 ml/7 fl oz vinegar

1 Put all ingredients together in a large pan and boil steadily for about 3 hours until a sauce-like consistency is reached. Stir from time to time to stop it burning and mash it down with a potato masher.

2 Liquidise the mixture and then sieve it if you prefer the pips removed.

3 Allow to cool and then bottle using vinegar-proof lids.

4 Keep bottles in a cool dark place.

Mary Hunter
Addingham, Yorkshire

Makes 600 to 750 ml/1 to 1¼ pints.

900 g/2 lb ripe tomatoes, quartered
1 onion, sliced
1 clove of garlic, crushed
100 g/4 oz granulated sugar
100 g/4 oz muscovado sugar
1 teaspoon salt
6 tablespoons vinegar
4 whole cloves
A pinch of cayenne pepper

1 Put the tomatoes in a 4 litre/7 pint mixing bowl with the onion, garlic and sugar. Heat on full power for 5 minutes, then stir well, mashing down the tomatoes.
2 Add the remaining ingredients and cook on full power for 10 minutes, stirring twice. Cool slightly. Cook longer for a thicker sauce.
3 Liquidise the mixture and then sieve to remove the pips.
4 Allow to cool completely and then bottle, using vinegar-proof lids.
5 Store in a cool dark place.

2 Stir in the egg yolk, rum, cream and the ground almonds or cake crumbs.
   Leave the bowl in a cool place for 10 minutes or so. Then, when the mixture is quite thick, shape into 12 balls. Finish as above.

Another Idea!
These can also be made substituting white chocolate for plain, and using desiccated coconut instead of ground almonds. Roll them in icing sugar, grated white chocolate or coconut.

Yvonne Hamlett
Haddenham, Buckinghamshire

RICH RUM TRUFFLES

These are so easy to prepare, and to make them look special, put them in little paper sweet cases. Makes 12.

75 g/3 oz plain chocolate
1 egg yolk
15 g/$\frac{1}{2}$ oz butter
1 to 2 teaspoons rum
1 teaspoon cream
2 teaspoons ground almonds or cake crumbs
Chocolate vermicelli

1 Put the chocolate into a bowl set over a pan of hot water and leave until it has melted. Stir in egg yolk.
2 Remove from the heat and stir in butter, rum, cream and ground almonds or cake crumbs.
3 Leave the bowl in a cool place for 10 minutes or so, then beat the mixture until it is quite thick. Shape into balls and roll them in chocolate vermicelli.

Miss R. Cawson
Fareham, Hampshire.

 Microwave

1 Put the chocolate and butter in a small basin and heat on full power for 1$\frac{1}{2}$ minutes, until melted.

FRUIT AND NUT SWEETS FOR CHRISTMAS

Children may enjoy helping to make these, because there is no actual cooking involved.

50 g/2 oz blanched almonds, finely chopped
50 g/2 oz dried apricots, finely chopped
50 g/2 oz dried figs, finely chopped
50 g/2 oz glacé cherries – red and green, finely chopped
2 teaspoons brandy
75 g/3 oz marzipan

1 Mix together the nuts, fruit and brandy.
2 Divide the mixture into two and roll each into a long thin sausage shape. Chill well.
3 Roll out the marzipan thinly into two strips just big enough to wrap around the fruit and nut rolls.
4 Press the marzipan around the rolls and seal the join with a little water. Return to the refrigerator until firm.
5 Cut into small pieces and put each sweet into a small paper case.

Grace Mulligan

ALL IN THE OVEN

These lists are to help you choose
a variety of recipes to cook in the oven at the
same time. It is one of the most popular features
of the television programmes when,
with careful juggling of dishes and cake tins,
we cook a main course, vegetables, pudding and a
cake all together.

GAS 8, 450°F, 230°C

Potato, Ham and Egg Pie

White Bread
Wholemeal Bread
Milk Bread
Poppy Seed Plait
Bridge Rolls or Batch Rolls

GAS 7, 425°F, 210°C

Salmon Parcel

Barbecue Spare Ribs

Pizza for 2
Apple and Mincemeat Parcel

Banana Alaska

Coconut Scones

GAS 6, 400°F, 200°C

Cod with Sweetcorn
Citrus Mackerel
Baked Grey Mullet
Mushroom-Stuffed Plaice
Crisp Lemon Sole
Salmon Savoury
Macaroni and Tuna Layer

Tasty Fish Pie
Sardines for Tea

Patti's Chicken for Two

Celery Pork Steaks
Pork with Chestnuts
Berkshire Moussaka

Scotch Eggs
Savoury Potato Bake with
   Frankfurters
Vegetables with Cheese
Cheese-Baked Potatoes
Savoury Pudding

Cheese and Leek Flan
Quick Egg, Bacon and Mushroom
   Pie
Sardine Pasties
Ham and Leek Flan
Chicken and Mushroom Pie
Fried Curry Puffs
Pecan Pie
Almond Mince Pies

Christmas Mincemeat Roll
Apple Pudding
Cherry Sponge Pudding

Hot Cross Buns
Bran Muffins
Australian Cakes

GAS 5, 375°F, 190°C

Teifi Salmon in a Sauce
Salmon and Potato Bake

Baked Lamb Chop with
  Courgettes

Cheese and Cauliflower Soufflé

Sausagemeat Flan

Baked Apple with Muesli
Savoury Baked Apple
Oaty Rhubarb Crumble
Oaty Apple Crunch

Harold's Fruit Cake
Yoghurt Cake
Cherry and Almond Slice
Lucy Cake

GAS 4, 350°F, 180°C

Bacon and Prune Rolls
Smoked Fish Soufflé
Chicken Pieces in a Cider Sauce
Baked Chicken with Pineapple
Nutty Lemon Stuffing

Savoury Hot Pot
Savoury Lamb Chops
Liver and Bacon Casserole
Liver Balls

Curried Meat Loaf
Potato and Bean Casserole
Hot Vegetable Pancakes

Casseroled Potatoes with Onions
  and Garlic
Cheese-Baked Potatoes

Fish Pie in Puff Pastry
Marmalade Flan
Apricot and Coconut Tarts

Old-fashioned Milk Puddings
Strawberries and Kiwi Fruit in a
  Cream-Filled Sponge

Honey and Malt Fruit Loaf
Spiced Carrot Tea Bread
Spicy Apple Loaf
Tom's Vancouver Carrot Cake
Grandmother's Ginger Fruit Cake
Walnut Flat Cake
Bran Biscuits
Muesli Bars

GAS 3, 325°F, 160°C

Belly Pork with Apple and Sage
  Coating
Hearts Braised in an Orange Sauce

Megan's Treacle Roll

Dumpling Loaf
Quick Lemon Cake
Wholemeal Chocolate Cake
Anzacs

GAS 2, 300°F, 150°C

Patti's Chicken for Two

Steak and Kidney Pie Filling

Baked Rice Pudding
Zarda or Sweet Saffron Rice

Wholemeal Gingerbread
Cumberland Shortbread

SPECIAL OCCASION MENUS

Stuffed Mushrooms
Chicken with Orange and Ginger
Chocolate Moulds

Celery Fritters with a Dip
Pork with Chestnuts
Chocolate Brandy Cake

Tuna Fish Pâté
Sherried Pork Chops
Fresh Peaches in Raspberry Sauce

Pear with Stilton Sauce
A Rich Beef Stew
Grapes with Muscovado and
Soured Cream

Pea and Mint Soup
Honolulu Chicken
Coffee Ice Cream

Quick Liver Pâté
Pork Stir Fry
Quick Fruit Puddings

Eggs in a Forest
Sea Bass with Clams and Herbs
Mandarin Surprise
(*Sally Wilson's winning menu – for the
title of 1987 Junior Cook of the Year*)

Quick Chilled Tomato Soup
Squid with Green Peppers
in a Black Bean Sauce
Chocolate Brandy Cake

Cheese and Leek Flan
Teifi Salmon in a Sauce
Apple Pudding
(*Lucy Barton-Greenwood's menu won her
second place in the competition*)

Smoked Fish Soufflé
Chicken Pieces in Cider Sauce
Banana Alaska

Minted Cucumber Mousse
Poached Salmon with Two Sauces
Strawberries and Kiwi Fruit in a
Cream-Filled Sponge
(*Simon Dunn's menu won him third place*)

Watercress Soup
Crisp Roast Duck with
Grapefruit Sauce
Christmas Mincemeat Roll
Ice Cream Christmas Pud

INDEX

(M) indicates that a recipe also has a microwave method.

181

Chicken and bacon omelette 97
Chicken fingers 57
Chicken and grape salad 108
Chicken mould 54
Chicken and mushroom pie 123
Chicken for one (M) 57
Chicken with orange and ginger 58
Chicken paste 33
Chicken salad 55
Chicken and sweetcorn soup 20
Creamed chicken with rice (M) 56
Creamy chicken with mushrooms (M) 55
Honolulu chicken 55
Mandarin chicken (M) 59
Patti's chicken for two (M) 61
To poach a chicken (M) 54
Quick chicken in a cream sauce 56
Steamed rice with chicken and Chinese mushrooms 60
Turkey or chicken in a cider sauce 63
Chilli con carne 79
Chilled soup with avocado 26
Chilled tomato and apple soup (M) 25
Chilled tomato soup, Quick 25

Chinese leaves
Quick stir-fried vegetables with oyster sauce 117
Stir-fried (M) 113

Chocolate
Cherry buns 160
Chocolate butter icing 161
Chocolate brandy cake 144
Chocolate fudge topping 160
Chocolate moulds 144
Chocolate mousse 144
Chocolate sponge 160
Steamed puddings (M) 160
Wholemeal chocolate cake (M) 161

Christmas
Almond mince pies 127
Apple and mincemeat parcel 126
Brandy or sherry sauce (M) 133
Christmas mincemeat roll 133
Crisp roast duck with grapefruit sauce 62
Fruit and nut sweets 176
Grandmother's ginger fruit cake 157
Ice cream Christmas pud 143
Sherry cake (M) 158

Simple Christmas pudding (M) 132
Turkey or chicken in a cider sauce 63
Turkey kebabs 64

Chutney
Red tomato chutney (M) 174
Sweet chutney 174
Cider with sausages 72
Citrus mackerel 44
Coconut scones 155

Cod
Cod baked with sweetcorn (M) 38
Cod with noodles in a leek and cheese sauce (M) 37
Fish Tikka (M) 39
Smoked fish soufflé (M) 40
Tasty fish pie 39
Coffee ice cream 143

Confectionery
Fruit and nut sweets for Christmas 176
Rich rum truffles 176
Cooking dried beans and peas 92
Corn raita 110

Cottage cheese
Cottage cheese and yoghurt dressing 107
Lentil and cottage cheese croquettes 94
Pizza for two 125
Cottage pie 78

Courgettes
Baked lamb chops with courgettes 81
Courgette omelette 97
Courgettes with tomatoes (M) 113
Eggs in a forest (M) 27
Vegetables with cheese (M) 103

Cream cheese
Hot savoury toasted snacks for one 30
Minted cucumber mousse 26
Cream of lentil soup 21
Creamed chicken with rice (M) 56
Creamy chicken and mushroom (M) 55
Crisp and buttery herrings 42
Crisp-fried fish pieces with a piquant sauce 42
Crisp lemon sole 44
Crisp roast duck with grapefruit sauce 62
Crispy noodles with beef 73

Crumbles
Oaty apple crunch (M) 137
Oaty rhubarb crumble (M) 136

183